THE FIRE OF VENTURE WAS IN HIS VEINS

An attacking Ndebele warrior with his weapons, which include the knobkerrie, assegai and throwing spears carried behind his cowhide shield. (Artwork by Patrice Courcelle © Helion & Company 2022)

A member of the Combined Column armed with his Martini-Henri rifle. (Artwork by Patrice Courcelle © Helion & Company 2022)

The Fire of Venture Was in His Veins

Major Allan Wilson and the Shangani Patrol
1893: Rhodesia's 'Custer's Last Stand'

David Snape

Helion & Company

Helion & Company Limited
Unit 8 Amherst Business Centre
Budbrooke Road
Warwick
CV34 5WE
England
Tel. 01926 499619
Email: info@helion.co.uk
Website: www.helion.co.uk
Twitter: @helionbooks
Visit our blog at http://blog.helion.co.uk/

Published by Helion & Company 2022
Designed and typeset by Mach 3 Solutions Ltd (www.mach3solutions.co.uk)
Cover designed by Paul Hewitt, Battlefield Design (www.battlefield-design.co.uk)

Text © David Snape 2022
Illustrations © as individually credited
Maps drawn by George Anderson © Helion & Company 2022

Cover: A member of the Combined Column armed with his Martini-Henri
rifle. (Artwork by Patrice Courcelle © Helion & Company 2022)

ISBN 978-1-914059-90-2

British Library Cataloguing-in-Publication Data.
A catalogue record for this book is available from the British Library.

For details of other military history titles published by Helion & Company Limited,
contact the above address, or visit our website: http://www.helion.co.uk

We always welcome receiving book proposals from prospective authors.

Contents

List of Illustrations

Preface

Whilst researching my book about the Jameson Raid,[1] I was interested as to how Doctor Jim could move from decorated hero to imprisoned villain in such a short time. Lauded for his work in the AmaNdebele War he was heavily criticised for the failure of his Raid. In truth, not all of the events of the War were successful and the most disastrous was the events of the Shangani Patrol which had cost the lives of over 30 men; massacred by an *Impi of* AmaNdebele almost within sight of a relieving force. Allan Wilson, the leader of the massacred patrol became a folk hero and an example of Victorian pluck.

I am grateful to my editor, Dr Christopher Brice and the proprietor of Helion and Company, Duncan Rogers, for allowing me to explore this precursor to the Raid. Without their experience this book would not have been completed.

I also hope that it might inspire my granddaughter, Amy, to take a little more interest in the history which fascinates her 'Grumpy'.

David Snape
Wellingborough
January 2022

---

1   David Snape, *The Rescue They Called a Raid: The Jameson Raid 1895-96* (Warwick: Helion & Co, 2021)

Introduction

The AmaNdebele War was part of the preparations for the Jameson Raid, although this was not known at the time. It enabled Cecil Rhodes and Leander Starr Jameson to acquire another part of Southern Africa in the name of the British Empire. The creation of the British South African Company (BSAC) and its attempts to exploit the land of Lobengula, King of the AmaNdebele, required the creation of a military force, many of whose members later took part in the Raid. The Company won the war, took over Lobengula's kingdom and it became part of the British Empire. Jameson was lauded as a hero and he, and Rhodes, set about planning to incorporate the South African Republic in a similar way.

However, there had been a small setback in bringing the war to an end. Jameson believed that it was necessary to capture Lobengula in order to make sure his people gave up the fight. Having captured GuBulawayo, Lobengula's capital, and finding that the King has escaped. Jameson decided to send out a Patrol with orders to capture the King and bring him back This was the Shangani Patrol, and it ended a miserable failure. The King escaped and 34 of the Patrol's members under the command of Major Allan Wilson were wiped out. Although not on the scale of Isandlwana, the heroic deaths of these men became an important part of the history of Rhodesia, where Shangani Day was a public holiday for many years.

The story of the Patrol is one of inefficiency, divided command, bravery, and massacre. It shows the Victorian Britons at their best and their worst. The view of these events has inevitably changed and many of the people of Zimbabwe are keener to point out the large numbers of AmaNdebele who were massacred during the War and the following uprising which occurred as a direct result of the Jameson Raid. This revolt which followed, known as the 'First Chimurenga', is seen as an attempt by the native people to regain their land and liberty from the control of Britain and its agent, the British South Africa Company.

1

'He is like a monkey that has its hands full of pumpkin seeds. If you don't beat him to death he will never let go'[1]

In 1882 Lobengula, second king of the northern AmaNdebele people, was warned by Piet Joubert, Commandant General of the South African Republic (ZAR), that the English were rapacious when it came to seizing land and could only be stopped by violence.[2] Joubert had no reason to love the English. Although of Huguenot descent, as a child he took part in the Great Trek from the British Cape Colony, where his fellow Boers felt that their way of life was threatened by British rule. In order to maintain their independence, they crossed the Vaal River and were able to continue to live their rural lives without interference.

Joubert became a successful farmer and a good lawyer. The Boer military system was based on the Commando structure which required every man be prepared to defend his district against threat. The structure was very informal, and its officers were elected by the members of their Commando. Joubert rose through the various levels of command until he was elected Commandant General in 1881, which gave him command over all the Boer forces and control of the distribution of arms and ammunition. Joubert's election by his fellow burghers was part of the Boer response to the annexation of the Transvaal by Britain in 1877 in furtherance of its plans to extend British dominance over southern Africa. The Boers were determined to restore the Republic by military means if necessary and the outcome was the Boer victory at Majuba Hill in 1881 and the signing of the Pretoria

---

1   Piet Joubert quoted in Martin Meredith, *Gold, Diamonds and War: The British, the Boers and the Making of South Africa* (London: Schuster & Schuster, 2007).
2   Throughout this book the name 'AmaNdebele' will be used to refer to the people and 'Matabeleland' to the country in which they live, which is now part of modern Zimbabwe. The AmaNdebele king's name has several spellings, but throughout the book 'Lobengula' will be used.

Piet Joubert, Commandant General of the South African Republic. (Open source)

Convention by which the South African Republic retained its independence under a nominal British suzerainty.[3] This control was mainly removed by the London Convention in 1887 and restricted to the ZAR's international relations.[4]

Joubert had truly beaten the monkey to death and his warning was a timely one for Lobengula. The AmaNdebele had once been part of the Zulu nation but their leader, Mzilikazi, originally a subordinate of Shaka, the great Zulu king, fell out with his monarch and left his lands to eventually conquer the Transvaal. However, confrontation with the Boers during the Great Trek forced Mzilikazi and his people to leave the Transvaal. They eventually settled on land that is now within present-day Zimbabwe, where he established a regime and military system similar to that of the Zulus.

In 1868 Mzilikazi gave miners and prospectors the right to mine gold on, but not own, land in the Tati district of his kingdom. This caused the first gold rush in the area, which at its peak saw 220 prospectors and miners active in the area. It became the first European settlement north of the Limpopo River and a base for hunters and traders. Mzilikazi died in 1868 and, after the customary violent jockeying for power that occurs when succession is in dispute, Lobengula, a son of Mzilikazi by a minor wife, became the AmaNdebele's second king. Lobengula maintained his father's military system and created an army of 150,000 men organised into 40 regiments based around his new capital, GuBulawayo.[5] Lobengula also confirmed his father's Tati Concession with the London and Limpopo Mining Company, run by Sir John Swinburne and Captain Arthur Lionel Levert, which allowed gold mining in the Tati River area (a strip of land between Matabeleland and the Bechuanaland Protectorate). In 1870 this Concession was revoked as the miners had little luck and Swinburne was unable to pay the annual fee to Lobengula.[6] The Concession was transferred to the Northern Light Mining Company, which was formed by returning miners who had been more successful in the diamond fields; it was eventually acquired by the Tati Concession Company.

In 1884 George Westbeech and George Arthur (Elephant) Philips, with whom Lobengula had spent time in their hunting camps, together with James Fairburn, a gold prospector, and Thomas Leask, another big game hunter,

3   The Pretoria Convention referred to the ZAR as the 'Transvaal Territories' but its title reverted to ZAR under the London Convention.
4   For details of the Annexation and the First Boer War, see John Laband, *The Battle of Majuba Hill: The Transvaal Campaign 1880–1881* (Solihull: Helion & Co., 2017).
5   Meredith, *Gold, Diamonds and War*, pp.207–208. Originally 'ko-GuBulawayo'.
6   John S. Galbraith, *Crown and Charter: The Early Years of the British South Africa Company* (Berkeley, CA: University of California Press, 1974), p.32.

Mzilikazi, King of the AmaNdebele and father of Lobengula. (Open source)

President Paul Kruger of the South African Republic. (Open source)

persuaded Lobengula to grant them a concession to dig for gold and other minerals between the rivers and allow them to employ a small number of European miners to assist them.[7] Lobengula, in granting these concessions, was prepared to take more risks in dealing with Europeans than his father Mzilikazi. He had continued the friendship established by his father with Robert Moffat, a Scottish missionary and member of the London Missionary Society. Kindly disposed to the missionaries, Lobengula always treated them well. It was this relationship that encouraged European travellers to attempt to settle in Lobengula's kingdom in order to exploit his country's natural resources. The AmaNdebele saw the Boers as enemies, but Kruger stated in his memoirs that in 1887 Lobengula asked for a Boer 'consul' to be appointed to Matabeleland and for it to be put under Boer protection.[8] Lobengula obviously would not let personal dislike interfere with political necessity. However, this may have been an offer made by Kruger himself rather than a request from Lobengula.

Sir Hercules Robinson, Governor of Cape Colony, wrote in a telegram to the Colonial Office: 'Transvaal has been trying to persuade Lobengula

---

7   Modern Gwaai and Manyame rivers. For the terms of the Concession, see Appendix II.
8   Quoted in Sarah Millin, *Rhodes* (London: Chatto & Windus, 1933), p.101.

to accept their protection and a Resident Consul, but he refused.[9] Given Kruger's ambition to extend his government's influence in the area, it would suggest that Robinson was correct in placing the initiative at feet of the Boers.

Robert Moffat's son, John Smith Moffat, the brother-in-law of David Livingstone, had previously been a missionary to the AmaNdebele but in 1879 he joined the British Colonial Service. Five years later he became Assistant Commissioner under Sir Sidney Shippard in Bechuanaland. In 1888, with the support of Cecil Rhodes, Smith, using his family connection, persuaded Lobengula to agree that he would only deal with Britain. No concessions were to be granted without the approval of Queen Victoria and, in return, Moffat promised King Lobengula that he would be under British protection. The Moffat Treaty, signed in February 1888, declared that 'peace and amity shall continue forever between Her Britannic Majesty, Her subjects, and the AmaNdebele people'.[10]

One of the visitors to Lobengula's kingdom has provided us with a description of the King. John Cooper-Chadwick, an Irish contemporary of Roger Casement at the Royal School in Armagh, went to South Africa and joined Methuen's Horse, a corps of mounted rifles made up of 600 volunteers mainly recruited in London.[11] The regiment was part of Sir Charles Warren's expedition to Bechuanaland in 1884, sent in order to assert British sovereignty in response to German annexation of South West Africa and the expansion of the ZAR. Warren was also charged with subduing the independent states of Stellaland and Goshen, which were supported by the Transvaal government and whose residents were stealing land and cattle from the local Tswana tribes. Known as the 'Warren Expedition', it consisted of 4,000 imperial and local troops and had the first three hot air balloons ever used by the British Army in the field as a means of improved observation. The venture was a success and Warren was recalled in 1885.

Cooper-Chadwick, having refused the offer of free passage back to England, joined Frederick Carrington's Bechuanaland Border Police (BBP), which had been raised in order to defend the area.[12] The BBP consisted of 500 mounted infantry and included an artillery troop.[13] The men were paid six shillings per day, and it was during this period that Cooper-Chadwick met Khama, one of the three Botswanan chiefs who shortly were to visit England in order to petition Queen Victoria and her Secretary of State for the Colonies, Joseph Chamberlain, to protect them from Cecil Rhodes' schemes to dominate their land.

After several other adventures, including mining and surveying and laying the telegraph line from Pretoria to Lichtenburg, Cooper-Chadwick formed a prospecting syndicate with his friend Benjamin Wilson and

---

9   NA Colonial Office, Africa (South) No. 358, 5633, No. 5.

10   For a complete version of the Moffat Treaty, see Appendix I.

11   John Cooper-Chadwick, *Three Years with Lobengula, and Experiences in South Africa* (London: Cassell & Co., 1894).

12   Frederick Carrington had commanded 'Carrington's Horse', which was part of Methuen's Expedition.

13   The BBP were to take part in the Jameson Raid in 1895–1896.

Alexander Boggie, a friend of Cecil Rhodes.[14] When the three had acquired sufficient sponsors to finance the syndicate, Cooper-Chadwick arrived at GuBulawayo in August 1888 to find it full of European fortune hunters. He sought an audience with Lobengula, whom he described as being dressed in a kilt of monkey skins and a pair of socks and wearing 'a wide awake hat with an ostrich feather in it'.[15] Over six feet tall but greatly overweight, Lobengula had a proud demeanour and stately walk, 'which gave him the bearing of a savage king'.[16] He had coarse features that exhibited cunning and cruelty, but these expressions were completely transformed when he smiled. Cooper-Chadwick described how Lobengula, of necessity, ruled his people by blood and fire and showed little mercy.[17] This is confirmed by Stafford Glass, who wrote that Lobengula 'exercised his control of his people with the same brutality that his father had shown'.[18] 'He was a savage in the fullest sense of the word.'[19]

However, the King displayed other characteristics that had not always been evident in his father, Mzilikazi. He was intelligent, cunning, a skilled orator and politician.[20] In spite of his apparent barbarity, Stuart Cloete sympathetically described Lobengula as 'a constitutional monarch, pleasing to his people, except when he was too prone to restrain them from war with the white men'.[21] The term 'constitutional' is strange in this context but it is true that Lobengula referred to a council of his *Indunas* who were often keen to ally themselves with the British.[22] Lobengula's hold on his throne was always tenuous as succession usually took place after an assassination and purge, which meant he could not totally ignore the opinions of his sub-chiefs.

The AmaNdebele were organised on military lines. A man's wealth was measured in cows and the king, with the largest herd, was the richest of them all. On an annual basis it was his duty to instruct his army as to which of their weaker neighbours they should attack in order to increase the national herd and gain a supply of slaves and concubines.[23] Not to do so would have put his throne in jeopardy but there is little evidence that Lobengula was genuinely reluctant to unleash his regiments of *Impis* in this way.

Cooper-Chadwick makes it clear that he and his colleagues had not just visited Lobengula out of curiosity but for specific reasons: first to obtain gold

14   Cooper-Chadwick, *Three Years with Lobengula*, p.63.
15   Cooper-Chadwick, *Three Years with Lobengula*, p.90. A 'wideawake hat' is a broad-brimmed felt casual hat with a low crown and resembles a slouch hat.
16   Cooper-Chadwick, *Three Years with Lobengula*, p.90.
17   Cooper-Chadwick, *Three Years with Lobengula*, p.90.
18   Stafford Glass, *The Matabele War* (London: Longmans, 1968), p.1.
19   Nancy Rouillard (ed.), *Matabele Thompson – His Autobiography* (Johannesburg: Central News Agency, 1957), p.59.
20   Chris Ash, *The If Man: Dr Leander Jameson – The Inspiration for Kipling's Masterpiece* (Solihull: Helion & Co., 2012), p.64.
21   Stuart Cloete, *African Portraits* (London: Collins, 1946), p.226.
22   Sidney Godolphin Alexander Shippard in a letter to Sir Hercules Robinson, High Commissioner for South Africa, dated 31 August 1888. Quoted in Philip Mason, *The Birth of a Dilemma* (Oxford: Oxford University Press, 1958), pp.121–122. '*Induna*' is a tribal councillor or sub-chief.
23   For a contemporary account of how the AmaNdebele were organised, see Charles Norris Newman, *Matabeleland and How We Got It* (London: Fisher Unwin, 1895), pp.155–157.

mining concessions and later to assist the representatives of Cecil Rhodes in gaining access to the wealth of Matabeleland.[24] Lobengula was very astute and recognised the threat the prospectors posed to his kingdom. Stuart Cloete described him as having a gift, 'not common among native Africans of being of being able to look ahead and see under the surface of events'.[25] Cloete could have been correct, but Lobengula may not have understood the real significance of dealing with these European visitors to his kingdom and their apparent harmless requests, especially as some of them represented Cecil John Rhodes, one of the most powerful men in Africa.

Rhodes had arrived in Africa on leaving school in order to improve his health. After several ventures, which included running a cotton plantation and prospecting for diamonds, he eventually became one of the richest men in South Africa and entered into partnership with Charles Dunnell Rudd. Rudd had been born in Norfolk, England, and, while Rhodes went to Oxford to make up for the early interruption to his education, Rudd managed their joint affairs. In 1880 Rhodes, Rudd and five other businessmen formed the De Beers Mining Company, which in 1888 merged with the companies of Barney Barnato to form De Beers Consolidated Mines. This company was soon to become the single owner of all diamond mining undertaken in the country. Rhodes' interests were not purely commercial. He was an arch imperialist who believed that the whole world would benefit if the British Empire expanded.

---

24   Cooper-Chadwick's stay in Africa came to a grisly end when he accidentally shot off both his hands and wrote his account with the pen attached to his elbow.

25   Cloete, *African Portraits*, p.228.

2

One of His Guiding Tenets was That Every Man had His Price

The Moffat Treaty opened the way for British entrepreneurs to attempt to persuade Lobengula to grant them concessions to search for gold despite previous failures to find the metal in significant quantities. Rhodes was convinced that the lands of the AmaNdebele were worth investigating for the ore and decided to send three of his associates to negotiate with the King.

The leader of these three, not surprisingly, was Charles Rudd, who was completely loyal and reliable as far as Rhodes was concerned.[1] Rudd was accompanied by a young South African, Francis (Frank) Thompson, who was to acquire the epithet 'Matabele'.[2] Thompson had acted as Rhodes' secretary in Bechuanaland and later worked for De Beers, organising compounds for African labourers in order to prevent them from selling stolen diamonds. During this occupation, he had learned something of the native languages and customs and, according to his autobiography, this allowed him to be the major spokesman during the negotiations with Lobengula.[3] He was something of a reluctant representative, however, for when Rhodes asked him to go to Matabeleland, he responded that he must first ask his wife. Rhodes, who knew his man,

Cecil John Rhodes, imperialist and capitalist. (Open source)

---

1   John G. Lockhart & Christopher M. Woodhouse, *Rhodes* (London: Hodder & Stoughton, 1963), p.141.
2   Gibbs (*A Flag for the Matabele* (London: Frederick Muller, 1955), p.29) described him as a 'mere South African'.
3   Rouillard, *Matabele Thompson*, p.67.

Charles Rudd, negotiator of the Concession with Lobengula. (Open source)

immediately produced Thompson's wife's written permission.[4]

The third member of the party was James Rochfort Maguire who had become friendly with Rhodes while they were at Oxford. Rochfort Maguire was elected a Fellow of All Souls in 1878 and called to the Bar in 1883. He was later to become Rhodes' 'alternate' on the board of the British South Africa Company and appear as a witness during the parliamentary inquiry into the circumstances of the Jameson Raid. He is described as being so impractical that he could not even open a tin of salmon.[5]

Lockhart and Woodhouse have suggested that Rhode's ability to assemble three such different characters to work as a team was evidence of his powers of persuasion.[6] Each had a different but important role: Rudd would look after the business aspects of the negotiations; Thompson would deal with the natives; and Rochfort Maguire would ensure that any agreement was written in the appropriate legal English and, bizarrely, coach the young Thompson in the Classics as compensation for him having failed to pass into Oxford. Strange bedfellows indeed.

However, before these three were able to arrive in Matabeleland, the Boers made a pre-emptive strike. In 1887 Paul Kruger, President of the ZAR, conscious that the British were anxious to negotiate with Lobengula, sent Pieter Daniel Cornelius Johannes Grobler to negotiate a treaty with the AmaNdebele. Grobler was an experienced trader but was greatly distrusted by Lobengula because he represented the ZAR, whom Shippard had previously warned might be planning an attack against the AmaNdebele.[7] Grobler overcame this suspicion and negotiated a treaty of 'friendship', written by Kruger, which declared there would be everlasting peace between the AmaNdebele and the Boers.[8] In return for recognising him as the paramount chief, Lobengula was committed to offering military support to the Boers when called upon. The treaty, dated 30 July 1887, did not, however, place a reciprocal commitment on the Boers nor was Lobengula offered anything tangible in return for signing it. Worse still, it seemed to allow the ZAR to have a resident consul in Matabeleland who would have criminal and civil jurisdiction over any Boer within Lobengula's lands and

---

4   Lockhart & Woodhouse, *Rhodes*, p.141.
5   Lockhart & Woodhouse, *Rhodes*, p.142.
6   Lockhart & Woodhouse, *Rhodes*, p.142.
7   Lewis Henry Gann, *A History of Southern Rhodesia from Early Days to 1934* (London: Chatto & Windus, 1965), p.72.
8   A. Schowalter (ed.), *The Memoirs of Paul Kruger as Told by Himself* (New York: Century Co., 1902), p.192.

joint jurisdiction in any dispute involving Boer and AmaNdebele. However, to Hugh Marshal Hole, who was to become Secretary for Matabeleland, the treaty 'bore the stamp of imposture from beginning to end'.[9] The only two European signatories to the treaty were Grobler and his brother Frederick. There were no other witnesses, and the document did not have a certificate signed by an interpreter indicating that it had been fully explained to the AmaNdebele signatories.[10] The names of these signatories did not seem to correspond with any real AmaNdebele names and the place where the treaty was made is unknown.[11] Moffat, however, claimed to have spoken to one of the *Indunas* who signed the treaty and explained that the unknown names were the result of Afrikaans attempting to phonetically transcribe AmaNdebele names, consequently resulting in different spellings from those produced by a similar attempt to transcribe them into English.[12] In return for his agreement to the treaty, Lobengula was given £140 by Grobler, together with a rifle and some ammunition. Perhaps Marshal Hole is somewhat ingenuous about Lobengula's statecraft as the treaty did prevent a major Boer incursion and was easily refuted during the negotiations with Rudd. It also explains why Kruger believed that Lobengula had agreed to a consul while the King could easily deny the fact.

Grobler had little opportunity to enjoy his appointment as consul. Some years earlier he had sold horses to Khama, Chief of the BaNgwato, which Grobler had claimed had been 'salted' against African Horse Sickness.[13] It is possible that Grobler genuinely believed the horses to be protected but, as indicated in a scientific paper of the time, 'true immunity in horses against this disease is never acquired'.[14] After the deal was done and Grobler left, the horses became sick and died. Khama feeling he had been tricked wanted revenge, and when Grobler was returning to the Transvaal with his treaty he was intercepted by a group of BaNgwato. A skirmish occurred during which Grobler was mortally wounded. Shippard, who came to investigate the affair, believed he had been shot accidentally in the leg by one of his own men, but it is likely that lack of medical care was the real cause of his death.

As a consequence of these events Rudd and his companions set off for GuBulawayo. Upon their arrival, the three found there were several other Europeans with financial backing and similar aims as well as resident missionaries such as Charles Daniel Helm and John Mackenzie who had great influence with Lobengula and his *Indunas*. Among these other visitors were Sam Edwards from Tati Mines; Cooper-Chadwick, Boggie and Wilson, who have already been mentioned; and James Fairburn, the keeper of Lobengula's seal without which no document could be considered 'legal'.

---

9   Hugh Marshall Hole, *The Making of Rhodesia* (London: Macmillan & Co., 1926), pp.61–62.
10   See Appendix III for an example of such a certificate.
11   Gann, *A History of Southern Rhodesia*, p.72; Lockhart & Woodhouse, *Rhodes*, p.136.
12   Mason, *The Birth of a Dilemma*, p.118.
13   Salted horses are ones that were previously infected and survived, so are therefore less susceptible to the disease.
14   Alexander Edington, 'South African Horse Sickness: Its Pathology and Methods of Protective Inoculation', *Proceedings of the Royal Society of London*, 67, 1900, p.305.

The negotiations proved somewhat protracted. Rudd and his companions decided not to follow the local custom observed by some Europeans of crawling on their hands and knees as they approached the King.[15] Walking boldly towards him caused surprise among his *Indunas* who lived in fear of their unpredictable monarch. After something of a delay, Lobengula asked who the three were and put certain questions to them. As a gift Rudd presented him with a bag of 100 gold sovereigns and the three were then told to go back to their camp and sleep.[16]

They returned to the royal kraal three days later and, according to Thompson's autobiography, the 'mere South African' took charge of the negotiations because of his knowledge of the language. Thompson says that the discussion took place in Sechuana (Setswana), the language of the Tswana people which only Lobengula and a few of his men understood.[17] Whether this was because it restricted the numbers of AmaNdebele knowing what was being said or that Thompson was not the complete linguist he claimed to be is hard to tell. Lockhart and Woodhouse indicate that it was the missionary Daniel Helm who acted as interpreter.[18] Lobengula seems to have been reluctant to talk about another concession. Gibbs believes that the discussions took many weeks with the King holding his own in debate with the Cambridge graduate and the Oxford Don.[19] It is also likely that he was assessing the reaction his *Indunas* might attempt to exert on him if he agreed to a new concession.

One of the causes for the delay in Rudd concluding the negotiations was the presence of Edward Ramsey Renny-Tailyour who was Eduard Lippert's agent. Lippert was a cousin of Alfred Beit but the two did not like one another. Renny-Tailyour was also anxious to obtain a gold concession from Lobengula and made offer and counteroffer in an attempt to persuade the King to favour his employer over the representatives of Cecil Rhodes. Daniel Helm had considerable influence over Lobengula and the King did not appreciate the fact that the missionary had become one of Rhodes's men. The AmaNdebele were aware that Sir Sidney Shippard was on the way to visit GuBulawayo with an '*Impi*' and many thought that they were going to kill AmaNdebele children.[20] Lobengula struggled to keep in check the *Matjaha* (unmarried warriors), who were describe as having 'insatiable vanity and almost incredible conceit'.[21] These young warriors wanted to kill all white men in GuBulawayo as a warning to others who might be thinking of coming. Wiser counsel from the *Indunas* was accepted by Lobengula, and Shippard was allowed to enter GuBulawayo unmolested, arriving on 16 October 1888, but even the Bechuanaland Resident Commissioner was kept waiting by the King. Shippard, while at Oxford, had discussed with Rhodes the latter's plans

---

15   Other sources claim that Dr Jameson was the first to be so bold in his approach to Lobengula.
16   Rouillard, *Matabele Thompson*, p.56.
17   Rouillard, *Matabele Thompson*, p.65.
18   Lockhart & Woodhouse, *Rhodes*, p.143.
19   Gibbs, *A Flag for the Matabele*, p.19. Gibbs seems to have undervalued Thompson's part in the discussions.
20   The '*Impi*', or army, consisted of 16 troopers of the BBP.
21   Sir Sidney Shippard, quoted in Mason, *The Birth of a Dilemma*, p.121.

for African expansion. It could hardly be a coincidence that, while discussing matters with Lobengula, Shippard argued that it would be better for the King to treat with one reputable company rather than several with doubtful reputations. Lobengula, despite his great fear of the Boers, also had worries about British intentions towards his country. He is said to have discussed these intentions with Missionary Helm who had also come under Rhodes' influence. In addition, the *Indunas* Lotjie and Sekombo, both of whom had been promised gifts by Thompson, also attempted to persuade Lobengula to grant Rudd's wishes.[22] The British were like a chameleon that advances very slowly on its prey. Suddenly the fly is swallowed up. To Lobengula his country was the fly and Britain was the chameleon.[23]

Shippard's persuasion did the trick, and shortly after he left on 30 October 1888, Rudd and his companions were given what they desired: a concession to mine for valuable minerals to which Rudd's name became synonymous.[24] Lobengula's agreement, according to Rudd, was obtained after a short conference between the King, Matabele Thompson and Lotjie.[25] In return, Rudd (Rhodes) agreed to pay Lobengula's price of £100 per month and provide 1,000 Martini-Henry rifles and 100,000 cartridges, and perhaps strangely, an armed steamboat on the Zambezi. Additionally, Lobengula, having acknowledged that he had been 'molested' by 'divers persons' who wished to obtain similar rights, authorised the Rudd (Rhodes) consortium to take steps to exclude any rivals from such a claim. Helm, who was less than open-minded, added his signature to the document claiming to have read its contents to the King several times.

Lobengula's grant of a concession seems to have disappointed the *Matjaha* who were hoping to be allowed to slaughter the whites. This had almost occurred when, just before the Rudd Concession document was agreed, Lobengula received a letter from the London Aborigine Protection Society which strongly advised him against granting a monopoly to any one organisation as, by doing so, he would risk AmaNdebele independence.[26]

It is unlikely that Lobengula fully appreciated the true significance of the document on which he had placed his mark. Helm's assertion that he explained the agreement to the King several times was meant to publicly ensure that there could be no suggestion that the Rhodes' group had tried to dupe the king. Lobengula had also discussed the concession with his senior *Indunas*, among whom there was a general agreement and similar arguments to those of Shippard had been made by some of them. Chris Ash argues strongly that Lobengula was not tricked into signing the Rudd Concession

---

22   Lotje (ILoché or Loshe) is described of being the equivalent of Matabele Prime Minister. Rouillard, *Matabelle Thompson*, p.68.

23   TNA, Colonial Office. 879/30/369/, no. 65. encl. 372, p.172. Reported by Sir Sidney Shippard to Sir Hercules Robinson, March 1889.

24   For the full content of the Rudd Concession, see Appendix III.

25   V.W. Hiller, 'The Commission Journey of Charles Dunell Rudd, 1888', in Constance E. Fripp and V.W. Hiller, (eds), *Gold and the Gospel in Mashonaland* (London: Chatto & Windus, 1949), p.202.

26   Howard Hemsley, *The History of Rhodesia* (London: William Blackwood & Sons, 1900), p.35.

and this is probably true.[27] Under its terms he gained access to a large number of guns and ammunition which colonial traders were forbidden to sell to him. He had taken his time to agree and had consulted his *Indunas*.

Sympathy for Lobengula's position is probably somewhat misplaced. Missionary Helm claimed that there were verbal promises made to Lobengula such as a limit on the numbers allowed to prospect for gold and an agreement to abide by the AmaNdebele laws that were not included in the document.[28] However, neither Thompson in his autobiography nor Lobengula in his messages refers to such restrictions, but this does not conclusively prove that there was no unwritten agreement between Rudd and the King. Frank Johnson suggested that Lobengula, though a canny negotiator, was ignorant of the world stage and of Rhodes' influence in it. The King believed that he had obtained a 1,000 rifles and Rhodes had only received a piece of paper. After all, the King had signed several such 'deals' in the past with little or no ill effects for him or his people.[29]

The Rudd Concession only gave Rhodes mining rights as, although the phrase 'win and procure' is ambiguous, it makes no reference to jurisdiction. This was in direct contrast to a similar concession granted to the Imperial British East African Company (IBEAC) by the Sultan of Zanzibar in April 1888, which not only afforded the IBEAC the right to search for precious metals and raw materials, but also gave it all powers and authority possessed by the Sultan in what later became known as Uganda and Kenya. This experiment proved unsuccessful and the IBEAC went bankrupt in 1895. Rhodes' voracity for wealth was tempered by as desire for power and the possession of valuable minerals such as gold was a manifestation of such power. Mashonaland was believed to contain gold, and Rhodes felt it should be occupied to secure this. But he seems to have wished to 'annex land and not natives'.[30]

Once in possession of his concession, Rudd left Matabeleland for Kimberley within four hours of gaining Lobengula's agreement. Thompson and Rochfort Maguire remained behind to ensure that Lobengula did not change his mind. Rudd's journey almost ended in disaster for, after a long ride in very hot weather and drinking alcohol to cool down, he was hurt when his horse fell. He lay delirious until rescued by bushmen who took him to the nearby village. Having recovered, he returned to the place of his accident where he had the presence of mind to hide the concession document in a hole in a tree and, having retrieved it, continued his journey, successfully arriving at Kimberley on 19 November 1888, 20 days after leaving GuBulawayo. Once in Kimberley, Rudd presented a delighted Rhodes with the concession. 'It is like giving a man the whole of Australia'.[31] The elated Rhodes and Rudd travelled to Cape Town and presented the document to an equally thrilled

27   Ash, *The If Man*, p.70.
28   Galbraith, *Crown and Charter*, p.72.
29   Frank William Frederick Johnson, *Great Days: The Autobiography of an Empire Pioneer* (London: G. Bell & Son, 1940), p.83.
30   Robert Rotberg, *The Founder: Cecil Rhodes and the Pursuit of Power* (Oxford: Oxford University Press, 1988), p.149.
31   Rotberg, *The Founder*, p.264.

Sir Hercules Robinson, Governor of Cape Colony. Robinson wanted to officially publish the document immediately but was counselled by Rhodes not to mention the promise of rifles being offered to Lobengula as this would greatly worry the Boers. The AmaNdebele's possession of an additional 1,000 rifles could upset the balance of power in the region. As a result, the news of the concession was published in the *Cape Times* and *Cape Argus*, the two most influential newspapers in the province, but stated that the price for obtaining it was 'valuable consideration of a large monthly payment in cash, a gunboat for defensive purposes on the Zambesi, and other services.'[32] Two days later the *Cape Times* published a notice, supposedly from Lobengula, which stated that, since the concession had allocated all the mining rights to Rudd, the presence of all other 'concession-seekers and prospectors' was abhorrent to the King and his people.[33] Clearly a strong warning suggested by Thompson and Rochfort Maguire.

However, the King quickly had second thoughts after receiving reports that he had been duped into selling his country. Such was the concern among the AmaNdebele that Moffat wondered whether Lobengula could handle the increasingly tense situation.[34] Thompson, the only remaining member of the Rudd trio still in Matabeleland as Rochfort Maguire had left heading south, endured a lengthy interrogation by the council of *Indunas* who demanded to know whether he had 'bought the country'.[35] There were even rumours that a force of whites with the help of a prominent *Induna* were about to invade and kill Lobengula.[36] Tensions rose to such an extent that Lobengula was forced to make a public gesture to save his throne and appease both the *Matjaha* and the suspicious *Indunas* by ordering the immediate execution of Lotjie, whom he accused of tricking him into signing the concession.[37] In the usual brutal way of demonstrating the King's anger, it was not only Lotjie who was killed, but his extended family and his followers, together with the destruction of his kraal and the seizure of his cattle; a total of some 300 men, women and children perished.[38]

Under the influence of George Phillips and others who had written on Lobengula's behalf to the local newspapers, *The Bechuanaland News and Malmani Chronicle*, to the effect that because there was a misunderstanding regarding the concession, it was suspended pending an investigation.[39]

---

32 Arthur Keppel-Jones, *Rhodes and Rhodesia: The White Conquest of Zimbabwe 1884–1902* (Montreal: McGill-Queen's University Press, 1983), p.81.

33 Keppel-Jones, *Rhodes and Rhodesia*, p.81.

34 Galbraith, *Crown and Charter*, pp.72–76.

35 Rouillard, *Matabele Thompson*, p.94.

36 Galbraith, *Crown and Charter*, pp.72–76.

37 Apollon Davidson, *Rhodes and His Time* (Pretoria: Protea Boekhuis, 2003), p.140.

38 Mark Strage, *Cape to Cairo: Rape of a Continent* (New York: Harcourt Brace Jovanovich, 1973), p.70; Lockhart & Woodhouse, *Rhodes*, p.152; Rouilliard, *Matabele Thompson*, p.178. Norris Newman (*Matabeleland and How We Got It*, p.23) limits the number to 70. Newman was in Matabeleland in 1894. Maund suggested that Lotjie's wealth was part of the reason for his death (Galbraith, *Crown and Charter*, p.73). Such a reason was not uncommon if an *Induna* was thought to have become too powerful.

39 See Appendix V.

It is possible that Lobengula needed little persuading since, as has been mentioned, there was considerable disquiet among his *Indunas*.

While this situation developed, Edward Arthur Maund, an explorer who had been in GuBulawayo working for the Exploring Company at the time of Rudd's visit, was keen to get Lobengula to grant him a concession of the mineral rights in the Mazoe Valley, which contained some of the richest land in South Africa. Such a grant would breach the Rudd Concession and so it was in Maund's interest to question its validity. Strangely, he suggested to the King that Queen Victoria might not actually exist since neither Lobengula nor any of his *Indunas* had ever seen her. Maund suggested that the King should send two of his trusted *Indunas* to England, both to prove her existence and to question the concession's validity. How could an imaginary monarch protect him? Lobengula was pleased with the suggestion and selected Mshete and Babayan, who were to be his eyes and ears, to accompany Maund, and promised to consider a Mazoe concession when they returned, to England.[40] The original draft of Lobengula's letter asked that Matabeleland become a British protectorate, but this paragraph was deleted by Missionary Helm, whom Lobengula trusted to examine Maund's letter, and a phrase requesting protection was substituted.

The four men, Maund, Colenbrander, acting as interpreter, and the *Indunas*, Mshete and Babayan, set off for Kimberley. They journeyed via the Transvaal rather than through Bechuanaland as Maund feared that Rhodes would be able to intercept the group. On arriving in Kimberley, Maund bumped into Dr Leander Starr Jameson, Rhodes' right-hand man, and was persuaded to visit Rhodes, who attempted to obtain information from Maund and asked to see Lobengula's letter – a request Maund politely refused. A frustrated Rhodes then attempted to bribe Maund by suggesting that the Exploring Company would let him down whereas he would ensure that Maund received benefits like those Rhodes had given to others.[41] Maund resisted the temptation and did not show Rhodes the letter. Rhodes's response was to journey to London with his fellow gold magnate and business partner, Alfred Beit, and purchase a large block of shares in the Exploring Company. So Maund and Rhodes were no longer on opposite sides but had become collaborators, and when Maund reached Cape Town the purpose of his mission had changed. He showed Rhodes Lobengula's letter which did not specifically criticise the concession. A delighted Rhodes felt that this was the 'very stick he wanted' to beat his opponents.[42]

Maund's party eventually left Cape Town with the permission of Sir Hercules Robinson, the High Commissioner, who, in telegrams to the Colonial Office, described Maund as both mendacious and dangerous, Colenbrander as hopelessly unreliable, and Babayan and Mshete as not genuine *Induna*.[43]

---

40 University of Witwatersrand Historical Research Papers Archive, ZA HPRA A77 *Maund Papers*: Memo by Maund of Meeting Held at King's Kraal, 24 November 1888, witnessed by Helm, Tainton and Johan Wilhem Colenbrander. Henceforth Witwatersrand: Maund Papers. Colenbrander would later accompany Maund and the Indunas to England as an interpreter.

41 Witwatersrand: Maund Papers, 17, p.11.

42 Lockhart & Woodhouse, *Rhodes*, p.110.

43 Galbraith, *Crown and Charter*, pp.77–78.

When the deputation arrived in London, they were introduced to Lord Knutsford, the Secretary of State for the Colonies, to whom they conveyed complaints about being beset by people demanding concessions. They then were received by Queen Victoria with whom they talked through their interpreter, Colenbrander. Peter Gibbs suggests that the two *Indunas* were somewhat overawed by the Queen's graciousness and modesty of dress, so they were less than forceful in putting forward their cause.[44] Victoria, who had taken part in similar meetings with representatives of foreign kings and had a taste for the exotic, received them courteously, took their letter and provided them with gifts to take back to Lobengula. They were then treated to a carefully stage-managed tour which, influenced by Rhodes, was meant to impress them as to the

Sir Hercules Robinson, High Commissioner for South Africa, 1895–1889. (*Illustrated London News*, 1896)

wealth and power of England as well as demonstrate her ability to protect the AmaNdebele. Among the many venues they visited was Aldershot, the headquarters of the British Army, where they witnessed some manoeuvres, including a demonstration of the power of machine guns. This was somewhat lessened by the guns' tendency to jam. They also visited the Bank of England's Gold Room in order to impress upon the *Indunas* the vast wealth of Britain. This was not necessarily a success as they wondered why Britons were prepared to travel to their land to obtain more.[45] The *Indunas* were well received by the curious British, and they attended several dinners held in their honour. As a warning they were shown the spear of Cestshwayo, King of the defeated Zulus, which hung on a wall in Windsor Castle.

The entire visit was a success, or so the AmaNdebele thought. They returned with a letter written by Lord Knutsford on behalf of Queen Victoria to the effect that those Englishmen seeking permission to dig for gold did not do so with her authority and Lobengula should not hastily grant permission to them. It would be wiser not to grant everything to one man, but to also consider the request of other deserving applicants.[46] The warning was too late, the Rudd Concession had been granted.

Rhodes told Maund to go back to Lobengula and keep him in a good humour. Rhodes still had to put in place another piece in his jigsaw to control Matabeleland.

---

44   Gibbs, *A Flag for the Matabele*, p.38.
45   Gibbs, *A Flag for the Matabele*, p.35.
46   Hansard, House of Commons Debate, Vol. 18, cc.543–627, 9 November 1893. See Appendix VII for the full text.

3

Who is Mr Rhodes?[1]

Cecil Rhodes had his concession, but he now had to get government support for his plans. Aspects of Rudd's agreement caused concern among government ministers. Lord Knutsford, Colonial Secretary, questioned Sir Hercules Robinson, High Commissioner in South Africa, as to whether 'there [was] any danger of complications arising' from the 1,000 rifles being part of the concession agreement.[2] Robinson agreed that this might be a possibility but felt it was better that Lobengula should get the rifles from Britain than from another country. If the native Africans are to be armed, it was better that these weapons came from Britain rather than any of her European rivals. This was an acknowledgement of the need to maintain the balance of power in two aspects: the European scramble for Africa, and the traditional rivalry between the various tribes.

Rhodes was very politically astute and realised that he had to gain the support of many different factions in order to obtain his fervent wishes: a charter granting him and his associates rights to exploit Matabeleland and other parts of South Africa, boosting the BSAC and expanding the Britain Empire. In order to achieve these aims, he canvassed the political parties and various influential individuals to get their support.

He began by 'squaring' his rivals in Matabeleland: the Bechuanaland Exploration Company and the Exploring Company. The 'squaring' meant 'getting them on his side' – an expression that frequently is used to describe Rhodes's business tactics. Lord George Gifford and George Cawston of the Bechuanaland Exploration Company were already interested in an incorporation under a charter that would permit them to exploit the mining rights of the lands of Lobengula and Khama as well as building a railway to the Zambesi. They had financial backing of £50,000, much less than Rhodes's and De Beers' combined resources from the goldfields. Amalgamation made sense to Gifford and Cawston, who realised they could not compete with such a powerful rival. They became co-directors first of the Central Search

---

1 Prime Minister, Lord Salisbury's question to Sir Harry Johnston, Commissioner and Consul-General for the Mozambique and the Nyasa districts. Harry Johnston, *The Story of My Life* (London: Chatto & Windus, 1923), p.221.
2 Millin, *Rhodes*, pp.107-108

Association and then the United Concessions Company. Other rivals and concessionaires were also bought out as Rhodes was prepared to undertake far more than anyone else would reasonably do.[3] The Colonial Office looked favourably upon such a plan since it was beset by the parsimony of the Treasury and so was likely to listen to any proposition that would expand the British Empire on the cheap.

George Cawston, Director of the United Concessions Company. (Wills & Collingridge, *The Downfall of Lobengula*)

When Rhodes arrived in London, he found opposition from both the Aborigines Protection Society and the London Chamber of Commerce. The former was determined to prevent the exploitation of native Africans and the latter perhaps because it feared a commercial imbalance that would put other companies at risk. There was also serious political opposition from both Houses of Parliament, and a parliamentary committee that included the Duke of Fife, Earl Grey and Joseph Chamberlain (who was soon to be Colonial Secretary) was created to prevent any charter being granted based on the Rudd Concession. The duke and the earl were soon 'squared' and became Rhodes' supporters and were to sit on the board of his chartered company. There was also the implacable Member of Parliament for Northampton, Henry du Prè Labouchère, who was influential in Commons' debates. Labouchère would not be 'squared' and remained an opponent of Rhodes for many years. On the other hand, Rhodes had powerful supporters, including Lord Rothschild, son-in-law of Lord Rosebery who would soon become Prime Minister, and Sir Hercules Robinson, the man on the spot in Africa, who was busy gathering Colonial Office support.

On 30 April 1889, Rhodes, Beit and Rudd applied for a charter that would permit them not only to develop minerals in the area of Mashonaland, but also to extend the railways and telegraph lines northwards in order to encourage colonisation and promote trade and commerce in the area. On

Cecil Rhodes and Alfred Beit, founders of the BSAC. (Open source)

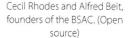

29 October 1889, almost a year after the signing of the Rudd Concession, Rhodes's company, the British South Africa Company (BSAC), was officially granted its Royal Charter by Queen Victoria.[4] The Concession's legitimacy was now safeguarded by the charter and, by extension, the British Crown, making it practically unassailable.[5] The charter came into effect in December 1889 and was initially meant to last for 25 years.

The charter empowered BSAC to treat with African rulers, own, manage, and grant or

---

3   Lockhart & Woodhouse, *Rhodes*, pp.159–161.
4   Rotberg, *The Founder*, pp.284–285.
5   Galbraith, *Crown and Charter*, p.86.

distribute land, and raise a police force (the British South Africa Police, BSAP). In return, 'The Company agreed to develop the territory it controlled; to respect existing African laws; to allow free trade within its territory and respect all religions'.[6] The charter attempted to ensure that the company developed peaceful relations with the local indigenous people, but it could make its own laws as long as they were approved of by the Secretary of State for the Colonies.[7] The British government used the charter as an opportunity to expand the empire at minimum cost but intended to retain overall control through its High Commissioner at Cape Town. The area concerned was known as 'Mashonaland' and bordered on Matabeleland.

While Rhodes's intrigues were progressing, there was also the need to ensure that Lobengula was still in agreement with the Concession, and to deliver the first batch of rifles. This would need a very capable ambassador, and Rhodes turned to his great friend, Dr Leander Starr Jameson, who had treated him during an illness and become his confidant. Jameson was described as a 'good surgeon, a man of charm, and a gambler', and these characteristics brought him into contact with the personalities of his age.[8] Good surgeons were scarce in Kimberley and his charm endeared him to the rich and adventurous. It is not clear whether Jameson was eager to go to GuBulawayo on this first trip (he had little experience of the native Africans) or whether he jumped at the chance. In February 1889, Jameson and Dr Frank Rutherfoord Harris undertook the hazardous two-month journey from Kimberley to GuBulawayo. Harris, who was to become Secretary of the BSAC in Kimberley, was a less than successful medical practitioner described as an 'incorrigible gas-bag'.[9] When the pair arrived on 2 April, they were greeted by James Maguire and Frank (Matabele) Thompson, Rudd's companions. The killing of Lotjie had made their lives in GuBulawayo even more precarious than normal. Jameson's role was to make sure that Lobengula did not repudiate the Concession and do all he could to assist the BSAC's occupation of Mashonaland. He also brought gold and 500 of the promised rifles in order to influence the King.

Discussions went very slowly regarding the establishment of a settlement in Mashonaland, which Lobengula claimed was part of his kingdom, and Jameson was forced to make two more journeys to meet with the King. On the final visit he was accompanied by a reluctant 'Matabele' Thompson, who had recently escaped from GuBulawayo, but was persuaded to return by Rhodes, who threatened not to pay Thompson what he was owed. However, Jameson's much-vaunted charm and his willingness to take risks were to pay off. Lobengula suffered from gout and Jameson successfully treated this with morphine. As Ash says, this was risky gamble as failure to provide effective treatment would probably have met with torture or worse.[10] The treatment was a success and endeared Jameson to Lobengula who even made him an

6   BSAC, *Rhodesia: South Africa Company 1892* (Cape Town: BDA, 1909).
7   Her Majesty's Government, *Charter of Incorporation*, 28 October 1889, Paragraph 10.
8   Millin, *Rhodes*, p.115.
9   Robert Blake, *History of Rhodesia* (London: Eyre Methuen, 1977), p.57.
10   Ash, *The If Man*, pp.79–80.

Induna and, during the awarding ceremony, gave him a black-plumed ostrich headdress, a shoulder cape, an ox-hide shield and two *assegais*.[11] In spite of this accolade, Jameson's discussions with Lobengula moved very slowly.

The Charter having been approved, the Colonial Office were determined to notify Lobengula with some ceremony and sent four soldiers from the Horse Guards, resplendent in their 'cuirassiers', with a coachload of gifts, to inform him.[12] Impressed by the soldiers' uniforms, Lobengula was convinced that Babayan had spoken the truth about what he had seen in England. Some of the *Matjaha* were less awestruck and thought that a warrior encasing himself in iron was a sign of a lack of courage. After a stay of some weeks, the soldiers departed, but not before their commander, Captain Victor Ferguson, presented Lobengula with his full-dress uniform.[13] Jameson, meanwhile, gained a remarkable success in his negotiations with the King. In order to begin mining in Mashonaland, Jameson had to persuade Lobengula to allow white settlers to enter the King's land. They would

Dr Leander Starr Jameson, friend and right-hand man of Cecil Rhodes. (Open source)

be in numbers and armed. Mashonaland had been chosen as a likely site for prospecting since it was some distance from GuBulawayo and away from AmaNdebele villages and thus less likely to experience a great deal of confrontation. The intrepid Jameson persuaded the suspicious Lobengula to agree and even to offer a group of AmaNdebele to work as labourers to construct a road upon which the group of prospectors and settlers, known as the 'Pioneers', could travel.[14] However, as happened many times before, Lobengula changed his mind when Jameson was absent and did not send men to help. They were provided instead by Khama, Chief of the BaNgwato, an enemy of Lobengula, who saw it as a method of limiting the AmaNdebele's king's power by assisting the white men to occupy part of his country.

Jameson set about raising a Pioneer Corps of 200 men both to construct the road and occupy Mashonaland. In doing so, Rhodes and Jameson sought advice from Frederick Courtenay Selous, an experienced big game hunter and acknowledged expert in all things African. Selous agreed to act as a guide and recommended that the Pioneers take a less direct route to Mashonaland that would avoid travelling through the Transvaal, the land of the Boers, and

---

11   G. Seymour Fort, *Dr Jameson* (London: Hurst & Blackett, 1903), p.89.

12   Captain V.J. Ferguson, Surgeon Major H.F. Melladew, Corporal Major White and Trooper Ross.

13   Robert Cary, *Charter Royal* (Cape Town: Howard Timmins, 1970), p.67.

14   Mason, *The Birth of a Dilemma*, pp.137–138; Peter Gibbs, *Blue and Gold: The History of the British South Africa Police, Vol. 1* (Salisbury: BSAP, 2009), pp.48–49.

a more direct route through Matabeleland. This was a fortunate decision since Lobengula's young men were angered at the prospect of an *Impi* of white men passing through their country.

The chosen route would require the construction of a road of some 460 miles long through forests, mountains, and swamps, along which a force of approximately 400 men would travel from the Macloutsie River to Mount Hampden.[15] Jameson hastily began assembling the Pioneers. They included farmers, miners, doctors, lawyers, cricket players, three parsons and a Jesuit.[16] They had all been promised 15 gold claims and a 3,000-acre farm, even though Lobengula had been told that they were only going to dig 'one hole'.[17]

The British government and the War Office were uneasy at the thought of a large body of Pioneers entering the hostile territories of Mashonaland and Matabeleland unprotected so Sir Henry Loch, High Commissioner for Southern Africa, put Rhodes under pressure to raise a force of 500 'police' who were in effect a troop of mounted infantry governed by military discipline that would eventually become the British South Africa Company Police. When Rhodes prevaricated, Loch threatened to revoke the charter which clearly indicates that it was the British government that demanded a military presence in Mashonaland, and it is possible that Rhodes resisted Loch's request because he did not wish the High Commissioner to interfere with the company's venture as well as increase the costs of the settlement. The officers of the BSAC Police were seconded from the British Army and their commander was Lieutenant Colonel Edward Graham Pennefather of the 6th Inniskilling Dragoons. He was an experienced 'Africa hand' and was described by Jameson as 'a capable fellow with plenty of dash'.[18] Pennefather was supported by his colourful adjutant, Captain Willoughby, who had dead-heated in the Derby. Willoughby was later to command the soldiers in the Jameson Raid, for which he was imprisoned.[19] The troops were well-paid, and this attracted a variety of recruits. 'Such a mixed lot I never saw in my life – from the aristocrat down to the street Arab, Peers and waifs.'[20] In spite of having such colourful characters as an unfrocked clergyman, a circus ringmaster, and an elderly survivor of the Charge of the Light Brigade, the majority of the troops were experienced soldiers in good physical shape, 'full of grit and dash'.[21] Marshal Hole agreed: 'No finer *corps d'elite* … had ever been raised.'[22] The same could not be said of the Pioneer

---

15 John Guille Millais, *Life of Frederick Courtenay Selous, D.S.O.* (New York: Longmans, Green & Co., 1919), p.177.

16 Lockhart & Woodhouse, *Rhodes*, p.180.

17 Mason, *The Birth of a Dilemma*, pp.142–143.

18 Ian Colvin, *The Life of Jameson* (London: Edward Arnold, 1922), Vol. 1, p.132.

19 See David Snape, *The Rescue They Called a Raid: The Jameson Raid 1895–96* (Warwick: Helion & Co., 2021).

20 Arthur Glyn Leonard, *How We Made Rhodesia* (London: Keegan Paul, Trench, Turner & Co., 1896), p.26.

21 Leonard, *How We Made Rhodesia*, p.79.

22 Hole, quoted in Lockhart & Woodhouse, *Rhodes*, p.180.

Officers of the Pioneer Column Corps. Left to right. Back row: Lt E. Farrell, Lt F. Mandy, Capt. A. Tabuteau, Lt J. Litchfield, Capt. J. Roach, Capt. H. Hoste, Lt H. Borrow, Capt. H. Campbell, Capt. R. Burnett, Rev. F. Surridge. Centre row: Lt W. Fry, Capt. A. Burnett, Capt. M. Heany, Maj. F. Johnson, Capt. F. Selous. Front row: Lt E. Tindale-Briscoe, Lt R. Nicholson, Lt R. Neale, Lt J. Brett. (Fry, *The Occupation of Mashonaland*)

Column's command structure. Although Major Frank Johnson was in charge, he was outranked by Pennefather. There was also Archibald Ross Colquhoun who was to be the Administrator of the soon to be occupied territory and the senior civil authority.[23]

As the Pioneer Column started to move, Lobengula again began to show signs of changing his mind and denied ever agreeing to allow the whites to enter his lands, and the King's mercurial character threatened to bring the whole project to a halt. Many of the natives hired to act as drivers and leaders of animals deserted in the face of a likely encounter with an AmaNdebele *Impi* which they felt was sure to attack the column once it entered Mashonaland. Jameson felt obliged to again to visit Lobengula, accused him of being a promise breaker and threatened a fight. Momentarily cowed, Lobengula denied that he had refused permission and Jameson returned to the column. There is little doubt that Jameson and Lobengula were friends of sorts, but the doctor demonstrated both his courage and powers of persuasion by tackling the African king in his own kraal in front of his *Indunas*. Lobengula, aware of what the British had done to the Zulus, was possibly afraid to confront them.

The column set off in June 1890 and continued without opposition but, on reaching the uplands, Pennefather was met with a message from Lobengula ordering him to go back. Lobengula, again wary of confronting the British, backed down once more and allowed the column to reach a spot that became known as 'Fort Salisbury'. Named for the British Prime Minister, which was

---

23   Colquhoun was a South African who had resigned from the Imperial Service having mixed up letters and sent the wrong one to his superior. It seems Rhodes liked this anecdote and offered Colquhoun a job.

an astute political move under the circumstances, Salisbury was to become the centre of future operations. The Pioneer Column had accomplished a prodigious feat and their efforts were described as 'a monument to British pluck and tenacity of purpose and the annals of British colonial history … can show nothing finer than this'.[24] Rhodes was reported to be the happiest man alive.

---

24   Howard Hensman, *History of Rhodesia: Compiled from Official Sources* (London: Blackwood, 1900), p.55.

4

The Way to War

Mashonaland was put under the jurisdiction of Sir Henry Loch, who had the authority to appoint all officials with legal powers. In practice, he simply endorsed the BSAC's nominees.[1] Colquhoun began to lay out the new town of Salisbury. The Shona people were pleased to have the Pioneers and the BSAC Police in their land as they hoped that they would provide protection against the AmaNdebele raids that Lobengula, as was customary, frequently ordered. Lobengula, on the other hand, believed that his authority over Mashonaland would continue unchanged in spite of the new arrivals. The raids against the Shona, which were a fundamental part of AmaNdebele life and a basis of Lobengula's power, would continue as before.

Colquhoun was not successful as Administrator and was quickly replaced by Jameson who had attempted to remain on good terms with Lobengula. However, in 1892, on the King's orders, two raids were made by AmaNdebele *Impis* on Mashonaland, but they had been given strict instructions not to harm any Europeans. Such raids heightened the fears of the Pioneers who, disappointed that there was little gold in Mashonaland, looked enviously on the rich grazing of Matabeleland and the possibility of lucrative cattle ranching. Their fears were further increased when, in 1891, Jameson reduced the protection available to them by decreasing the numbers of BSAP from 650 to 150 men. The BSAC was not making the profits it had expected to, and its shares were described as 'wastepaper'.[2] The reduction in the BSAC Police numbers was mainly to save money, but it also suggests that Jameson believed that his powers of persuasion would avoid serious conflict with Lobengula in the future. In order to the silence Pioneers' protests and form a sort of flimsy bulwark, Jameson raised the Mashonaland Horse – a group of volunteers who formed a 'paper regiment' but had little real interest in military duties.[3] Further problems occurred in December 1892 when the Shona cut the telegraph wires that linked Jameson in Salisbury to Rhodes in Cape Town. To the Shona, the 500 yards of copper wire made perfect body ornaments and although the wire was never recovered, it was quickly

---

1   Glass, *The Matabele War*, p.278.
2   Cloete, *African Portraits*, p.238.
3   Keppel-Jones, *Rhodes and Rhodesia*, p.325.

Sir Henry Loch. (*Review of Reviews*, 1891)

Archibald Ross Colquhoun, First Administrator of Mashonaland. (Open source)

established that the culprits had been led by a headman named Gomalla. The Shona were ordered by Jameson to hand over the offenders for trial or pay a hefty fine in cattle. They chose the latter, but the cattle with which they paid the fine belonged to Lobengula. The King, who had previously been informed of the crime, was assumed by Jameson not to have been involved but wanted Lobengula to use his influence to prevent any repetition.

Lobengula was on the horns of a dilemma. He claimed suzerainty over the Shona so could not let them steal from an ally or pay the fine with his cattle. The King's authority was further challenged by a second theft in May 1893. There followed another fine, again paid with the King's cattle. The situation was further complicated because the headman responsible craftily informed Lobengula that Jameson had simply taken the cattle in an attempt to divert the blame from his tribe for their loss. When Jameson realised who the cattle's real owner was, he ordered them returned and both cases of wire theft were settled in ways that maintained workable relations with the AmaNdebele rather than damaging them.[4] It is clear that up to this point at least Jameson was keeping within the rules set out by the charter. He did, however, make it clear that the border between Mashonaland and Matabeleland must be respected by both sides; neither the Pioneers nor the AmaNdebele *Impis* must cross it.

The idea that there was a border between Mashonaland and Matabeleland became a serious cause of controversy between Jameson and the King. Lobengula acknowledged the border as a demarcation line between

---

4   Glass, *The Matabele War*, p.66.

Mashonaland and Matabeleland but ignored it when it suited him. This greatly frustrated Jameson, who had on a number of occasions defended Lobengula's treatment of settlers who crossed into Matabeleland without permission. There seems to have been two views of the border.[5] Lobengula saw it as a line beyond which the settlers should not cross, while the doctor, on the other hand, saw it as the genuine limit of Lobengula's authority and a barrier for his *Impis*. There is some naivety in Jameson's view since the annual attacks by Matabele against Shona were a well-established tradition and important to maintaining Lobengula's position. Such was the 'disappointment' of the Shona that the settlers were content only to remonstrate against AmaNdebele atrocities; they vehemently protested that the Company had promised that

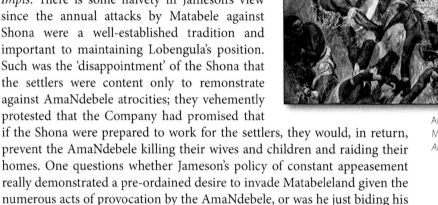

An AmaNdebele raid on the Mashona. (Creswicke, *South Africa and the Transvaal War*, Vol. 1)

if the Shona were prepared to work for the settlers, they would, in return, prevent the AmaNdebele killing their wives and children and raiding their homes. One questions whether Jameson's policy of constant appeasement really demonstrated a pre-ordained desire to invade Matabeleland given the numerous acts of provocation by the AmaNdebele, or was he just biding his time? His lack of punitive action, however, made him unpopular with the settlers and the Shona.[6]

Lobengula was clearly affronted by the 'theft' of his possessions, which implied he was being accused of stealing the wire and, unconvinced that Jameson would punish the culprits in the way he would expect, he sent a small *Impi* of 70 warriors in June 1893 to attack the kraal of the Shona Chief, Bere, whom Lobengula accused of stealing some of his cattle. Bere's kraal was some ten miles from Victoria, one of the first townships established in 1890 by the settlers who had been persuaded by The British South African Company to venture into Mashonaland. The arrival of this war party caused further panic among the Shona and the settlers alike. The local magistrate, Captain Lendy, with typical Victorian phlegm, and accompanied by three policemen, rode to investigate and discovered that the AmaNdebele had torched the kraal, killed a number of Shona, and seized the women and children.[7] Lendy and his small troop gave chase and the *Impi* scattered, claiming to have only intended to punish the Shona for stealing Lobengula's cattle and not to harm anyone else. Lendy acted with commendable restraint probably because of his precarious position and reminded the AmaNdebele that they must respect the border but exacted no punishment; it is true that

---

5   J.V. Woolford, 'The Matabele War', *History Today*, 28(8), 1978, p.541.

6   Gibbs, *A Flag for the Matabele*, p.12.

7   Captain Charles Frederick Lendy RA had been seconded to join the Pioneer Column and commanded an artillery platoon. When the column was disbanded, Lendy claimed his promised reward of land.

Captain Frederick Lendy RA, Commander of the Artillery in the Victoria Column. (Wills & Collingridge, *The Downfall of Lobengula*)

he was heavily outnumbered. Captives were freed but the cattle were not returned. Lendy reported the affair as an 'inter-tribal dispute in which it was not [his] business to interfere'.[8] There was no suggestion of 'recklessness and undue harshness' in Lendy's actions, which was an accusation that was to be made about him subsequently. Jameson described Lendy's treatment of the AmaNdebele as a 'judicious action'.[9] Again, if Rhodes and Jameson were really looking for an excuse to simply invade Matabeleland, it would seem that this was an opportunity missed.

It is possible that Lobengula genuinely believed that either the border was porous for his *Impis* or was simply unimpressed by the fact that the company had shown weakness in responding to the attack on Bere's kraal, which was extremely modest compared with the normal AmaNdebele response to offenders. It is also very possible that the King was conscious of the feelings of his younger warriors who blamed him for his lack of resolve when dealing with such outrages as the cattle theft by the Shona. In July he sent two more larger *Impis*, totalling 2,500 warriors, into the area surrounding Fort Victoria. They were also given instructions not to touch Europeans, but they took this not to include the Shona servants who worked for the Pioneers. The *Impis* scoured the district, killing, raping, and destroying property. 'The whole Country swarmed with them.'[10] They also collected cattle, some of which belonged to the white settlers, and when their terrified owners retreated to the safety of Fort Victoria, the AmaNdebele destroyed their empty farms.[11] This was the most serious raid so far and the AmaNdebele surrounded Victoria and 'swaggered through the streets with their bloody spears and rattling shields'.[12] Newton commented that as the AmaNdebele had taken cattle that were clearly the property of white settlers they must have known that there would be consequences.[13]

There is some suggestion that Lobengula attempted to forewarn Lendy and Jameson of his intentions, but it seems that his letters did not arrive in time for them to react. When they did arrive, however, it was clear from

---

8   Ash, *The If Man*, p.171.
9   Mason, *The Birth of a Dilemma*, p.156.
10   PA C 7555 I Report by Mr P.J. Newton upon the Circumstances Connected with the Collision between the Matabele and the Forces of the British South Africa Company at Fort Victoria in July 1893, p.4. (Henceforth Newton Report).
11   Cloete, *African Portraits*, p.238.
12   Melina Rorke, *Her Amazing Experiences in the Stormy Nineties of S. Africa's Story* (London: Harrap, 1939), p.120.
13   Newton Report, p.5.

the sights that greeted them that the border meant nothing to the King. Whatever his real intentions, Lobengula's warriors 'only' seemed to have committed atrocities within the confines of the town on the first day, 9 July, and subsequently turned their attention to the surrounding farms and kraals. On 10 July, the leader of the *Impi*, Manyao, entered Victoria to discuss removing the Shona fugitives who had sought sanctuary in the town. Lendy was absent and the company was represented by Charles Vigers, the resident Civil Commissioner. Vigers, keen to keep Manyao occupied until Lendy's return, treated the *Induna* with respect and showed him the guns available to the settlers that could be used against the *Impi* if necessary. In doing so, Vigers also allowed Manyao to see the very Shona he wanted to take, which proved they were there. When Lendy returned Manyao, perhaps aware of European sensibilities, offered to drag the Shona beyond the confines of the town and slaughter them out of sight in the bush. Lendy refused to accept this subterfuge and offered to try the culprits if Manyao was prepared to lay charges against them.[14] Unsurprisingly, Manyao refused Lendy's offer and left empty-handed to continue his carnage elsewhere.

Jameson, still in Salisbury, was somewhat sceptical of the seriousness of the affair and warned Lobengula that Lendy would demand the return of the stolen cattle and the *Impis* must return across the border. This demand was given a cutting edge by Jameson who said he would order Lendy to take his police and expel the *Impis*, no matter how numerous they might be.[15] His telegram said that if these demands were ignored, Lendy should demand restoration and use a display of force if necessary. However, Doctor Jim was aware of the cost and unexpected outcomes of combat – after all, Lendy had limited numbers at his command – so Jameson made it clear that he expected Lendy to use his tact 'to get rid of the Matabele without any actual collision'. Both these pieces of correspondence indicate that the policy of tolerance and appeasement continued if only to prevent excessive expenditure the company could ill afford.

Harris and Lendy tried to contradict any press reports about the AmaNdebele presence near Victoria they considered to be exaggerated. In 1892 *The Financial Times* had stated that: 'The Chartered Company is doing all in their power to provoke Lobengula.'[16] Opponents of the BSAC claim that Rhodes and Jameson were fortunate that the AmaNdebele were so obstinate that they wouldn't respond to Jameson's admonitions regarding their traditional behaviour in respect of such raids and were playing into their hands. Jameson's actions, however, seemed to be a further attempt to play down the negative impact of AmaNdebele raids on both public opinion and the company's investors. However, these attempts did little to reduce the fears of the settlers in Victoria who saw the company as being weak and ineffective

---

14   Newton Report, p.5.
15   Jameson's telegram to Rutherfoord Harris, 10 July 1893, quoted in Colonial Office, *South Africa: Copies and Extracts of Correspondence to the British South Africa Company in Mashonaland and Matabeleland* (London: HMSO, 1893), p.50.
16   L. Michell, *The Life and Times of the Rt Hon. Cecil John Rhodes* (London: Arnold, 1910), Vol. 2, p.85.

in protecting them. Jameson assured Rhodes that: 'The Victoria people have got the jumps. I hope to get rid of the Matabele without trouble.'[17]

Such was Jameson's confidence in Lendy's ability to handle the situation that it was not until the attacks had been running for three days that he decided to leave for Victoria. The journey was roughly 188 miles and, while on the road, Jameson was able to see the damage the *Impis* had inflicted on both the Shona's kraals and the settlers' farms. Victoria was in a poor state of military readiness; there were only seven police officers, but Lendy had recruited a force of 400 volunteers from among the settlers. The lack of horses, however, meant that this scratch force could only be used as infantry to defend the fort and not to drive the AmaNdebele away. Even the artillery had to be manoeuvred by hand. This poor state of affairs again questions whether Rhodes and Jameson were hell bent on genuine conquest, which might turn out badly and was sure to be expensive.

War was still not inevitable. Henry Loch enquired whether there would be enough ammunition if things deteriorated but Jameson replied that this was merely a raid against natives round Victoria and not against whites. 'I hope to get rid of them without trouble.'[18] Jameson seems to have decided that driving the AmaNdebele *Impis* back across the border was the priority and that Lobengula could be dealt with later according to whatever explanation he eventually offered for the attacks.[19]

When Jameson arrived in Victoria on 17 July, he called an *Indaba* (a council or conference) and sent for the AmaNdebele *Indunas*. The *Indaba* began with the usual courtesies, but Jameson made his possible intentions very clear as two Maxims and a Gatling gun were well in view of the AmaNdebele. They had previously been told to lay down their weapons before the *Indaba* could start and they had done so. Jameson told the *Indunas* that he was perfectly capable of keeping order in Mashonaland without AmaNdebele help; there was no need for them to send *Impis* to do so. Manyao, their leader, claimed that the Concession had only given the company the right to dig in Mashonaland and not to govern it: Lobengula was King of Mashonaland. Jameson, by lounging in a kitchen chair, displayed his coolness by asking Manyao whether he had, in fact, lost control of his men. Somewhat surprisingly, the *Induna* admitted that this was the case. This was an excellent riposte in an attempt to divert responsibilities for the atrocities since it suggested that the AmaNdebele hot heads were not acting under proper orders. During this exchange, Manyao's second in command, a much younger *Induna* named Umgandan, shouted at Jameson that he was following Lobengula's orders and would not be stopped by white men. Jameson ordered him to be silent and told him he 'only spoke with men, not boys'.[20] There is no doubting Jameson's bravery at his moment, even if supported by the Gatling gun.

17   Phillip B.S. Wrey, 'The Collision at Victoria', in Wills & Collingridge, *The Downfall of Lobengula*, p.60.
18   Wrey, 'The Collision at Victoria', p.60.
19   Wrey, 'The Collision at Victoria', p.60.
20   Colvin *The Life of Jameson*, Vol. I, p.254.

Jameson gave Manyao an hour to get his men moving towards the border or face being driven across, with the time period being explained by gesture. Umgandan, unbowed, shouted that they would have to be forcibly moved. The *Indaba* lasted around 20 minutes and afterwards Jameson and Lendy collected 40 mounted men with which to enforce the ultimatum. Captain Lendy's troop did not leave the fort until well after the expiry of the stipulated hour.[21] He was told to approach the *Impi* and, if it was on the move, drive it on, but if it had not done so, attack. After a few miles, Lendy surprised a large group, led by Umgandan, plundering and killing at a Mashona kraal. There was a brief exchange of shots and one of the first fatalities was Umgandan himself.[22] He was shot by Captain Bastard who kept Umgandan's shield and *assegai* as a souvenir.[23] The warrior's head was presented to Dr Brett, who had the flesh boiled off it.[24] The remaining AmaNdebele fled but Lendy, suspicious of a trap, did not follow.

Jameson's *Indaba* at Victoria. (Wills & Collingridge, *The Downfall of Lobengula*)

Captain Lendy's actions came under scrutiny almost immediately. He claimed he had been fired upon and had simply returned fire. There were also accusations that the Shona had killed a wounded AmaNdebele and that a captured AmaNdebele had been shot by an English officer. Such accusations were given very short shrift by the Colonial Office, but it did think an official inquiry was required. Lendy's actions were examined by the Newton Commission that was held in 1894 and charged with discovering what happened at the *Indaba*. It addressed whether the AmaNdebele had been given a fair time to retire, whether they had fired first and whether Lendy's men had killed a AmaNdebele who was in the act of surrendering.[25]

The mention of the commission is important since its findings had relevance to Jameson's intentions regarding war with the AmaNdebele. The Newton Commission concluded that the AmaNdebele had been given sufficient time to begin heading for the border, and that Lendy's men had been the first to fire but had ceased fire immediately the order was given and did not pursue the enemy on horseback. The commission also concluded that there was no evidence to support the claim that a AmaNdebele was shot while surrendering.[26] The attack was well ordered, executed, and a successful

---

21 Hans Sauer, *Ex Africa* (London: G. Bles, 1937), p.222. Newton states that it was 1¾ hours (Newton Report, p.6).
22 Keppel-Jones, *Rhodes and Rhodesia*, p.243.
23 Roger Marston, *Own Goals, National Pride and Defeat in War: The Rhodesia Experience* (Rothersthorpe: Paragon, 2010), p.57.
24 Thomas Victor Bulpin, *The White Whirlwind* (London: Nelson, 1961), p.185.
25 Francis James Newton, Resident Commissioner in Bechuanaland, 1895–1897.
26 Newton Report.

dismounted action – not a blood bath as Jameson's opponents claimed. Lendy, whose account was utterly believed by Jameson, was unable to defend his claim of being fired upon as, before the commission met, he died through over-vigorous attempts to put the shot.

There seems little doubt that the Shona, whose kraals had been burned, women and children captured, and cattle stolen were much less magnanimous than Captain Lendy had been. It was they who killed a number of AmaNdebele, mutilated Umgandan's body and generally enjoyed the defeat of their traditional enemies. The white settlers were even less reassured after the marauding *Impi* had returned to GuBulawayo. 'Everybody is for declaring for war, and the only fear expressed is that the matter may be smoothed over.'[27] In Victoria, after a public meeting, a committee was appointed to tell Jameson that they did not believe that Lobengula would ever keep his word and they would either leave the settlement or solve the AmaNdebele problem themselves. On hearing Lendy's exaggerated claim to have killed 300 AmaNdebele, Jameson is said to have responded, 'I hereby declare war on the Matabele.'[28]

27   *Glasgow Herald*, 12 September 1893
28   Ivon Fry's account, quoted in Keppel-Jones, *Rhodes and Rhodesia*, p.244. Fry was one of Lendy's men and his memoirs, although written long after the event, nevertheless give the spirit of the time.

5

The March of the Columns

Jameson realised that appeasing the AmaNdebele was no longer an option. The settlers, upon whom the new territory depended, were close to leaving or refusing to accept the BSAC's authority. Both Rhodes and Jameson were acutely aware that the value of BSAC shares was under threat and their plans to expand the British Empire in Southern Africa were beginning to flounder. Lobengula seemed unwilling or unable to control his young men, who saw the BSAC's protection of the Mashona people as a challenge to their traditional way of life and a threat to the prosperity of their nation. It would be impossible for Rhodes, with his belief in the superiority of the British nation, to ignore AmaNdebele behaviour or to expect the settlers to tolerate what they saw as AmaNdebele barbarism.

Jameson was genuinely reluctant to go to war. He had tried to avoid a major conflict in the face of considerable provocation and even attempted to support Lobengula when he felt the King was in the right. The final 500 rifles of the Rudd Concession had been delivered to Lobengula in June 1893, only a month before the Umgandan incident. There had been no plans for a major conflict, not least because the military strength available to Jameson was small when compared to the huge numbers of AmaNdebele warriors at Lobengula's command. After all, Jameson had recently reduced the numbers of the BSAC Police, and Lendy's patrol of 70 men consisted of almost half of those troopers available after their numbers had been reduced from 650 in 1891. The Mashonaland Horse was really a group of Friday-night soldiers drawn to military glamour rather than its discipline.[1] There were only roughly 100 riding horses in Mashonaland and only 38 of these were in the proximity of Victoria.[2] There have been suggestions from both Jameson's contemporaries such as Henry de la Prè Labouchère,[3] owner of the inappropriately named *The Truth*, and more recently from organisations

---

1   G.H. Tanser, *A Scantling of Time: The Story of Salisbury, Rhodesia (1890–1900)* (Salisbury: Stuart Manning, 1965), p.88.

2   Mason, *The Birth of a Dilemma*, p.164; Frederick Courtenay Selous, 'Introductory Review of the War', in Wills & Collingridge, *The Downfall of Lobengula*, p.4

3   Labouchère was MP for Northampton. Between 1893 and 1894, he asked questions and made speeches in the House of Commons that were critical of the BSAC's involvement in Mashonaland and the First Matabele War on no less than 21 occasions.

such as '*The Rhodes Must Fall*' movement that Jameson was on the lookout for an armed conflict even though at this stage of his career he had little if any military experience.[4]

Jameson needed the official support of Sir Henry Loch and the British government since what he intended to do was in fact a declaration of war against a nation that had been officially recognised by Britain. On 18 July Jameson spent several hours in telegraphic correspondence with his chief, Cecil Rhodes, and Sir Henry Loch. Jameson had previously been told by Hans Sauer, another pioneering medical man, that the local Boers, who were fighters experienced in native skirmishes, believed that only 700–1,000 men would be required to conquer Matabeleland.[5] Rhodes was somewhat cautious and suggested that even 1,000 Britishers would not be sufficient to tackle Lobengula's 20,000 warriors.[6] In one of the telegraphic exchanges, Rhodes asked Jameson to read Luke 14:31, a verse in the Bible suggesting that it is foolish to attack a large force with a much smaller force.

George Robinson, 1st Marquess of Ripon and Colonial Secretary. (Open source)

The BSAC had little cash to spend on a war as it had already spent vast sums of money on acquiring Mashonaland. Loch was in favour of putting an end to AmaNdebele raids and taking over Lobengula's country, and in a telegram to Jameson on 24 July he told the doctor that he could 'rest assured that the authorities were fully alive to the urgency of the situation and will not be backward in taking action in order to preserve both the present and future safety of the country'.[7] Loch was able to persuade a reluctant government to support and partially fund a war against the AmaNdebele and gave Jameson permission to prepare. Lord Ripon, the Colonial Secretary, made it clear that the government was the senior partner in this venture, and nothing should be done without Loch's permission.[8]

It took Jameson a relatively long time to get things ready – not least because of the need to obtain many additional horses, repair saddles which were kept in store, and obtain enough waggons to carry supplies and ammunition. His plan was to attack GuBulawayo with three columns of troops approaching from three different British settlements: Salisbury, Victoria, and Tuli. He was assisted in these preparations at Salisbury by Major Patrick Forbes, second in

4   Meredith, *Diamonds, Gold and War*, p.280.
5   Sauer, *Ex Africa*, p.224.
6   Hensman, *History of Rhodesia*, p.80.
7   Newton Report, p.123.
8   Hensman, *History of Rhodesia*, p.82.

Hiram Stevens Maxim and his machine gun. (Open source)

command of the BSAC Police, who was described as 'a typical British bulldog with as much sense'.[9] In order to get volunteers for this dangerous venture, and because money was short, recruits were only offered 7/6d a day, and promised that their existing claims in Mashonaland would be protected until six months after the war. They were also offered a farm of 6,000 acres, 20 gold claims in Matabeleland and a share in half of the cattle captured.[10]

Despite this potential generosity Forbes was only able to recruit sufficient men to form three troops which were to become known as the 'Salisbury Column'.[11] Forbes was able to obtain a significant amount of firepower consisting of a 7-pounder cannon and a Nordenfeldt[12] as well as a galloping Maxim,[13] which he regarded as a clumsy weapon. It was the Maxim that proved key to the future confrontations with the AmaNdebele.

While Forbes was busy in Salisbury, Jameson was making similar preparations in Victoria. Lendy had declined the offer of commanding the Victoria Column in preference to being in charge of the artillery that was to accompany it, so Jameson chose Captain (later Major) Allan Wilson to take over.[14] The size of this column (414 men) meant that only 170 men could be

---

9   Rotberg, *The Founder*, p.313. Much later, after the war was over, Forbes was described by a reporter from the *African Review* as being 'short, squat with a very strong physique and a martial air … a stout, strong travelled stained soldier of a useful type'.

10   Charles H.W. Donovan (*With Wilson in Matabeleland: Or Sport and the War in Zambesia* (London: Henry & Co., 1894), p.203) suggests that the unmounted men from Johannesburg, who had been recruited by Sir Henry Loch to join the invasion, were only offered five shillings.

11   P.W. Forbes, 'Organising the Forces', in Wills & Collingridge, *The Downfall of Lobengula*, p.66. See Appendix V.

12   The Nordenfeldt was a multiple-barrelled gun that was fired by pulling a lever back and forth. The ammunition was gravity-fed through chutes for each barrel.

13   A type of belt-fed machine gun with the capability of firing up to 600 rounds per minute.

14   Wilson was born in Glen Urquhart, Scotland, in 1856 and emigrated to South Africa in 1878 after completing his apprenticeship as a bank clerk. He joined the Cape Mounted Riflemen and was discharge after three years with the rank of Sergeant. He then became a gold prospector and trader, and later joined the Basuto Police. Returning to the search for gold he joined the

Major Allan Wilson. (*Illustrated London News*, 6 January 1894)

mounted, and the shortage of horses also affected the third column at Tuli. The Victoria Column also had the benefit of an artillery troop, commanded by Captain Lendy, who was an ex-Royal Artillery officer who clearly felt more at home with his guns than leading a larger body of men.

Forbes' original plan was that the three columns would operate separately and approach GuBulawayo from different directions which, he hoped, would weaken AmaNdebele morale as they would have to fight on three fronts in order to defend the approach to the King's kraal. However, should they retreat towards it, this would mean that the three columns would be able to come together and concentrate on this major target. The biggest worry was that the *Impis* would withdraw and take up a strong defensive position that could only be taken by a direct assault, which might be hindered by the coming rains. Forbes conjectured that the AmaNdebele felt they were so strong numerically that they would not use such a defensive tactic but rather attack the columns directly and consequently suffer large numbers of casualties from the rifle and Maxim fire the troopers would bring to bear.[15]

The AmaNdebele army consisted of 20 *Impis* but these were of varying quality. The constant attacks on neighbouring peoples resulting in the capture of boys and women to provide male offspring who, when grown, would join the *Impis* seems to have diluted the fighting spirit of the AmaNdebele. They had also recently suffered from an outbreak of smallpox that cost many lives.[16] However, in spite of a dilution of fighting qualities and the decline in numbers, the AmaNdebele still possessed a massive numerical superiority. Despite Rudd's 1,000 rifles, most AmaNdebele warriors fought with the *assegai* and carried a cowhide shield, and their tactics, similar to that of the Zulus, involved approaching the enemy as quickly as possible and engaging in hand-to-hand combat.

The Salisbury Column with Forbes at their head left town at 1500 hours on 5 September to the hearty cheering of the inhabitants and under the lenses of several photographers. It headed towards Fort Charter where it

Bechuanaland Exploration Society as Chief Inspector and was sent to Fort Victoria as its representative. As Forbes ('Organising the Forces', p.70) comments: 'Wilson had seen a considerable amount of service in the native wars in the colony.' Wilson was described as 'a man among men, tall, square-shouldered, and fine looking with a heavy moustache' who never drank anything other than ginger ale (Neville Jones, *Rhodesian Genesis* (Bulawayo: Rhodesia Pioneers' and Early Settlers' Society, 1953, p.82). Clearly this was somewhat unusual in a place and time when heavy drinking was often the norm. On the outbreak of the war, Wilson was promoted to major and began training the Victoria Column of 414 men.

15   Forbes, 'Organising the Forces', p.75.
16   Keppel-Jones, *Rhodes and Rhodesia*, p.251.

would pick up the extra horses.[17] The column was slow-moving and made about 12 miles a day, taking six days to complete the journey. Forbes found that only 59 horses had arrived and many of them had horrible sores on their backs because they had been poorly ridden on the journey from Victoria by men who he judged not able to distinguish between a cow and a horse.[18] There had originally been 171 horses but over 30 percent of them became sick or disabled and it was not until 22 September that a further 109 horses arrived, thereby enabling the Salisbury Column to be fully mounted.

Major Wilson and Dr Jameson organised the Victoria Column in a similar manner but were also delayed by the lack of sufficient horses as well as the extra 150 men Jameson had organised to come from Johannesburg.

The Tuli Column, or Southern Column, commanded by Major Hamilton Goold-Adams, head of the BBP, and Commandant Pieter Raaff,[19] a Boer, of the Raaff Rangers, was also delayed because of a shortage of horses. Khama, King of the BaNgwato, who had been an enemy of Lobengula for some years, also offered 150 of his men to join this invasion force which was to be the largest of the three columns consisting of 130 mounted men and 1,000–1,800 on foot. Hensman indicates that there were an additional 400 Africans in the Tuli Column, which suggests that some Shona were also willing to take revenge against the AmaNdebele.[20] Half of these warriors were armed with Martini-Henry rifles.[21] It seems that Raaff's instructions from Rhodes and Jameson was to delay the Southern Column's departure to ensure that the BSAC forces from Salisbury and Victoria reached GuBulawayo first.[22] The column played a fairly insignificant role in the invasion of Matabeleland, being somewhat hampered by Sir Henry Loch's instructions that it should only act in defence.

It was decided, in spite of Forbes' original plan, that the Salisbury and Victoria Columns should combine, probably because it was finally realised that they would be vastly outnumbered by the AmaNdebele. Forbes proposed that Jameson, the military amateur, had important input into this decision, which suggests that the doctor saw his role as more than a civil servant. A similar problem was to arise during the Jameson Raid when Jameson initially ignored the advice of his military commander, Sir John Willoughby.[23] Captain Willoughby was also to be Jameson's military adviser in this venture, and he

Major Patrick Forbes Leader of the Column. (Wills and Collingridge)

---

17 Forbes, 'Organising the Forces', p.71.
18 Forbes, 'Organising the Forces', pp.72–73.
19 Raaff had served with distinction in the Zulu War and was the Resident Magistrate in Tuli.
20 Hensman, *History of Rhodesia*, p.86.
21 'Goold-Adams Report, 21 November–18 November 1893', in Wills & Collingridge, *The Downfall of Lobengula*, p.217.
22 Ash, *The If Man*, p.192.
23 Snape, *The Rescue They Called a Raid*, pp.66–67.

Some of the officers of the Victoria Column
Left to right: standing: Lt Stottard, Capt. Judd, Maj. Wilson, Capt. Napier, Capt. Fitzgerald. Lt Hamilton, Lt Williams;
seated: Lt Simpson, Adj. Kennelly.
(Wills & Collingridge, *The Downfall of Lobengula*)

and the doctor arrived in Fort Charter to inspect the preparations Forbes had made and agree a joint strategy for the Victoria and Salisbury Columns. Jameson and Willoughby returned to Victoria to inform the waiting Wilson about the new plan.

These somewhat lethargic preparations had not escaped Lobengula's notice as he had used spies to discover what the whites intended. Since it was clear that some form of military invasion was planned, the King employed four somewhat opposing strategies in response: first, he used his wizards to 'doctor' the roads in the hope that magic would slow down the columns' advance; second, he began assembling his *Impis*; third, he attempted to appeal directly to Queen Victoria and chose Mshete, who had been a member of the earlier delegation, to do so; and finally, he sent one of his half-brothers, Ingugbogubo, together with two *Indunas* – Mantusa, commander of the Mabokotivani *Impi* and Inguba of the Matchovini – accompanied by the trader James Dawson, who was to act as interpreter, to journey to Palapye where the Reverend John Moffat, Assistant Commissioner and friend of Lobengula, resided to ask that two white men return with them to GuBulawayo to investigate the border outrages in which Lobengula continued to strongly deny involvement.[24] This mission was in response to a

Sir John Willoughby, Jameson's chief staff officer, wearing his Sudan Medal and Khedive's Star. (*Illustrated London News*, 1896)

---

24   PA C 284, Correspondence Respecting the Death of Two Indunas at Tati, October 1893. No. 3 Enclosure 6. Moffat to Loch including Ingubogubo's Statement, 24 October 1893

letter from Henry Loch that invited Lobengula to discuss how things might be resolved peacefully.

What happened next was subject to an official inquiry ordered by Sir Henry Loch and carried out by his military secretary Major Sawyer.[25] Both Lord Ripon and Sir Henry were aware of public opinion in certain quarters that was volubly in support of the AmaNdebele. Although these were events that happened thousands of miles away from Britain, the British people were not unaware of the goings-on in Matabeleland. Lobengula had sent ambassadors to Queen Victoria at Windsor Castle complaining about the numerous Britons who were coming to his country attempting to exploit his kingdom, and this visit had been reported in the popular press and received with some sympathy.

The tragedy began when Dawson and the three *Indunas* arrived at Tati at 1600 hours on 18 October and dismounted in the mine's yard which was about a mile from Major Goold-Adams's camp across the Tati River. Goold-Adams was present in the yard and talking to William Kirkby, the Tati mine manager. Dawson was surprised to find a military camp at Tati and, although he spoke to Goold-Adams, he did not realise that he was the officer in charge, and so did not explain the reason for the presence of the three AmaNdebele *Indunas*. Instead, Dawson asked Alfred Taylor, the Tati mine's foreman, to take charge of the three envoys.[26] Tired and thirsty after his long ride, Dawson then left the yard accompanied by his old friend Frederick Selous, who was acting as scout for the column, to obtain refreshments and they were later joined by Kirby at dinner.[27]

The *Indunas* were sensitive regarding their status as envoys of Lobengula and conscious of their authority as military commanders so did not appreciate the dismissive way in which they were being treated. They refused to answer questions about the reason why they had come to Tati and their behaviour, especially in the case of Mantusa, was very arrogant. Kirby, frightened by their demeanour, sent Taylor to fetch the colonel and, shortly afterwards, Goold-Adams arrived and instructed the foreman to disarm the *Indunas* and, with the help of some troopers, the AmaNdebele were marched across the Tati River to Goold-Adams' camp where they were told they would be interrogated the next morning. Goold-Adams, again, using a trooper as interpreter, addressed the envoys saying that no harm would come to them unless they tried to escape whereupon they would be shot. Corporal Horace Harboard, part of the picket occupying the yard, allocated Troopers Knox, Griffiths and Leroux as their guards. The time was around 1845 hours and Dawson was still enjoying his dinner.

The *Indunas* were increasingly indignant at the treatment they had received and suddenly, without warning, Mantusa snatched a bayonet from Knox's scabbard and stabbed Griffiths in the chest. He then stabbed Corporal Harboard in the shoulder and attempted to escape. Knox, recovering from

25 Glass, *The Matabele War*, p.200.
26 Glass, *The Matabele War*, p.200.
27 Frederick Courtney Selous has been suggested as H. Rider Haggard's inspiration for his character Alan Quartermain.

the shock of the attack, shot Mantusa in the back as he was running away, killing him instantly. Inguba, seeing his chance, also attempted to escape and but was clubbed about the head with a rifle by Griffiths and died of his injuries shortly afterwards. Lobengula's brother, Ingubogubo, made no attempt to run as he seemed 'thunderstruck at the whole fatal occurrence'.[28] One version of the events suggests that it was after the two *Indunas* had attempted to escape that the King's half-brother was immediately bound hand and foot. However, Ingubogubo's version was that it was the sight of him being bound that prompted Mantusa to react so violently.[29]

Meanwhile, having finished his meal, Dawson started to go to Goold Adams' camp but before he arrived, he was told that something serious had occurred in the yard. During his evidence to Sawyer, Dawson claimed that this was the first time he had heard that the *Indunas* had been physically detained. Kirby refuted Dawson's statement, however, by saying that he had told him of the *Induna*'s detention, and they had discussed it at dinner.

Lieutenant Colonel Hamilton Goold-Adams when Governor of Queensland, 1915. (Open source)

The following day, another three AmaNdebele post boys were shot in suspicious circumstances while attempting to escape. After interviewing witnesses, Sawyer concluded that no one was to blame for the deaths of the AmaNdebele.[30] Sawyer, perhaps sensitive to critics such as Labouchère, also felt that while there was no actual evidence that either the *Indunas* or the post boys were attempting to escape, it was reasonable to assume that they were doing so in order to pass on information about the Tuli Column to the AmaNdebele *Impis*.[31] Sawyer concluded that it was the delay in bringing the three *Indunas* to Goold-Adams while Dawson was taking refreshment to which the 'subsequent deplorable occurrences may chiefly be attributed'.[32] This seems a little unfair on Dawson's need for refreshment, but Goold-Adams, whose orders led to their deaths, concurred and even Dawson agreed that if anyone was to blame, it was he.[33] Glass has suggested that the real blame should rest on the shoulders of Kirby, who had taken fright at the sight of armed AmaNdebele in his yard and called for Goold-Adams, whose treatment of the AmaNdebele

28   Norris Newman, *Matabeleland and How We Got It*, p.106. Ingubogubo was actually being held by an NCO so was not free to runaway unhindered.
29   Glass, *The Matabele War*, p.201.
30   PA C 7284, W.H. Sawyer's Report upon the Circumstances Leading to the Death of Indunas on 18 October 1893. Dated 9 January 1894, p.10. Henceforth Sawyer Report.
31   Sawyer Report.
32   Sawyer Report, p.11.
33   Glass, *The Matabele War*, p.203.

led to their deaths.[34] Lobengula realised that his attempts to prevent a major collision were doomed to failure no matter what he did but, in fairness to Jameson, these attempts could be seen just another example of Lobengula's vacillations.

On 2 October the Salisbury Column left Fort Charter and made slow progress towards Matabeleland. Forbes took the precaution of sending out scouts to obtain information about the AmaNdebele *Impis'* movements, but none was available. The column moved on, but Forbes returned to Fort Charter on 4 October to discuss further developments via telegraph with Allan Wilson who was still at Fort Victoria.[35] Wilson indicated that the last of his column was about to leave and since the plan was that the Victoria Column and the Salisbury Column would combine, Wilson and Forbes agreed that they would meet at Iron Mine Hill, which was roughly halfway to GuBulawayo, and 75 miles from Fort Charter and 86 miles from Fort Victoria.

The Salisbury Column set off again on 6 October but having found that the road passed through some densely wooded areas and being

A glamourised depiction of troopers from the Salisbury Column waiting to move from Fort Charter. (Wills & Collingridge, *The Downfall of Lobengula*)

wary of attack, Forbes decided that it should proceed in a more direct line across open country. Jameson's orders, which Forbes had received at Fort Charter, indicated that he should proceed towards GuBulawayo, that the Tuli Column under Goold-Adams was underway and that Jameson would be with it until it reached GuBulawayo. Forbes swiftly began to move forward, and the Salisbury Column travelled 10–12 miles a day in two stages to avoid the midday heat. Although it was the dry season there were heavy showers, which indicated that the columns should move as quickly as possible while they could.

On 9 October Forbes reached the Umniati River, which was the physical boundary between Mashonaland and Matabeleland.[36] The river was very shallow, and the column had little difficulty crossing it with the assistance of the accompanying natives who cut shallow paths through its bank. Aware that they were now in AmaNdebele country, Forbes sent out scouting parties. One party, under Captain Owen Williams, was to explore the country down towards the waggon road to see if an *Impi* was attempting to move towards Salisbury now that it was almost completely depleted of defenders, while the other party was to scout towards the Iron Mine Hills to detect any opposition as well as find the best route for the column. Forbes and his main party crossed another river, the Umvumi. The scouting party from Iron Mine Hills

---

34 Stafford Glass, 'James Dawson, Rhodesian Pioneer', *Rhodesiana*, 16, July 1967, p.73.
35 Fort Charter was to remain the nearest telegraph line to GuBulawayo throughput the war.
36 Now the Munyati River.

returned on the evening of 12 October with native guides who reported that there were no AmaNdebele in the vicinity. On 14 October, as agreed, the Salisbury Column laagered at the Iron Mine Hills, named after the numerus mine workings in the area. Forbes went up the hill and tried to contact the Victoria Column by heliograph but failed, and although Forbes was looking over a flat plain Wilson's men could not yet be seen.

There was a large herd of cattle in the area, however, some of which had been stolen from Victoria, and Forbes felt that recapturing the cattle would be a useful activity while awaiting Wilson's arrival. One should not be surprised at Forbes' decision since cattle were symbols of AmaNdebele wealth as well as being one of the inducements to encourage the volunteers to join the columns. While gathering this information, the Victoria Column's scouts arrived, accompanied by Jameson and Lieutenant Colonel Willoughby. Forbes sent out a party of 60 men to capture the cattle and they were accompanied by Jameson and Willoughby. The doctor was never one to miss an opportunity. The party captured over 3,000 cows and their calves and began to make their way back to the camp. Shortly afterwards, Forbes who had ridden forward, encountered a small group of armed AmaNdebele who remained at a distance. Forbes, concerned that there might be a large *Impi* close by, made his way back towards the Iron Mine Camp taking care to watch whether he was being followed. It was when Forbes returned to the camp that he found that a disaster had happened.

The main body of his men who were returning with the cattle had been ambushed by some AmaNdebele hiding behind rocks. During the ensuing skirmish, Captain John Campbell was shot in the left thigh.[37] The wounded Campbell was helped to return to the camp and Jameson, with the assistance of two other medical men, successfully amputated the leg at the hip joint which had been completely shattered. Campbell, however, did not recover and died the next day.[38] He was given a funeral with full military honours and the service was conducted by the Right Reverend George Wyndham Hamilton Knight-Bruce, Bishop of Mashonaland, who left a description of the events:

> This afternoon Captain Campbell died. Humanly speaking, his reckless courage cost him his life, and he rode nearly two miles with his hipbone badly broken. I was thankful to have got here, and to be with him, though I had no idea the end was so near. About five hundred men attended the funeral; three volleys were fired, and I said a few words.[39]

---

37   John Alexander Livingstone Campbell was born in Argyllshire, Scotland, in January 1865. He joined the Royal Artillery in 1876 and retired in 1888. Realising that the BSAC would offer good prospects to an ex-military man, Campbell joined the company as a mining inspector in the Lo Mogunda Goldfield District and was then appointed its magistrate. When the columns were assembled, Campbell was quick to volunteer to join the Salisbury Horse as ordinance officer.

38   P.W. Forbes, 'Leaving Mashonaland for the Front', in Wills & Collingridge, *The Downfall of Lobengula*, pp.92–93

39   G.W.H. Knight-Bruce, *Memories of Mashonaland* (London: Edward Arnold, 1895), p.244.

Forbes was somewhat more thoughtful: 'I think there were a good many standing around the grave that evening who realised for the first time that what we had undertaken was no child's play, but stern reality, and that poor Campbell's fate might at any time be the fate of one or all of us.'[40]

Campbell was the first of the party to die, but Forbes was relieved when Williams's scouting party returned unharmed, having not discovered large numbers of AmaNdebele advancing on Salisbury.

40   Wills & Collingridge, *The Downfall of Lobengula*, p.245.

6

Major Wilson and the Victoria Column

Having taken command of the Victoria Column, Major Wilson began ensuring that these amateur soldiers were properly drilled, organised and instructed while Lendy concentrated on organising the artillery consisting of Maxims, a 7-pounder, and Hotchkiss guns.[1] On 5 October having received a stirring address from Jameson, who had the 'remarkable gift of being able to say the right thing and no more', they marched out of Victoria to join up with the Salisbury Column.[2] Many of the Mashona kraals provided provisions for the column as it made its way towards Matabeleland, possibly to prevent the whites from 'looting', but also to demonstrate their support of its mission to punish the marauding AmaNdebele, the signs of whose attacks were visible to the marching men.[3] The first part of the column's journey was on the main 'road', and it then turned off across country as the way became difficult for the heavy waggons.

On 14 October, the Victoria Column heard that there were five AmaNdebele *Impis* in the area and began to take greater precautions as it moved. Consequently, Wilson ordered his men to take extra care and remain within the column's laager at night. Large numbers of armed natives passed the troopers, seemingly on their way deeper into Matabeleland with warlike intentions, but soon returned travelling in the opposite direction back towards Mashonaland. Donovan claims that the only natives who actively engaged in the upcoming fighting were the levies provided by King Khama.[4]

During their march, the Victoria Column was guided by Selous and a AmaNdebele *Induna* named Man-yéze who had once been a powerful adviser to Lobengula. However, as often occurred when the King began to fear that an *Induna's* influence and status had reached a threatening level, Lobengula had the old man's family and followers slaughtered, his cattle confiscated, and his kraal destroyed. Man-yéze offered his services to Jameson and

---

1   Another form of rapid-fire gun.
2   Donovan, *With Wilson in Matabeleland*, p.190.
3   Donovan, *With Wilson in Matabeleland*, p.203.
4   Donovan, *With Wilson in Matabeleland*, p.211.

supported Matabele Wilson as a useful guide since the *Induna* 'knew every stick and stone in the country'.[5]

The Victoria Column arrived at Iron Mine Hills on 16 October after minimum difficulty but Forbes, who was in overall command, decided to keep the two columns several hundred yards apart while on the march as he was worried about his seniority since Wilson was also a Major and the Victoria Column was the larger of the two. The two groups did, however, camp side by side in the evening to provide mutual protection. Forbes need not have feared as he was quickly acknowledge as being in overall command after making an ultimatum that Wilson and Lendy either accept him as leader or they should return home. The Honourable Captain Charles White was in charge of the scouts and Lendy of the combined artillery.[6]

The Victoria Column was given little time to rest as Forbes ordered the now-designated 'Combined Column' to set off on the following day and advance towards the place where the Salisbury men had captured the cattle. Friendly natives told Forbes that they had seen small numbers of AmaNdebele but were not aware if there were any *Impis* in the area. The Combined Column continued their march the next day but were hindered by having to cross several streams, one of which, the Umgusa, had very steep banks that the waggons could not safely descend so time was spent finding suitable drifts or passing places through which to cross.[7]

Moving a horse-drawn Maxim across a drift. (*The Graphic*, 1893)

The two sections of the Combined Column were now forced to divide, having found two drifts about a mile apart and had to laager separately as a result. Shortly after leaving the Iron Mine Camp many Mashona arrived to join the column. They had been recruited on the instructions of Major Wilson by Arnold and Quested, who were well known among the Shona. The total number of Africans involved was now 900. The relationship between the various groups of Mashona was not always amicable and they often set up separate laagers. These new arrivals were deployed to drive the increasing number of cattle the columns had captured.

Wilson's ever-vigilant scouts fanned out while the Victoria Column was preparing to laager and claimed to see, on a group of hills to their front, a large mass of AmaNdebele, which they estimated to number around 4,000. Wilson ordered this news to be carried to Forbes' Column, which, like that of Wilson, deployed the various machine guns covering the valleys that led

5   Donovan, *With Wilson in Matabeleland*, pp.215–216.
6   Norris Newman, *Matabeleland and How We Got It*, p.90.
7   Now the Umguza River.

to the river down which the AmaNdebele would have to approach the two camps. However, the scouts had been mistaken; they had confused Mashona for AmaNdebele as well as greatly exaggerating their numbers.

On the evening of 19 October, another scouting party under the command of Captain Williams almost stumbled onto the military kraal of the Insukameni *Impi* around which there were roughly 60 AmaNdebele who were attending to a large heard of cattle. They also observed a considerable number of warriors within the kraal itself. Sensibly, the scouting party withdrew and returned to inform the Combined Column the following evening.[8] A somewhat top-heavy probing force of 120 men with two Maxims was organised, commanded by Wilson and accompanied by Jameson and Willoughby, which set off to at midnight to attack and destroy the kraal but when they arrived, they found it deserted. Forbes had wanted to lead the force, but Jameson insisted he should stay with the main body – a fact that suggests that Jameson was the real person in charge. Forbes comments on Jameson's desire to constantly put himself in harm's way whenever the opportunity arose despite military advice to the contrary.[9]

The AmaNdebele had obviously foreseen the possibility of a night-time attack on the kraal and retreated into the bush. The party took a few prisoners and burned the kraal, which was quite new and capable of holding up to 3,000 warriors. It is interesting that, when describing the kraal, Donovan comments that it was built on a reef that had indications of gold – the real reason for the BSAC's interest in Matabeleland.[10] The withdrawal of the Insukameni further benefitted the raiding party as, on hearing what had happened, another *Impi* that was hiding in the Somabula Forest also decided to withdraw rather than directly attack the party and ensconced itself behind defensive *scherms* or screens – in this case, made of thorn bushes. Had Wilson's party attempted to enter the forest they would have faced stiff resistance in a confined space. Donovan also points out that the absence of Wilson's force and the two Maxims weakened the Combined Column, and it was fortunate that the AmaNdebele did not attack it at that point.[11] Wilson's party set off to return to the Combined Column disappointed, fatigued, and riding weary horses, not arriving until after dark at about 1800 hours.

In the meantime, the Combined Column, with Captain John Bastard in temporary command of the Victoria Column, continued in a southwest direction through dense vegetation which hampered progress, and had to be cleared so that the column could proceed.[12]

The route then led through the Somabula Forest which, since it was very dense, put the Combined Column at greater risk of attack as it was unable to laager. As Forbes wrote: 'It was a very anxious time.'[13] The column was aware

---

8   Norris Newman, *Matabeleland and How We Got It*, p.90.

9   P.W. Forbes, 'From Sigala Mountain to the Shangani', in Wills & Collingridge, *The Downfall of Lobengula*, p.103.

10   Donovan, *With Wilson in Matabeleland*, p.123.

11   Donovan, *With Wilson in Matabeleland*, p.224.

12   Bastard was an ex-Royal Navy officer in command of No. 2 Troop of the Victoria Rangers. He had been mining in the Victoria District but was to transfer to Matabeleland after the war.

13   Forbes, 'From Sigala Mountain to the Shangani', p.102.

that the AmaNdebele were also in the forest and probably poised to attack. However, the Combined Column passed well to the left of the AmaNdebele's prepared ambush and escaped unscathed.[14] The fact that a dense fog had descended on the forest not only confused members of the column, but also seems to have deterred the AmaNdebele from attacking as they believed that it was caused by the 'white man's magic'.[15] The 5,000 strong *Impi*, commanded by the *Induna* Mjaan, thus missed an almost perfect opportunity to destroy their enemy.

The Combined Column reached the Vungu River and laagered while Jameson and Forbes sent two native runners back to Salisbury with news of their progress. The Vungu was wide, but at that time of year it was almost dry, and the column crossed it without difficulty. Captain White's scouts, searching ahead, encountered a group of AmaNdebele warriors with whom they exchanged fire. Dense fog, unusual in those parts, descended again and the column's guide confessed to be lost. Forbes ordered the Combined Column to halt and form its two laagers until the fog cleared with everyone expecting an AmaNdebele attack. Perhaps this anticipation is why Forbes' orders to laager took only six minutes to complete.[16]

Just before the fog had fallen, Forbes had sent out a party led by Captain Williams and five others including Captain Albert Burnett,[17] who was a first-rate scout and had taken over the scouting duties during Selous' absence. William's task was to search for the kraals of the Maholi who were thought to be friendly to the Europeans because of the treatment they had received from the AmaNdebele. William's group also became lost in the fog but continued their search when it finally cleared. They came across a small kraal where an elderly couple informed them that there were no AmaNdebele in the area, only Maholi.

Captain Burnett had dismounted and walked towards another small kraal, which he believed was deserted, in search of grain for his horse. Suddenly, a shot from the interior of a hut hit him in the stomach. The scouting party blindly returned fire into the hut but were unaware as to their fusillade's effectiveness until a woman, hidden behind it, called out that the attacker had run off. This proved to be a ruse, for when the suspicious scouts set fire to the hut, the sniper ran out and was shot dead.[18] As it would have been unsafe for them to remain in the kraal, Wilson's men struggled to get Burnett back on to his horse. While they attempted to return to the Combined Column, Maurice Gifford[19] set off to bring a doctor. Sadly, Burnett quickly succumbed

---

14   PA C 7290, Further Correspondence Relating to the Affairs in Matabeleland, Mashonaland and the Bechuanaland Protectorate; Sir John Willoughby's Account of the Battle of Shangani, 24 November 1893 (henceforth Willoughby's Account); Norris Newman, *Matabeleland and How We Got It*, pp.219–226.

15   Forbes, 'From Sigala to the Shangani', p.102; Donovan, *With Wilson in Matabeleland*, p.218; Gibbs, *A Flag for the Matabele*, p.133.

16   Forbes, 'From the Sigala to the Shangani River', pp.102–103.

17   Burnett was a Londoner and had served with the Warren Expedition and later as a member of the BBP before joining the Pioneer Column.

18   Forbes, 'From the Sigala to the Shangani River', pp.103–104.

19   The Honourable Maurice Raymond Gifford served in the Egyptian Campaign of 1882, and as a scout in the Red River Rebellion in 1885. He later went to South Africa and became general

to his wounds and was buried by Bishop Knight-Bruce that evening when the scouting party returned to the Combined Column.[20]

When news of Burnett's wounding reached Forbes, he ordered that a 20-man patrol under the command of Captain John Spreckley proceed to assist the scouting party. Before this could happen, however, the impetuous Jameson, accompanied by Willoughby and others, set off in the supposed direction of the incident. They soon were lost and fired upon by AmaNdebele. While one can admire the bravado of Jameson and Willoughby, one should not forget that they were travelling through unfamiliar territory with few landmarks to assist them. The dense bush was populated by many hundreds of AmaNdebele who were familiar with their surroundings and, as we have seen in the case of Burnett, could suddenly appear and cause havoc. Forbes, who was supposedly in command of his irregular forces, frequently found himself challenged by these eccentrics who believed they had a gift for military tactics. Jameson was of course, one of the worst and neither Forbes nor Willoughby were able to contain him. Not unexpectedly, Jameson's party returned to the Combined Column long after Burnett's body had been brought back to camp. As Forbes observed, the column had lost two good men 'with nothing at all to show for it'.[21]

On 24 October the Combined Column reached the Shangani River where the *Induna* Man-yéze had predicted the AmaNdebele would attack in numbers.[22]

      manager of the Bechuanaland Exploration Company before joining the Pioneer Column as a scout.

20   Forbes, 'From the Sigala to the Shangani River', pp.104.

21   Forbes. 'From the Sigala to the Shangani River', pp.104.

22   Chris Ash, *Matabele: The War of 1893 and the 1896 Rebellions* (Pinetown: 30 Degrees South, 2016), p.88.

7

The Battle of Shangani River

The Shangani River posed the most difficult obstacle the Combined Column had so far faced. The column slowly made its way towards a track that was on the far side of the Shangani and between several bushy *kopjes*, or small hills. The track would take it towards the kraals where Burnett was ambushed and between the *kopjes*. The column laagered a mile from the river and the numerous women and children who had been captured from the AmaNdebele on the journey were repatriated to their own people. There was also a large herd of cattle which, according to Donovan, numbered 700, that had to be driven alongside the men and waggons.[1] Forbes and Wilson went to investigate a suitable place to cross the river, the banks of which were heavily covered in bush that would have to be cleared for the column to cross. To make matters more difficult, *dongas*, or gullies caused by running water, ran towards the river which would make driving the waggons difficult. The two column commanders decided that, with some effort, their men could create two drifts after clearing the bush and continue beyond the river where there was a clear space large enough to accommodate both columns in their separate laagers and prevent a surprise attack by the AmaNdebele.

The Combined Column had arrived at a most dangerous point in its journey. It was clear that getting the waggons across the Shangani would be a difficult and, more importantly, a slow process during which the column would be very vulnerable to attack. The men would be engaged in challenging work to create the crossings, so it was important that every precaution was taken in order to protect them. The ground was covered with dense bushes, gullies, and rocky *kopjes*, which prevented the men from having a clear field of fire if attacked. The density of the bush might also allow the AmaNdebele to creep close to the column and suddenly burst out to attack with overwhelming numbers. The AmaNdebele, who were experts in hand-to-hand combat, would then have a very distinct advantage. Forbes ordered the column to form a strong defensive laager and dispatched two mounted troops, two Maxims, and a 7-pounder to take up elevated positions on the near side of the river to protect the men and waggons as they crossed.

---

1   Donovan, *With Wilson in Matabeleland*, p.213.

Two more mounted troops patrolled further along the Shangani's banks to prevent surprise attack from any AmaNdebele who had crossed the river at a different point. Adding a belt to his braces, Forbes also sent two more troops across the river with orders to destroy kraals and capture cattle.

Creating the drifts took the best part of the day before the 16 waggons of the Victoria Column and 21 waggons of the Salisbury Column were made ready to cross. The Combined Column customarily constructed two drifts as close as possible to one another. Those designated to work on them placed stones to shore up the banks and, where necessary, cut out their sides to widen the passage and then laid bushes where the ground was soggy.[2] Despite these efforts, the drifts were not of the best, but the two halves of the Combined Column made strenuous efforts to construct them and cross the Shangani. Forbes indicates that the crossing was completed, and the columns laagered within an hour and a half. They were closer together than usual with a thick hedge of thorn bush constructed between them that provided a secure place in which to place the oxen without which the men would be stranded without food.[3] The speed of the crossing, given the difficulties the column faced, was quite remarkable, Donovan suggests that this was because it was accomplished through the efforts of the men and not by using the oxen.[4] Forbes has suggested that the oxen of the Victoria Column were in poor shape and, instead, long rope was attached to the tow chain of each waggon and they were pulled, one by one, across the river by every man available and this made flogging and swearing at the beasts unnecessary.

The position of the Combined Column's joint laager was not a strong one but had been chosen because of the time of day. Willoughby suggests that it was the relative weakness of the site that encouraged the AmaNdebele to attack because it was fairly open and 'much in favour of an attacking force'.[5] Shortly after the column had finally laagered, the two patrols Forbes had sent across the river returned with large numbers of captured cattle, sheep, and goats. The evidence of burning kraals in the distance gave further proof of their effective clearance of the land immediately across the Shangani. They also brought back a few Maholi who had taken the opportunity to run away from their AmaNdebele masters as well as several women and children who had been captured during AmaNdebele raids in the region of Victoria. This group of former captives were keen to remain with their liberators, but their presence added to the column's problems for, as Forbes remarked, they could not be left 'to the mercy of the AmaNdebele'.[6] Neither patrol had seen any sign of the enemy but did find a little grain which was in short supply in the column.

Continually aware of the column's danger, even when in a protective laager, Forbes placed pickets with four groups to the front and back of

---

2   Donovan, *With Wilson in Matabeleland*, p.226.

3   Forbes, 'From Sigala Mountains to the Shangani', pp.104–105.

4   Donovan, *With Wilson in Matabeleland*, p.226.

5   Willoughby's Report on the Battle of Shangani, November 1894, in Norris Newman, *Matabeleland and How We Got It*, Appendix A., p.200. Henceforth Willoughby's Report.

6   Forbes, 'From the Sigala to the Shangani', p.105.

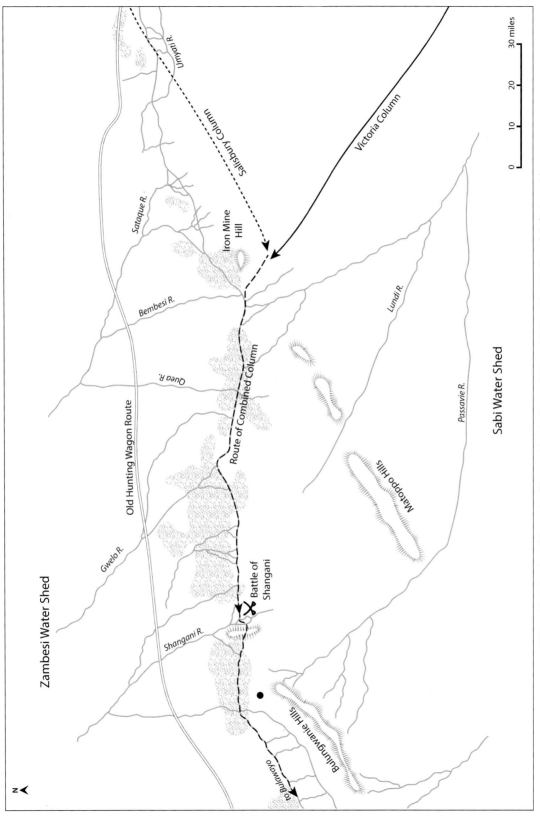

N

Umyati R.

Salisbury Column

Sataque R.

Iron Mine Hill

Bembesi R.

Victoria Column

Lundi R.

Oueu R.

Route of Combined Column

Old Hunting Wagon Route

Matoppo Hills

Passavie R.

Gwelo R.

Battle of Shangani

Shangani R.

Sabi Water Shed

Bulungwane Hills

Zambesi Water Shed

to Bulawayo

0   10   20   30 miles

Willoughby's drawing of the route of the combined columns. (Wills and Collingridge, *The Downfall of Lobengula*)

57

the laagers and one group on either flank to prevent a surprise attack. He issued orders that the men in each laager would stand to at 0400 hours each morning since this was thought to be the AmaNdebele's preferred time to attack. Forbes, like a conscientious officer, inspected the laagers that evening to ensure they were as secure as possible. He also released two signal rockets at around 2000 hours in case any of the scouts from the Tuli Column were in the neighbourhood. Forbes rockets were seen as further examples of the 'white man's magic' and delayed an AmaNdebele attack to around 2200 hours on the night of 24 October.[7]

Perhaps Forbes was unaware that Jameson had telegraphed Commander Raaff to persuade Lieutenant Colonel Goold-Adams not to begin the Tuli Column's march until a week after the Victoria Column had departed to ensure that it was the company and not the Goold-Adam's troopers who arrived first at GuBulawayo. Both Rhodes and Jameson were keen to ensure that Matabeleland become a company asset rather than an extension of the Bechuanaland Protectorate. High Commissioner Loch had other ideas and had telegraphed Goold-Adams on several occasions in October encouraging him to move faster, but the lieutenant colonel continued to lead the Tuli Column at a snail's pace with the probable expectation that this might be a long campaign. It was not until 23 October that the impatient and frustrated Loch gave Goold-Adams a direct order to get a move on towards GuBulawayo. This message, however, was also delayed and by 29 October, Goold-Adams was still in ignorance of Loch's wishes, by which time it was too late for his BBP to win any race.[8]

Forbes' precautions with regards to the laagers and the necessity of manning the barricades from early in the morning proved their worth when firing was heard at 0355 hours on the morning of 25 October from the direction of the native contingent which had laagered to the rear of the Salisbury Column and was under the command of Lieutenant Quested.[9] The AmaNdebele under the command of the *Induna* Mjaan had launched an attack on the native laager because, according to Hensman, the Shona had spent the night in reverie at being reunited with previously captured relatives and the AmaNdebele feared that they would not be able to launch their attack under the cover of darkness as the Shona were wide awake.[10] The waggons of the Combined Column's two laagers were quickly manned and Forbes and his men returned fire. Such was the weight of fire the Combined Column was able to bring to bear from every side that 'the whole laager became an instant sheet of flame'.[11] Forbes' men were initially to regret the fact that the Rudd Concession had placed 1,000 rifles into the hands of the AmaNdebele – a regret that would have been much greater if the AmaNdebele had been given proper instruction in their use. It appears that Lobengula's warriors believed

---

7   Willoughby's Account.
8   Mason, *The Matabele War*, p.211.
9   Burnham suggests it was around 0230 hours (Frederick Russell Burnham, *Scouting on Two Continents* (New York: Garden City Co., 1926), p.76); Donovan (*With Wilson in Matabeleland*, p.229) states 0400 hours.
10   Hensman, *A History of Rhodesia*, p.89.
11   Hensman, *A History of Rhodesia*, p.89.

that the higher the sights were set, the greater the speed and power of the bullets they fired. This misconception greatly interfered with the accuracy of their marksmanship.[12] They had, however, been able to get very close to the laager and, as the attack was made in the dark, the individual AmaNdebele positions could only be seen by the flashes of their rifles. Perhaps as, Donovan, Gibbs, and Burnham have pointed out, the AmaNdebele would have been much more successful if they had relied on their traditional fighting method of creeping up on the enemy and then launching a devasting attack.[13] It was even suggested in the South African press that the AmaNdebele had not intended to use their rifles but rather to employ their traditional method of attack, but this intention was spoiled when a warrior of the Maven *Impi* discharged his rifle by accident and the rest of the AmaNdebele, believing that it was an attack signal, opened fire.[14]

The Combined Column's initial response was less than controlled; it was still dark and the AmaNdebele's rifle flashes were all that could be seen. The defenders needlessly expended a large amount of ammunition, but it was sufficient to give the AmaNdebele 'a warm time of it'.[15] It took the officers in charge some time to control their men and persuade them to cease firing into the darkness. Forbes states that it was impossible to order a ceasefire since the noise was too great and the amount of firing from the AmaNdebele also made it unsafe to do so.[16] Donovan suggests that Wilson was able to bring his men under control, but this may have been because of the way that Wilson's reputation was established after the events to come.[17] However, Donovan's praise for Wilson's men is confirmed by Willoughby, who described the control Wilson exercised in the Victoria laager as 'excellent'.[18] Burnham described it as one of the most spectacular night fights he had experienced.[19] Forbes comments that this was the first time that he or most of his men had been under fire and he was pleased how steady everyone had been with little or no excitement and less wild shooting.[20]

The battle consisted of three separate attacks by the AmaNdebele. During the first and most threatening attack, which lasted roughly three-quarters of an hour, Quested, who had overseen the friendly natives, forced his way into the column's laager. His own Maholi laager was the first to be attacked and was overwhelmed, although his Shona had 'stood their ground well'.[21] Willoughby was less complimentary about the performance of those Shona under the command of Lieutenant John Brabant, whom he claimed were 'panic stricken' and ran towards the Victoria Column's laager

12 Forbes, 'From Sigala to the Shangani', p.110; 'The Shangani Fight', *The Queenslander*, 3 February 1894, p.231.

13 Donovan, *With Wilson in Matabeleland*, pp.237–238; Gibbs, *A Flag for the Matabele*, pp.134–135; Burnham, *Scouting on Two Continents*, p.76.

14 *Johannesburg Star*, 23 December 1893; Donovan, *With Wilson in Matabeleland*, p.229.

15 Donovan, *With Wilson in Matabeleland*, p.229.

16 Forbes, 'From Sigala to the Shangani', p.107.

17 Donovan, *With Wilson in Matabeleland*, p.229.

18 Willoughby's Report, p.221.

19 Burnham, *Scouting on Two Continents*, p.78.

20 Forbes, 'From Sigala to the Shangani', p.111.

21 Willoughby's Report, p.221.

across the Maxim's line of fire.[22] Consequently, some were hit by their own side. The AmaNdebele attacked the Maholi with their customary ferocity, indiscriminately killing men, the rescued women, and their children.

> Here a young woman and her baby lay pinned to the ground by an assegai. There a poor little boy who had tried to hide himself in an ant-bear hole with half a dozen wounds in his miserable black body.[23]

The shrieks and yells of these friendly natives were said to sound over the noise of the intense firing.[24] Quested had tried to resist the AmaNdebele onslaught but had eventually been forced to flee to the protection of the Combined Column's laager. He had not escaped unscathed, however, having been shot in the left thumb, left side and left arm.[25] Forbes' pickets also managed to retreat to the laager uninjured.[26] The Maxims proved very effective, especially since somewhat unusually they did not jam throughout the attack.[27] The guns caused a considerable number of casualties and checked the AmaNdebele's first rush at the laager. The 7-pounder and the 2-pounder Hotchkiss, which only fired 7 and 28 shells, respectively, came as an even greater surprise to the AmaNdebele.[28] This first attack lasted about 30–40 minutes and the AmaNdebele returned to the cover of the bush.

Forbes was conscious that some of the friendly Africans who had been in their own laager might not have gained the security of the Combined Column's laager, so he sent out Captain Spreckley[29] with a patrol of 20 mounted men to see if any were in hiding close by. Spreckley's troop were able to rescue a number of the Maholi and, although fired at from the bush, all were able to return to safety.

The AmaNdebele's second assault on the laagers was somewhat bizarre. Forbes, while observing the surroundings through his binoculars, noticed a group of 200–300 AmaNdebele quietly assembling on a nearby *kopje*. Such was their demeanour that he believed that they must be some of the missing friendlies, and despite a suggestion by Paul Chappé that they were

---

22 Willoughby's Report, p.221. Brabant was to reach the rank of Major General and in the Second Anglo-Boer War commanded the Colonial Division in 1900 and the Colonial Defence Force of Cape Colony in 1901.

23 Donovan, *With Wilson in Matabeleland*, pp.239–240.

24 Burnham, *Scouting on Two Continents*, p.136.

25 *Johannesburg Star*, 23 December 1893.

26 Forbes, 'From Sigala to the Shangani', p.107.

27 Forbes, 'From Sigala to the Shangani', p.111. The AmaNdebele called the Maxims 'J'kuton'kuto' – an attempt to onomatopoeically imitate their sound when firing.

28 When a shell exploded in their midst, the warriors fired at the site of the explosion. It seems they believed that the shell contained diminutive white men who sprang out when it exploded and the AmaNdebele were trying to kill them in this way. (Forbes, 'From Sigala to the Shangani', p.112) They were equally perplexed as to how their opponents were able to wrap their bullets in a blanket (shell case) and shoot them at them. (Donovan, *With Wilson in Matabeleland*, p.233).

29 John Anthony Spreckley arrived in Africa in 1881 and having worked on an ostrich farm, served a year in the BBP. He then became an unsuccessful gold prospector in Matabeleland. He was commander of C troop in the Salisbury Horse during the AmaNdebele War and was killed in the Second Anglo-Boer War.

The Battle of Shangani showing the troopers using the waggons as defensive positions. (Open source)

AmaNdebele, Forbes would not permit any firing at them.[30] Chappé's hunch was correct, for when the AmaNdebele reach the bottom of the *kopje*, they sat down and began firing at the column's laager. Forbes response was immediate, and rifle and Maxim fire soon forced the warriors to retire. There is no disguising the fact that Forbes had admiration for his enemies' bravery at his point; they were, as Forbes points out, the Insukameni *Impi*, which was 'the best regiment there'.[31]

When the Insukameni had retired out of sight, Forbes sent out a patrol again, under Spreckley, to the east, and one under Captain Maurice Heany to the northeast. He instructed Wilson to send out a similar patrol to the south led by Captain Bastard. These patrols soon found AmaNdebele secreted in the bush or hiding in watercourses within a few hundred yards of the laager. Each patrol had a brisk exchange of fire with the loss of four valuable horses. Forced to retreat, the three patrols fell back onto the laager pursued by the AmaNdebele who were again driven off by the Maxims.

Shortly afterwards, a group of AmaNdebele were seen gathering on a *kopje* some 2,000 yards to the west of the laager but they were dispersed by three accurately aimed shells from the Salisbury Column's 7-pounder.[32] Similarly, Lendy was using the 1-pounder Hotchkiss at a range of 1,300–2,000 yards to bombard small groups of AmaNdebele gathering to the south and southwest of the laager. Forbes indicates that one such shell killed 12 men.[33] The time was 0830 hours, and the battle was virtually over. Forbes considered that

---

30   Paul Chappé had been a storekeeper in East Griqualand but served as a volunteer officer during the Griqualand Rebellion. He had also served in the Basuto and Zulu Rebellions as a volunteer officer. He joined Jameson's Raid as a Veterinary Sergeant and Trumpeter. After the AmaNdebele War he was appointed a First Native Commissioner to Matabeleland. He was to interrogate the AmaNdebele survivors of the Shangani Patrol.

31   Forbes, 'From Sigala to the Shangani', p.108.

32   Willoughby in his Account describes them as AmaNdebele Reserve under the *Induna* Manlevo who, unusually, was on horseback.

33   Forbes, 'From Sigala to the Shangani', p.109.

Captain Owen Williams. (Wills & Collingridge, *The Downfall of Lobengula*)

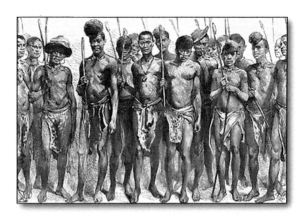

Warriors of the Royal Imbezu *Impi*. (*The Graphic*, 1893)

'the result of the engagement' was 'very satisfactory' since it had given his inexperienced men confidence.[34] It also reduced the AmaNdebele reputation as fighting men as they had previously been compared to the Zulus. Even the oxen had remained calm, although several were killed by AmaNdebele fire.

Bishop Knight-Bruce drove his custom-built waggon around the battle site and ensured that all the AmaNdebele wounded were collected and cared for.

Norris Newman reports the casualty list as follows: one trooper killed; 27 of the friendly Shona and a native driver killed and 26 Shona wounded; and six men, including Captain Quested, wounded. He estimates that the AmaNdebele lost 500 killed.[35]

During the fighting Manonda, the *Induna* in charge of the AmaNdebele attacking force, was wounded and later committed suicide, probably in anticipation of Lobengula's reaction to the defeat. It seems that other *Indunas* had similar thoughts and one is reported to have fallen on his own *assegai*.[36] Rhodes was pleased when he heard of the victory and the effectiveness of the Maxims, and in a letter to Sir Gordon Sprigg, four times Prime Minister of Cape Town, Rhodes said that: '[T]he shooting must have been excellent. … It proves the [BBP] men were not only brave, but cool, and did not lose their heads, though surrounded with the hordes.'[37] Willoughby, in his report of the battle, regretted that the victory had not been followed up more effectively but argued that this was impossible because of the broken terrain that lay in front of the column.[38]

---

34   Forbes, 'From Sigala to the Shangani', p.111.
35   Norris Newman, *Matabeleland and How We Got It*, p.94.
36   This was recorded in the notebooks of Jack Carruthers, a scout in the Victoria Column.
37   Rotberg, *The Founder*, p.442.
38   Willoughby's Report, p.226.

8

Towards GuBulawayo

Forbes was keen to further demoralise the AmaNdebele and decided to continue the trek that same afternoon. There was a large open plain three miles ahead and if the Combined Column could reach it safely the improved visibility it provided would mitigate any further major attacks. However, the route the column had to followed to reach the open plain narrowed as it passed between *kopjes*, which meant that if an attack occurred, a defensive laager would provide a clear target for AmaNdebele who were secreted on the *kopjes* above. The two parts of the Combined Column moved closer together with men on each flank to prevent surprise attack. Forbes claimed that this was his most anxious moment in the whole campaign, but he need not have feared as they reached the wide space and laagered in its centre without any opposition.

The next day, 26 October, the column travelled a further five miles until it reached the Manzamnyama River and laagered close to it.[1] There were several abandoned kraals nearby, some of which contained large amounts of much needed grain which the column commandeered. The native guides warned Forbes that there were military kraals of the Jingen and Zinyangene *Impis* close by and Captain Heany, with a troop of 21 men, was sent to destroy the latter kraal as it was only six miles away. The patrol burnt the kraal but noticed a large number of AmaNdebele warriors advancing towards it, so the men quickly began to return to the safety of the laager.

They were forced to retreat very rapidly which put so much strain on their mounts that two riders were forced to abandon their horses and continue on foot. Heany sent a messenger to warn Forbes, whose column had travelled a further 4½ miles, of the impending fight and the Major ordered 40 men and two Maxims to move forward to cover Heany's retreat. Captain Williams, accompanied by five others who had been on patrol, rode to meet Heany as he was riding towards the laager. William's men had a lucky escape having been almost cut off by many AmaNdebele. They had only managed this by riding through the warriors and their subsequent hail of fire. Williams' horse panicked at the noise and bolted, carrying its struggling rider towards the

---

1   Now known as the Nata River.

nearby *kopjes*. This somewhat perplexed the AmaNdebele seeing Williams apparently riding towards them, so they shot his horse through both hind legs forcing him to dismount and take cover in nearby rocks. Williams had a Lee Metford magazine rifle and was able to keep the warriors at bay for some time but once out of ammunition he was forced to use his revolver, which had a shorter range and allowed the AmaNdebele to get closer. The end was inevitable, and Williams was shot through the head.[2] The AmaNdebele stripped his body and removed anything of value. The weapons were sent on to GuBulawayo for the King's approval. Forbes claims that they did not mutilate Williams' body as was the usual custom, probably because they admired his courage.[3] Heany and his men, less the two 'knocked up' horses, arrived safely back at the column.

On the 29 October the Combined Column again started to move forwards and Forbes sent out scouts with Captain White to find the way to GuBulawayo or contact the Tuli Column, which he felt would be not far away. The column passed several kraals, some of which contained large amounts of ammunition, indicating that the AmaNdebele occupants had left in great haste. This was collected and the kraals burned in a continuation of Forbes 'scorched earth' policy. A scout returned reporting that there was a very large force of AmaNdebele in the bush three miles ahead of the Combined Column and that Captain Henry White had remained to observe what they were doing. Forbes sent out a troop from both halves of the column, but they were unable to draw the AmaNdebele out from cover. Keen to move on, Forbes led the column a further two miles before laagering. When this was almost completed a large number of AmaNdebele were seen coming through gaps in the *kopjes* ahead, and some of them populated the high ground to the column's front. Lendy, who commanded the Victoria Column's artillery, was ordered to run out its 7-pounder with its range of 4,000 yards and fire at the approaching warriors. Lendy's first shot fell short but the next two landed in the middle of the assembled AmaNdebele. The missiles caused a considerable number of casualties and the AmaNdebele began to retreat, which was hastened by two further accurately placed shells.

The Combined Column continued to move towards Lobengula's capital, fighting small skirmishes on the way. Its start on 1 November was delayed until 0800 hours because of a thick fog. Scouts had been deployed as usual and reported that the way ahead was clear of AmaNdebele. The column came to the Imbembezi River which the scouts suggested should be crossed. Forbes decided not to do so and turned the column away from the riverbank. During this manoeuvre, scouts returned to report they had failed to reach GuBulawayo because they came across large numbers of AmaNdebele who chased them for some distance. The mounted scouts had escaped but while doing so caught two women who provided them with important news.

---

2   Norris Newman, *Matabeleland and How We Got It*, pp.93–94.
3   Williams, who had formerly been an officer in the Royal Horse Guard, was the eldest son of Lieutenant General Owen Williams and his military experience was a loss to the column's amateur officers.

Lobengula had left GuBulawayo! There were some AmaNdebele left in the capital and the Tuli Column had not yet arrived.

The Combined Column proceeded unmolested until it came within ten miles of a distinctively shaped hill, known as '*Intabas Induna*', that they knew was roughly eight miles from GuBulawayo. Forbes decided to laager but the spot he chose was not a good one; one wonders if he was becoming overconfident as he approached the King's kraal in the knowledge that Lobengula had fled. The disadvantages of the site Forbes had chosen were mainly that it was within 500 yards of dense bush and about a mile from the nearest water. The former issue meant that the AmaNdebele could approach unseen to within a relatively short distance from the column and the latter made it necessary to remove the precious horses and oxen from the protection of the laager. While Forbes was organising his camp, he saw a group of AmaNdebele in the distance, some of whom were mounted, driving a few cattle on what he assumed was the main path to GuBulawayo. Forbes ordered the 7-pounder crew to attempt to shell the group, which was about 1,400 yards away. This activity may have distracted various sections of the column since a large group of AmaNdebele suddenly erupted out of the nearby bush. Trooper Thompson, one of two dismounted pickets who were preparing a meal, was caught completely by surprise because of this lack of attention. Having tried to climb a tree in order to escape, Thompson was pulled down and stabbed to death. The other trooper, Trooper White, was able to hastily mount his horse but soon fell off, and horse and man rushed back to the camp while being covered by his comrades' fire. He arrived completely exhausted but safe.

The AmaNdebele continued to advance towards the laager in the traditional method of attack copied from the Zulus; they were the 'Chest of the Buffalo' and contained the two royal *Impis*, the Imbezu and Ingubu, who had mocked the defeated warriors that returned to GuBulawayo after their defeat at the Shangani. Other *Impis*, acting as the 'Horns of the Buffalo', broke out on either flank of the laager. This was a determined attack on the Salisbury half of the laager, made by the best of the AmaNdebele army and their fire was very intense. Forbes believed that it was initially almost as heavy as the fire of the Combined Column's even though all its rapid-fire guns were being worked. Again, however, the warriors were firing too high and continually missed their targets.[4]

Wilson, realising that the Victoria section of the laager was under little threat, deployed his rapid-fire guns and sent troopers to the flanks on each side to assist the Salisbury half of the column. As Willoughby was to report: 'Notwithstanding the fire of three Maxims, one Gardner, one Nordenfeldt, two shell-guns, besides some 400 rifles, the enemy continued to reinforce his first line (though latterly to a lesser extent) up to 1.25 p.m.'[5]

---

4   P.W. Forbes, 'The Downfall of Lobengula', in Wills & Collingridge, *The Downfall of Lobengula*, p.121.

5   Willoughby's Account of the Battle of Imbembezi Fought Near the Head Waters of the Bembezi River, November 1, 1893', in Norris Newman, *Matabeleland and How We Got It*, p.231. Henceforth Willoughby's Account of the Battle of Imbembezi.

The Chest of the Buffalo got to within 300 yards but could advance no further. After 40 minutes the attack slackened and the AmaNdebele withdrew 'in a sulky sort of way'.[6] The two royal *Impis*, not used to defeat, were clearly reluctant to acknowledge that it had finally happened to them even though they had been practically annihilated.[7] A further weakness of Forbes' chosen laager site was that there was a strip of 'dead ground' into which five AmaNdebele snipers secreted themselves and were thus able to direct accurate fire into the laager. They were eventually forced to retreat, leaving two of their dead comrades behind.

Forbes lost no time in making sure that the AmaNdebele had actually withdrawn by sending out a number of patrols. One patrol, under Captain Bastard, strayed too close to the nearby bush and several AmaNdebele who had been in hiding dashed out in the hopes of capturing Bastard's Patrol. Lieutenant Edward Tyndale-Biscoe[8] opened up with a Maxim and the attackers quickly scattered, but not before Bastard's horse had been shot twice.

The horses that were being watered a mile away, stampeded and headed towards the AmaNdebele and away from the laager. If they were lost, so too would the patrol be as the men on foot would have been quickly overwhelmed by the superior numbers of the AmaNdebele. Willoughby and Henry Borrow prevented this disaster by leaping on two of the few horses that had been kept back in the laager and, under the cover of the Maxims and rifles, managed to reach the stampede and head the horses towards the laager and away from the advancing AmaNdebele. Ash describes this as a 'remarkably courageous act'.[9] Willoughby, an Imperial Officer, was more suitably modest.[10]

The Battle of Imbembezi was virtually over and the troopers began to collect the wounded AmaNdebele. Clearly, they had lost many warriors, perhaps as many as 1,000 killed and wounded.[11] The Imbezu *Impi* had lost over 70 percent of its number, but the column had only lost three troopers killed and eight wounded. Perhaps as important, it had only lost four horses killed. The expenditure of ammunition by Forbes' men was huge and included 8,600 Martini-Henry rounds used by both the men's rifles and the Maxims, 570 rounds of Gardner ammunition, 25 7-pounder shells, and 30 from the 2-pounder Hotchkiss. However, unlike the Battle of Shangani, the Shona contingent played little part in the action.

Ash is keen to point out that the Battle of Imbembezi was not a case of the typical 'rifles against' spears battle.[12] The AmaNdebele had many more rifles

---

6   Forbes, 'The Downfall of Lobengula', p.122.

7   Willoughby's Account of the Battle of Imbembezi.

8   Tyndale-Biscoe was a sailor and had been harshly treated, having been discharged from the Royal Navy because of his stammer. Before his discharge, he had been mentioned in despatches for his work in the Sudan Campaign. He was one of the original pioneers in 1890 and was to go on to fight in the Second Anglo-Boer War where he gained a mention in despatches and special promotion for his part in the defence of Ladysmith.

9   Ash, *Matabele*, p.109.

10   Willoughby's Account of the Battle of Imbembezi.

11   Willoughby's Account of the Battle of Imbembezi.

12   Ash, *Matabele*, p.110.

The Battle of Imbemezi: 1 November 1893. (*Illustrated London News*, 17 March 1894)

than the Combined Column and possessed a collection of more unusual weapons, such as muskets and even four-bore elephant guns. While searching the battlefield, Forbes' men also discovered several .303 rifles, which were superior to the Martini-Henrys. Where these rifles originated is uncertain, but three years later, in 1895, Boers, who believed that they had interests in the area, were caught smuggling such weapons into Mashonaland.[13]

Imbembezi was a more important victory than the Battle of Shangani. The best of the AmaNdebele *Impis* had been crushed and the war seemed almost to be over. All that remained was to capture Lobengula and his capital. Forbes was initially anxious to take GuBulawayo by sending 100-man flying squad to the settlement. Again, he had second thoughts because of the very poor condition of the horses. The following morning, 2 November, the column continued its slow progress but, on 3 November, it heard an enormous explosion and saw a huge cloud of smoke from the direction of GuBulawayo.

Typically, Jameson and Willoughby could not wait for the slow-moving column to reach its goal and rode ahead towards GuBulawayo. The Combined Column, its waggons decorated with makeshift flags, marched into GuBulawayo on the afternoon of 4 November led by Pipe-Major MacDonald of Captain Dallamore's foot soldiers playing the 'GuBulawayo March' on his bagpipes.[14] Lobengula had fled his capital and much of the kraal had been destroyed. The King had stored a large amount of ammunition and black powder there but, when he decided to flee, he ordered his men to collect up his 80,000 rounds of Martini-Henry ammunition and 2,000 pounds of black powder and follow him. They were so panic-stricken, however, they set fire to the kraal. The fire spread to the stored ammunition resulting in the large explosion the column had heard the previous morning. However, despite the destruction it was clear that the huts of the white traders who lived in the settlement had been spared and the column's scouts found James Fairburn

---

13   A.E. Heyer, *A Brief History of the Transvaal Secret Service System from Its Inception to the Modern Times* (Cape Town: William Taylor, 1899), p.15.

14   Donovan, *With Wilson in Matabeleland*, p.272.

and William Usher sitting unharmed on the roof of their store.[15] The column also found that Colenbrander's compound was undamaged, and its buildings were suitable to use as a hospital and store. Consequently, it was decided to laager there.

Forbes had still not received any definite news of the Tuli Column. Lobengula had sent his son-in-law, the *Induna* Gambo, with an *Impi* of 3,000– 4,000 warriors to attack Goold-Adams but had only given Gambo ten Martini-Henry rifles. It appears that Lobengula did not trust Gambo and was worried that he would join forces with the Tuli Column rather than attack it. Rumours flew and it was said that Gambo's *Impi* had attack the Tuli Column and killed several of Goold-Adams's men.

There were plenty of knick-knacks for the members of the Combined Column to acquire; some might say loot. In particularly, among the ruins the men found Lobengula's silver elephant which had been presented by the Tati Mining Company. This was a valuable object and was raffled off.[16] Despite appearances, the occupation of GuBulawayo by the Combined Column was a relatively orderly affair, and the controlled behaviour of its men was probably, if reluctantly, welcomed by the AmaNdebele whose expectations were no doubt based upon the brutal unpredictability of Lobengula.[17]

Jameson was anxious to let his chief, Cecil Rhodes, know that they had finally captured GuBulawayo and sent the American scouts, Frederick Burnham and Pear Ingram (a Montana cowboy), accompanied by a Zulu boy who knew the way and was 'known for his personal courage and ability to ride' to Tati where they hoped to find a telegraph in order to wire the news.[18] This was, as Forbes points out, a dangerous endeavour as Gambo's *Impi* might well have been between the small party and Tati. Forbes admiringly believed that the three men 'could be depended upon to get through if it were possible for anyone to do so'.[19]

Forbes was correct in his assessment about the scouts' courage and ability. Burnham recounted how they came upon a couple of AmaNdebele who were packing up the camp of Gambo's departed *Impi*. These were quickly captured and held at gunpoint. The Zulu boy, described as being adept at obtaining information without the use of force, interviewed the captives.[20] The good news was that Gambo's *Impi* had attacked Goold-Adam's Column but had failed to defeat it. The bad news was that the warriors provided by King Khama had fled to Botswana because of an outbreak of smallpox. Their flight had left Goold-Adams with his original 400 BBP who, said the captives, 'would soon be roasted like pheasants before the fire'.[21]

After a very precarious journey with several near misses, they reached Goold-Adams' Column and were reunited with the scout, Frederick Selous,

15 Norris Newman, *Matabeleland and How We Got It*, p.97.
16 Donovan, *With Wilson in Matabeleland*, p.276.
17 Ash, *Matabele*, p.112.
18 Burnham, *Scouting on Two Continents*, p.84.
19 P.W. Forbes, 'The Occupation of GuBulawayo', in Wills & Collingridge, *The Downfall of Lobengula*, p.129.
20 Burnham, *Scouting on Two Continents*, p.84.
21 Burnham, *Scouting on Two Continents*, p.84.

said to be Ridder Haggard's inspiration for Alan Quartermain. Selous, although wounded in 'a bit of a fight', was still able to continue to act as a scout for the Tuli Column.[22] Burnham and Ingram continue towards Tati and encountered Colenbrander carrying despatches for Goold-Adams and Jameson. A disappointed Burnham, on arriving at Tati, discovered that the telegraph line had yet to reach the settlement and only an unreliable heliograph was available to contact the outside world. The nearest place for effective long-distance communication was Palapye. Undaunted Burnham and Ingram set off to travel the further 100 miles in order to inform Rhodes about Jameson's and Forbes' success. The news appeared in the English newspapers on 10 November, with Burnham and Ingram having completed the 200-mile journey in four days.

Francis Burnham photographed in 1901 showing his DSO, Matabele, and Boer War Medals. (Elliott and Fry Photography Studio, London. Open source)

---

22   Millais, *Life of Frederick Courtenay Selous*, p.201.

9

In Pursuit of Lobengula

While Burnham and Ingram were carrying Jameson's despatches, the doctor sent out messengers in search of Lobengula, asking him to return to his capital and so put an end to the fighting.[1] The message was in English, Dutch, and Zulu, and stated:

> I send this message in order, if possible, to prevent the necessity of any further killing of your people or burning of their kraals. To stop this useless slaughter you must at once come and see me at GuBulawayo, where I will guarantee that your life will be safe and that you will be kindly treated. I will allow sufficient time for these messengers to reach you and two days more to allow you to reach me in your waggon. Should you not then arrive I shall at once send out troops to follow you, as I am determined as soon as possible to put the country in a condition where whites and blacks can live in peace and friendliness.[2]

Lobengula's reply was as follows:

> I have heard all that you have said, so I will come, but let me to ask you where are all my men which I have sent to the Cape, such as Moffatt and Jonny and James, and after that the three men – Gobogobo, Mantose and Goebo – whom I sent. If I do come where will I get a house for me as all my houses is burn [sic] down, and also as soon as my men come which I have sent then I will come.[3]

Forbes suggests that Jameson gave Lobengula two days to consider his position.[4] The time expired, so Jameson instructed Forbes to take 200 men to follow and capture Lobengula but, since this would be a very risky strategy and there was much opposition among the members of the column, Jameson had second thoughts and changed his mind.[5]

---

1   Donovan, *With Wilson in Matabeleland*, p.276.
2   Quoted in Hole, *The Making of Rhodesia*, p.317.
3   Quoted in W.D. Gale, *One Man's Vision: The Story of Rhodesia* (GuBulawayo: Books of Rhodesia, 1976), pp.198–199.
4   Forbes, 'The Occupation of GuBulawayo', p.132.
5   Colvin, *Life of Jameson*, Vol. 1., pp.283–284; Forbes, 'The Occupation of GuBulawayo', p.132.

The messengers to Lobengula were delayed because they had been taken prisoner and handed over to the Imbezu *Impi* from whom they were able to discover that the *Impi* was reluctant to fight any more as they had lost many men in the battles of Shangani and Bembesi. They were also able to confirm the death of Captain Williams by showing Jameson's messengers Williams' compass and chain and describing the 'pictures' on his arms.[6] In another message Lobengula repeated his request that two men whom he trusted, Fairburn and Asher, be sent to him so that he might discuss matters with them. Lobengula also sent a third message that included a gift of gold for Jameson.[7] This letter fell into the hands of two troopers, Daniel and Wilson, who kept the gold and did not forward the message. Their crime was discovered, and they were initially sentenced to 14 years imprisonment. It was the failure to receive this letter that influenced Jameson's decision to wait no longer.[8]

On 12 November Goold-Adams and the Tuli Column began to arrive at GuBulawayo, and the following day Commandant Raaff and his men arrived. Things were becoming less dangerous, and Forbes was able to allow some men to return to Salisbury. Furthermore, Bishop Knight-Bruce, who had conducted a church parade just before the arrival of the Tuli Column, decided to leave. Realising that time was of the essence and that Lobengula's liberty might turn into a guerrilla war given his tendency to constantly change his mind, Jameson decided not to wait any longer for the King to return and arranged with Goold-Adams to authorise 210 men with four Maxims and a 7-pounder drawn by ten mules be sent to bring back Lobengula by force. This flying column consisted of 90 BBP and 60 'Riff Raaff' from the Tuli Column as well as 60 men from the Victoria Column; the whole force was to be under Forbes command.[9] The troopers would be supported by 200 native carriers organised by Lieutenant Brabant.[10]

Somewhat uncharacteristically, Jameson, normally the first to move towards the action, together with Lieutenant Colonel Goold-Adams, the senior imperial officer, decided to remain at GuBulawayo. Hence the need to delegate command of the flying column to subordinates. Burnham suggests that Jameson, realising that the action he was proposing was fraught with danger since there were still large *Impis* in the area that could easily wipe out a small party, however well-armed, refused to take responsibility for ordering men to go in pursuit of Lobengula, but rather asked for volunteers to do so.[11] This might explain the column's confused command structure. One wonders whether this is an accurate assessment or an attempt to exonerate Jameson from blame for the disaster that resulted. Whether the men were volunteers

---

6   Forbes, 'The Occupation of GuBulawayo', p.133. The 'pictures' were Williams' tattoos.
7   Hensman, *A History of Rhodesia*, p.100.
8   See Chapter 16.
9   Glass, *The Matabele War*, p.227. Raaff's men were generally considered to be the dregs of Johannesburg.
10   John O'Reilly, *Pursuit of the King* (GuBulawayo: Books of Rhodesia, 1970), p.156.
11   Burnham, *Scouting on Two Continents*, p.86.

or not, it seems there were plenty to choose from and a selection was made for a force to make a dash to capture the King and end AmaNdebele resistance.[12]

The officers under Forbes were undoubtedly handpicked but their very presence was a potential source of tension. As one has already noted, Forbes was conscious that Wilson also held the rank of Major. Wilson was older than Forbes, with a good deal more experience and had commanded the Victoria Column, which had been much larger than Forbes' Salisbury command.[13]

Commandant Raaff, who was Wilson's junior in rank, was appointed second-in-command of the flying column and, to make matters worse, placed in command of the BBP who were imperial troopers and not the amateurs who made up the rest of the column.[14] Captains Tancred and Coventry of the BBP seem to have accepted Raaff being appointed to command the BBP over their heads with little demur. Things were even more complicated since Jameson had instructed Forbes to consult with Raaff before making any offensive or defensive decisions.[15] Ash suggests this virtually made Raaff the actual commander of the column.[16] Raaff had fought in the Basuto War in 1865 when Forbes was only four years old, and he had been made a Companion of the Order of Saint Michael and Saint George (CMG) for his work in the Zulu War. Clearly, the Forbes–Wilson rivalry was made worse by Raaff's position, and the situation was described by Colenbrander as a question of three 'pocket generals [who] could never agree with each other'.[17] This is perhaps an unfair assessment of Raaff who offered his views in an experienced and controlled way, but nevertheless seemed to annoy Forbes.[18] If 'action man' Jameson had accompanied the flying column it is possible his charm could have held things together, but he dared not leave GuBulawayo in case Lobengula returned and was greeted by Goold-Adams, an imperial officer, rather than Jameson, the BSAC official. It was a question of putting the BSAC's interests first rather than taking part in a thrilling adventure.

In preparation for its departure, the flying column was allocated provisions to last three days, together with 100 rounds per man.[19] This, in retrospect, seems to be an extraordinarily meagre allocation. Did Forbes and his superiors think that these would be sufficient resources for the members of the flying squad to capture the King whom they might intercept as he was journeying back to his capital? Or did they feel that taking additional supplies would slow them down? A third possibility is that they expected to be able to commandeer more supplies from the kraals they passed on their way. None of these reasons seems convincing. It is possible, of course, that someone did not think through the logistics required and was anxious to

12   Burnham, *Scouting on Two Continents*, p.87.

13   Ash, *Matabele*, p.138.

14   Some authorities suggest that Wilson was actually second in command but the fact that Raaff's group had been selected by Goold-Adams seems to make it unlikely that he was meant to be out-ranked by Wilson.

15   Robert Cary, *A Time to Die* (Cape Town: Howard Timmins, 1968), p.40.

16   Ash, *Matabele*, p.138.

17   Colenbrander, quoted in O'Reilly, *In Pursuit of the King*, p.33.

18   Cary, *A Time to Die*, pp.30–40.

19   For the composition of the patrol, see Appendix IX [AQ5].

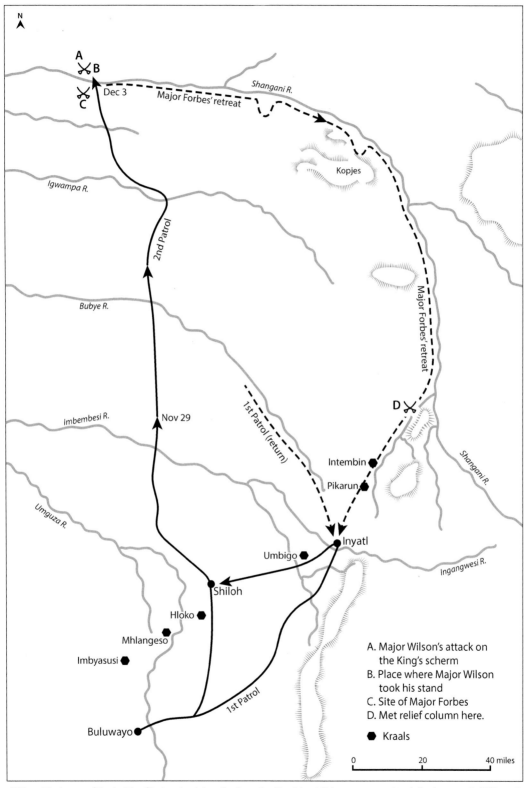

N

A
X B
X
C
Dec 3
Major Forbes' retreat
Shangani R.

Kopjes

Igwampa R.

2nd Patrol

Bubye R.

Major Forbes' retreat

Imbembesi R.

Nov 29

1st Patrol (return)

D X

Umguza R.

Shangani R.

Intembin

Pikarun

Inyatl

Umbigo

Ingangwesi R.

Shiloh

Hloko

Mhlangeso

Imbyasusi

A. Major Wilson's attack on
   the King's scherm
B. Place where Major Wilson
   took his stand
C. Site of Major Forbes
D. Met relief column here.

⬢ Kraals

1st Patrol

Buluwayo

0   20   40 miles

Willoughby's map of the battle of Imbembesi showing how the Combined Column prepared to defend an attack. (Wills and Collingridge, *The Downfall of Lobengula*)

send the flying column on its way on what was assumed would be a very short venture. One would have thought that the 200 bearers would easily be able to transport more rations, but this would probably slow the flying squad down. The bearers would, however, move more quickly than waggons.

The squad's leaders were aware that an *Impi* stood between them and the likely hiding place of Lobengula and that it would have to be dealt with before they could capture the King. The squad was directed to proceed to the nearest royal kraal and then to Shiloh via Emalangeni Hill. The weather, which was later to play a significant part in the outcome of the venture, was very fair when the flying column, which has gone down in history as the 'Shangani Patrol', left GuBulawayo on 14 November at 1930 hours, before the last sections of Goold-Adams' Column arrived

The Shangani Patrol's first halt was at the Koce River, where it set up camp in the form of a square since it had no waggons with which to form a laager. The Salisbury men took the front face and the Victoria men the right. The left side was formed by the men from the Tuli Column while the rear was made up of BBP. A Maxim was placed at each corner of the square. Forbes was conscious that he needed to protect the horses from over-exertion for, even though care had been taken to choose the best available, they were still not very fit.

Earlier in the day, the Shangani Patrol had been joined by the two American scouts, Burnham and Ingram, who had returned from Palapye with despatches for Jameson. They volunteered to catch up with Forbes' men and did so after darkness had fallen at around 1830 hours. Forbes was aware that there was a large group of AmaNdebele hidden in the bush close by and 'ordered' the two scouts to do something that would either disperse or at least distract them. Burnham's account of how this was accomplished is typical of a Boy's Own comic. He took some rockets and, using an improvised launcher made from a tree sapling, launched one into the sky. The effects were startling to the superstitious AmaNdebele who thought this was yet another example of Jameson's magic. Burnham launched a second rocket with even greater effect as, by this time, the sapling 'launcher' had become weakened and, instead of shooting up into the sky, the rocket travelled horizontally into a kraal full of warriors. 'The result was particularly gratifying.'[20] O'Reilly advises caution when examining Burnham's version of events and points out that he was considered an expert at telling tall tales.[21] Forbes, however, confirmed the incident with the rockets in his version of the event.[22]

The commanders of the Shangani Patrol decided that it should travel by night and rest in the bush during the day in order to prevent it being ambushed.[23] This would also mean that the men should reach Umhlangeni early in the morning and be able to launch an attack in daylight. The patrol

---

20   Burnham, *Scouting on Two Continents*. p.88.

21   O'Reilly, *Pursuit of the King*, p.36.

22   P.W. Forbes, 'The Pursuit of the King', in Wills & Collingridge, *The Downfall of Lobengula*, p.144.

23   It is interesting, given the fractured command structure of the patrol that Forbes ('The Pursuit of the King', p.136) does not say by whom the decision was made.

recommenced its journey at 0100 hours when the temperature was lower but just before it continued the pursuit, it was joined by John Willoughby, always anxious to be in the thick of it, and on this occasion accompanied by James Murray Gourlay, a gold prospector, who was later to become the Managing Director of Gourlay's Rhodesian Management Company Ltd.

The Shangani Patrol continued another eight miles, some of which was through dense bush, and came to the Elebeni *kopjes* where there was a small royal kraal of extremely well-built huts that were sufficient for three of Lobengula's queens. It was deserted but contained large amounts of 'kaffir corn' and mealies.[24] Given the few rations with which the Shangani Patrol had begun its journey, it is not surprising that it paused for half an hour in order to give its horses a good feed. Forbes and Colenbrander took the opportunity to climb onto the roof of one of the huts and see as far as Emalangeni and the whereabouts of Shiloh. The patrol then continued and passed two more kraals but saw no AmaNdebele. The weather began to change; there was a heavy shower in the afternoon and the night would prove to be very squally. As darkness fell, their camp was two miles from the Imbembezi River and set up as on the previous night, but Forbes also ordered that each face of the square be made up of a double rank of men, which reduced the camp's size.

The moon rose at around 2200 hours and the patrol set off again at 2300 hours crossing the Imbembezi through a wide, sandy drift that was 'then quite dry'.[25] Before crossing the next river, the Inkwekwesi, the patrol became aware of another kraal from which the sound of barking dogs and the smell of wood fires clearly indicated that it was occupied. The patrol therefore crossed the river avoiding the kraal and camped, waiting for sufficient light to attack it. One might suggest that this was a brave but perhaps foolish strategy since Forbes did not know how many AmaNdebele were actually in the kraal, and it would require a frontal assault. On the other hand, to have a group of AmaNdebele in the patrol's rear could well have been asking for trouble. It is an example, however, of Forbes, underestimating the abilities of the AmaNdebele – a fault which would contribute to the calamity to come.

Forbes divided his force into three groups. The largest group under Wilson consisted of 145 men and two Maxims and they were to attack the right flank of the kraal. Raaff's Rangers were to attack the left flank and Heany, with 45 men and the 7-pounder, was to advance down the 'road' directly towards the kraal. The two flanking groups were guided by Charles Acutt and Johannes Colenbrander. Forbes suggests that the kraal was an ideal place to attack, and his deployment of attackers was well carried out. The attack was, however, a disappointment. There was no *Impi*, just a few AmaNdebele families and their cattle, who put up a little resistance before eventually running away. Eleven AmaNdebele men were killed, a few women and children taken prisoner and 1,000 cows taken. Forbes learned from the captured women that Lobengula had moved towards the Bubye River, which was roughly ten miles north of Emalangeni. His train included four waggons although

---

24   Sorghum and sweet corn.
25   Forbes, 'The Pursuit of the King', p.137.

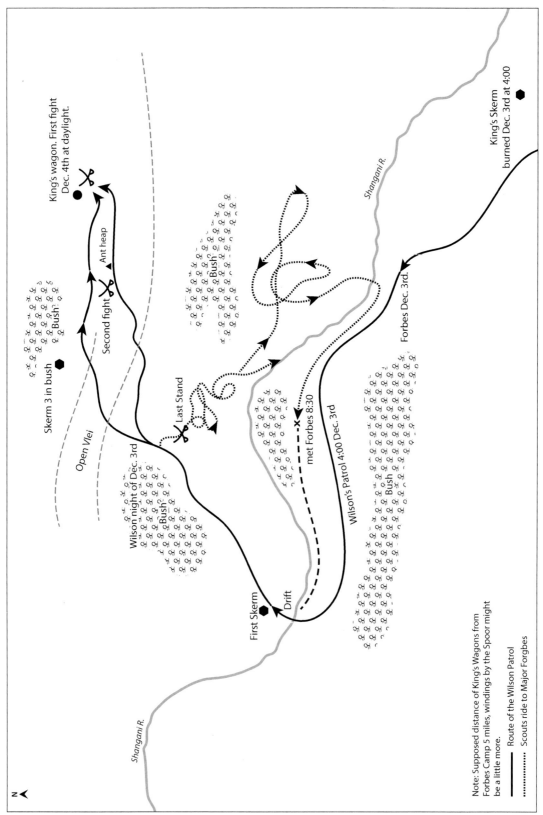

King's wagon. First fight Dec. 4th at daylight.

Ant heap

Second fight

Skerm 3 in bush

Bush

Open Vlei

Last Stand

Bush

Wilson night of Dec. 3rd

Shangani R.

Shangani R.

First Skerm

Drift

met Forbes 8:30

Wilson's Patrol 4:00 Dec. 3rd

Bush

Forbes Dec. 3rd.

King's Skerm burned Dec. 3rd at 4:00

Shangani R.

N

Note: Supposed distance of King's Wagons from Forbes Camp 5 miles, windings by the Spoor might be a little more.

— Route of the Wilson Patrol

······ Scouts ride to Major Forbes

The route of the Shangani Patrol. (Wills & Collingridge, *The Downfall of Lobengula*)

there originally seemed to have been seven.[26] His oxen were exhausted, and the waggons were now being pulled by his followers, but these were few in number. The prisoners claimed that Lobengula's people were sick of fighting and Forbes' Patrol had completely caught their kraal unawares.

This information was good news for Forbes: Lobengula was not too far away and not hidden in dense bush. The Shangani Patrol continued and reached its first objective, the Emalangeni, which was 40 miles from GuBulawayo by the morning of 16 November.[27] Lobengula's 'spoor' had been initially easily followed but the 50,000 cattle that had been driven behind completed obliterated any trace of the King's waggons.[28] The patrol occupied a mission station that belonged to Reverend William Alan Eliot and the Reverend Bowen Rees. Although it had been ransacked by the AmaNdebele, there was some excellent grass close to a large dam Rees had built that offered excellent grazing for the horses, which was very welcome.[29]

It had been Forbes' intention to continue during the night as he did not want to waste any time in the pursuit of the King but, following Jameson's instructions, he consulted with Commandant Raaff who advised caution. Perhaps Ash is correct in believing that the Major tended to always believe what the natives told him.[30] Raaff suggested that Forbes send out scouts to discover whether Lobengula had really crossed the Bubye. Forbes' account indicates that he agreed, but only reluctantly, to follow Raaff's advice.[31] Forbes asked Burnham to check the intelligence he had been given and the American set off with John Grootbanum, a member of the Fingo people for whom Burnham had much praise as he was brave and spoke good English.[32] Usually, Burnham had little positive to say about the indigenous people, but he compared Grootbanum to Umslopogas, the Zulu companion of Alan Quartermain.[33]

After a difficult journey through thick bush where it was necessary to lead the horses, Burnham came to a kraal next to the spot where Lobengula was supposed to have crossed the river. They arrived in the middle of the night and, rather than scouting the riverbank, Burnham decided it would be better to capture one the of the kraal's inhabitants. Burnham describes how he and Grootbanum crept into a hut and quietly dragged a man out and carried him into the bush. The captive was then questioned, and he confirmed that Lobengula had crossed the river. Not wishing to be duped, Burnham, keeping hold of the captive, examined the river and found the tracks of Lobengula's waggons. The truthful prisoner was then released and Burnham and Grootbanum crossed the river and followed Lobengula's spoor

26 Burnham, *Scouting on Two Continents*, p.89.
27 Umhlangeni was also known as Inyati.
28 Burnham, *Scouting on Two Continents*, p.89. 'Spoor' meaning 'track' was frequently used in accounts of the patrol.
29 Rees had been a witness to the second concession awarded to Leask in July 1888.
30 Ash, *Matabele*, p.140.
31 Forbes, 'The Pursuit of the King'.
32 The Fingos were a South African people descended from a group of refugees who had been driven southward in native wars and later settled east of Great Fish River.
33 Burnham, *Scouting on Two Continents*.

until they came across a burnt-out waggon, which indicated that the King was abandoning anything that slowed down his escape. Forbes' version had less of the 'daring do' about it.[34] He records that it was another pair of Raaff's men who went to the river and took a prisoner. This could be a case of Forbes mixing up the events of the two scouting parties or Burnham, always a teller of tall tales, taking the credit for the most daring version. It is hard to decide at this distance in time which was the truth, and Forbes was convinced that no spoor of the King's waggons had been discovered. Both men had a hidden, or perhaps not so hidden, agenda.

Later that night, the patrol was approached by a AmaNdebele named Makasa carrying a white flag. He claimed to have been left in charge of Shiloh by the Reverend Eliot but was unable to prevent the looting of the mission by the defeated warriors returning from the Battle of Imbembezi. Makasa agreed that Lobengula was heading towards the Bubye, and a prisoner was brought into the camp who also confirmed the story. Galvanised into action, Forbes sent runners back to Jameson in GuBulawayo relaying his intention to pursue the King.

Before leaving the mission, Forbes divided his force, leaving 80 men under Captain Frederick Fitzgerald with one of the Salisbury Column's Maxims and the 7-pounder. Forbes and his 200 men set off that night and travelled through dense bush in the darkness. The patrol marched in two columns with the two Maxims to their front. Finally, having marched ten miles and reaching open ground, they occupied a deserted kraal and waited until daylight. By this time, they had eaten all the rations they had carried from GuBulawayo but had plenty of cattle they could slaughter as well as the small amount of kaffir corn they had found in the kraal.

Moving off at daylight, the now reduced Shangani Patrol travelled four miles and reached the Bubye, which had been reduced to a series of large pools of water. As they neared the river, Forbes saw a large herd of cattle and sent instructions to Commandant Raaff to send men to capture them. Raaff chose Captain Lloyd M. Francis to lead a party of 12 men to secure the cattle.[35]

During the halt at the Bubye, the patrol continued to seize cattle and captured several AmaNdebele. The information these prisoners provided confirmed that Lobengula had reached the river but was about 20 miles lower down. He was being followed by the Imbezu and Ingubu *Impis*, whom, the captives claimed, did not want to fight but would not surrender unless ordered to do so by their King. To confirm how near Lobengula's entourage was to the patrol, Forbes discovered that five of his queens had stayed at a nearby kraal. Forbes released five of his prisoners and sent them with messages to both Lobengula and to the Imbezu *Impi*. Forbes' message to the King indicated that there was no escape and that he would be followed

---

34   Forbes, 'The Pursuit of the King'.

35   Forbes ('The Pursuit of the King', p.139) mentions Francis that had a reputation as an experienced fighter but that his own knowledge of Francis's military activities in Natal suggested that he was unreliable. Forbes wrote his account to defend the actions of his patrol and it might be that this observation was based on hindsight rather than an impression he held at the time. It also added to his criticisms of Raaff who obviously held Francis in high esteem.

no matter where he went. To prevent further bloodshed Lobengula should surrender to the patrol and, as an act of good faith, Forbes not only promised to ensure that the King would come to no harm, but he also promised not to fire on any AmaNdebele until he received Lobengula's answer. The message to the Imbezu was very similar. Forbes confirmed that he would continue to follow the King, who had broken his promise to surrender, but as he did not want to fight the *Impi* the warriors should surrender, after which they would be allowed to return to their homes.

It was Forbes' intention to quickly move down the river in pursuit of Lobengula since he was aware that every hour lost meant that the King moved further away. Raaff intervened once again and persuaded the Major to send out scouts before the patrol continued. Although Forbes was clearly resentful of the Commandant's apparent excessive caution, he agreed to send out the scouts. He reasoned that not to do so would cause Raaff to stir up his Rangers and it was important for the various sections of the Shangani Patrol to think as one.

It is interesting to speculate as to which of the two men's decisions was correct. Forbes was keen to complete his mission and bring in the King. This meant pressing on without a moment to lose. Raaff was conscious that the patrol had already been reduced in number and so was increasingly vulnerable. If it did encounter a large *Impi* such as the Imbezu, especially in dense bush without the ability to set up a defensive laager, it could easily be overwhelmed. Throughout the direction of the war until this point, the split command had not been much of a problem. Forbes' authority had not been seriously questioned but Jameson's instructions to consult the Commandant at every step and the background of Raaff's Rangers meant that Forbes' decisions were always under scrutiny. At this point, Forbes did not feel that his position was strong enough to go against Raaff and reluctantly concurred, sending scouts ahead before moving off, fearing that if he did not do so 'morale might suffer'.[36] The following morning, Forbes sent Burnham and Armstrong downriver to see whether there were large numbers of AmaNdebele between the patrol and the fleeing King.[37]

Forbes had guessed correctly that there was discontent among his men and that some were reluctant to continue the hunt. He claimed that it was later that he discovered that this unrest had started among Raaff's men because the Commandant had told them that they should return to GuBulawayo as soon as possible, perhaps because their supplies were depleted. Forbes had previously warned Wilson that Raaff 'could not keep anything to himself' and did a great deal of harm by gossiping with his junior officers and men.[38] Again, one can see Raaff's point. The patrol had reached the last kraals at the river, and it was uncertain whether there were more Kraals downriver that might contain food. If the patrol, which was almost out of provisions, were to proceed into the unknown, it could reasonably be seen as a foolish step.

---

36 Forbes, 'In Pursuit of the King', p.141.
37 Bonar Armstrong was to become Native Commissioner in Mangwe and played a significant part in the Matabele Uprising.
38 Forbes, 'In Pursuit of the King', p.154.

For some time, the men had been living on captured food found in the kraals they had passed and were unsure where the next meal would come from. To try to judge the willingness of the men to proceed, Forbes called a conference with Wilson and Raaff. The Commandant pointed out the situation as he assessed it: they were on a very dangerous mission and were not a large party. Apart from shortage of food, the patrol had limited ammunition and, without waggons, had no means of carrying any wounded.

The differences between the Commandant and the Major may have been based on their different views of the current state of the war. Forbes seems to have seen his expedition as a mopping-up operation in a war that was already won. Raaff, with greater experience of native warfare, thought the AmaNdebele believed that for them there was 'no retreat'.[39] Forbes suggestion that if they came across a strong AmaNdebele force then the patrol should retire appalled Raaff, who believed this would lead to a panic among the amateur soldiers and result in their slaughter.

The relationship between Forbes and his officers seems to have been somewhat distant. While holding Wilson in great esteem, Forbes treated others such as Heany (who had graduated from West Point) and Spreckley, the commanders of A and C Troops of the Salisbury Horse, as having worthless opinions on military matters, even though they were loyal to him.[40] Forbes was very conscious of his insecure authority. Cary argues that he knew that if things went wrong, Jameson would want to know if Raaff had approved of the decisions Forbes had made.[41] Other officers such as Tyndale-Biscoe seemed to have their ears closer to the ground concerning the men's views and wrote in his diary: 'We are now living on anything we can pick up, mostly meat and kaffir corn. [The result of this was] a good deal of discontent among the men on account of the rations.'[42] Spreckley was even more critical of Forbes' leadership style and wrote: 'The men were bullied when they were really doing well.'[43] Forbes, not unnaturally, blamed Raaff for not keeping him informed about the men's feelings.

The three senior officers agreed to call a separate parade of the three sections of the patrol to discover whether they were prepared to continue the hunt. Since the contract with the BSAC was that the troops should be properly fed and this was not being fulfilled, Forbes argued they should be allowed to decide whether they wanted to proceed with the mission or not. After all, most of them were volunteers. Forbes impressed upon Wilson and Raaff that they must not let the men know the reason for the parades since he did not want 'barrack room gossip' to work against him. Forbes' decision was made despite Raaff's suggestion that there should be a conference at which all the officers were present – not just Forbes, Wilson, and himself. The men were not to be pressured either way but given a free choice. Cary records a slightly different version of the arrangements for the parade. He suggests

---

39   O'Reilly, *In Pursuit of the King*, p.127.
40   Cary, *A Time to Die*, p.41.
41   Cary, *A Time to Die*, p.40.
42   E.C. Tyndale-Biscoe RN diary, quoted in Cary, *A Time to Die*, p.42.
43   John Spreckley, quoted in Cary, *A Time to Die*, p.42.

that Spreckley reported to Forbes that he had heard rumours that Raaff's men were anxious to return to GuBulawayo to get supplies. A furious Forbes ordered a parade at 1100 to discuss the ration situation.

While the three leaders were coming to their decision, Armstrong and Burnham arrived back from their scouting mission and reported that they had travelled six miles down the river and seen large numbers of natives and thousands of cattle moving eastwards. None of the natives had attempted to stop them. The scouts concluded that the patrol was safe to proceed for a further five to six miles downriver.

The first parade was duly called at 1100 as arranged and Forbes spoke to the members of the Salisbury Column whom he had led in the first stage of the war. After explaining that he could no longer guarantee a food supply, he asked those who were discontented with the situation to step forward. To his astonishment, 74 men including those under Captain Borrow, who were the escorts for the Maxim, did so. Forbes then announced that those who had stepped forward would be sent back to GuBulawayo but those who had remained 'loyal' would continue to pursue Lobengula come hell or high water. Forbes then stormed off to speak to the next group. Heany, horrified by Forbes' inept questioning of the men, hurriedly followed the Major and pointed out that the men had not understood the original question to mean that they would be sent back, and Forbes had forced them to unwittingly refuse to do their duty. Before dismissing his troop, Heany explained to them that the officers were unaware of the way in which Forbes would put his question to them and if they had done so he was sure that the result would have been different. Raaff's men gave an even worse response when asked – only four wanted to continue. It was only Major Wilson's men from the Victoria Column who responded positively, with all 60 opting to stay in the hunt for the King. Wilson was admired by his men in a way that Forbes was not, and this may have been the deciding factor in their decision. On the other hand, Forbes, who believed that discontent had first occurred among the Victoria men, suspected that Wilson had put pressure on his men not to vote to return. Seeing a way to re-establish his authority, Forbes instructed Raaff to return with his men, but the Commandant refused to do so. He was a soldier he argued and besides, he also had command of the BBP. There is some confusion as to whether the 'soldiers' (the BBP) in the Shangani Patrol had also been asked their opinion. If this was the case, as O'Reilly suggests, it must have been something of a novelty to be given a choice rather than being ordered to do something.[44]

Many officers seemed to have thought that Forbes' had completely misjudged the morale of his men and if he had offered to send for food and medical supplies, they would have been happy to continue the chase. Clearly, as a result of the 'vote' and Forbes' reaction to it, the relationships between the three senior officers deteriorated even further. Forbes sent a message to Jameson regarding the patrol's failure to catch Lobengula and the general dissatisfaction among his men.

---

44   O'Reilly, *In Pursuit of the King*, pp.43–44. Forbes suggests they were not asked but may have been when the question was put to the volunteers.

While waiting for Jameson's reply, Forbes decided that the patrol should return the next day to Shiloh. An AmaNdebele warrior from the Imbezu *Impi* suddenly appeared and claimed that his colleagues had received Forbes' message offering terms but did not trust it until they had checked its veracity for themselves. The AmaNdebele said that there were several of his fellows hidden in the nearby bush waiting to hand over their arms. During this conversation Forbes suddenly saw his native drivers running towards the camp as a group of AmaNdebele were busy driving away a large herd of cattle that had been recently captured. The patrol took up defensive positions and Forbes told Raaff and Wilson to send men out to retake the cattle. The parties successfully recaptured the cattle and killed 11 or 12 of the rustlers. It was clear the Imbezu warrior who had entered the camp had been a decoy and many of the men wanted him shot because of his deception. Forbes, again perhaps taken in by the warrior's story, refused to allow him to be harmed as the Major was convinced that it was true that the *Impi* wished to surrender but the sight of so many cows with too few guards was too much and they couldn't resist the temptation. The result of this attempted coup was that Forbes, fearing that a return to Shiloh would seem like retreat, and heeding Raaff's warning, ordered an advance of a few miles down the river the next day but planned that the patrol should return in the afternoon.

Forbes sent the seven men who had fallen sick and all the cattle back towards Shiloh. The following morning the Shangani Patrol moved eastwards down the banks of the Bubye but, despite many signs that large numbers had recently passed through, it did not see any AmaNdebele. Having reached the end of the open country, Forbes ordered the men to set up camp. There was another clash between Forbes and Raaff during this rest period. Raaff had seen an unknown rider galloping into the nearby bush and had sounded the alarm, but the rider turned out to be one of the patrol's outriders. Forbes was furious either at Raaff's mistake or at what the Major felt was the usurpation of his authority. Forbes argued that the men were nervous enough and such silly mistakes just added to their unease. Forbes was now totally convinced that the patrol must return as quickly as possible. Raaff's faint-heartedness and that of some of the other officers was affecting the men's morale and the thickening bush put them at increasingly greater risk of attack. In fairness to Raaff he was very ill at this time and given the energy and commitment required during the mission, it is hardly surprising that he seemed eternally pessimistic.

While Forbes was contemplating these ideas, Jameson's message arrived. As one might expect, because of the doctor's keenness to capture Lobengula, which he believed would put an end to the expensive war, the message directed that the men should return to Shiloh where Jameson would send 'what food he could spare' together with reinforcements and more ammunition.[45]

---

45 Forbes, 'The Pursuit of the King', p.145.

10

On Lobengula's Heels

The Shangani Patrol limped through heavy rain into Shiloh on 23 November. They had been away from GuBulawayo for four days and, apart from capturing cattle, the importance of which should not be underestimated, they had failed to achieve their mission. Lobengula was still free. The men were bedraggled, dispirited and had been going in the wrong direction. Their food was exhausted, their horses, in the terms of the time, were 'knocked up', and they were low on ammunition. Their morale was undoubtedly at rock bottom.

Forbes used the next day to take stock of the situation. The support Jameson had sent included ten waggons of supplies but the oxen of five of them could go no further. The Major calculated that, with the remaining five waggons he could take food for 300 men on three-quarter rations which should last them 12 days.[1] Jameson had also sent around 200 men under the command of Captain William Napier but most of them were without horses.[2] Napier also brought a small amount of brandy, enough for a tot per man. Such small things can improve morale and it was so in this case.

It was clear to Forbes that he needed to reduce the size of his party if he were to have any chance of capturing Lobengula. Speed was of the essence and slow-moving men, horses, and waggons would not achieve this. Accordingly, he chose the following groups to attempt to capture Lobengula for the second time: Captain Borrow and 22 mounted men from the Salisbury Column; Captain Wilson and 70 mounted men and 100 men on foot from the Victoria Column; and Commandant Raaff and 20 mounted men together with 78 mounted BBP under Captain Coventry.[3] This made a total of 190 mounted men and 100 on foot.

---

1   Forbes, 'The Pursuit of the King', p.147. Cary (*A Time to Die*, p.47) suggests that it was enough for 268 men for 13 days. O'Reilly (*In Pursuit of the King*, p.45) also quotes 12 days. It is not clear whether Forbes took the full 300, which might account for the extra day. The additional members could have been native bearers.

2   Napier was born in Scotland and served with the Natal Carbineers at Isandlwana. After a period as a gold prospector, he was employed by the BSAC and joined the Victoria Rangers in 1882. After serving throughout the Matabele War and the Matabele Rebellion he became a farmer but returned to the Colours and served in the Second Boer War.

3   These are the figures quoted by Forbes.

The reorganised patrol also included four waggons, two of which were loaded with a Maxim. The two other Maxims were horse-drawn as was the Hotchkiss, which Napier had brought from GuBulawayo. Forbes was reluctant to take any waggons at all because the heavy rains had made the ground very muddy but did so 'because they were there'.[4] This seems a strange way to make a decision and one wonders if there were outside opinions like Raaff's at work since the waggons could transport the wounded if it became necessary. Forbes hinted as much when he indicated that he would only use the waggons for a few days. A few natives were also included in the reorganised patrol.

The remainder of the men, including some who had accompanied Napier, were sent back to GuBulawayo with Bastard and Heany in charge. They went with a message from Forbes to Jameson pointing out that the rations, though welcome, were only sufficient for 12 days. Forbes' reorganised patrol would go as far as it could in that time but would expect to be back to the Shangani on the main road to Mashonaland by the twelfth day. Jameson was asked to send more food to the Shangani. Forbes also asked Jameson if he could create a diversion on the road to the Shangani, but Jameson was unable to help with this.

The heavy rain continued, and it was not until 25 November that Forbes began the second search with only 30 men fewer than the original number who had left GuBulawayo. Forbes' men quickly found the spoor of Lobengula's waggons and followed it for eight miles before they made camp, having passed several *scherms* and kraals on the way. They did find some grain and were careful to burn the kraals. Their laager made use of the waggons by having one at each corner with the oxen securely held on its inside along with the cattle that would be used to feed the men.

The next morning 'Matabele' Wilson arrived with welcome brandy for the sick and a message from Jameson indicating that the Shangani Patrol had been within three miles of Lobengula when they had turned back towards Shiloh. The message also emphasised that it was important to capture the King. 'Matabele' Wilson commented on the condition of the men in the reconstituted Shangani Patrol as being wet and cold and in need of basic supplies such as matches and tobacco which were in short supply.[5] He declined the offer to join the patrol and continue the search, and together with Charles Acutt, who was sick, returned to GuBulawayo. Forbes continued his march having lost two horses which had strayed into the bush and the patrol halted after four miles of heavy going. Colenbrander came into the camp with a large number of cattle and two small native boys who had been in charge of the cows. Forbes' pickets came in to say that a group of AmaNdebele warriors had approached them asking to speak to the Major. The warriors had been polite but refused to be disarmed. Forbes had all the horses collected together as a precaution but, when he reached to spot where the warriors had been seen, he found the birds had flown and, even though Raaff conducted a search, they could not be found. Forbes complains that

---

4   Forbes, 'The Pursuit of the King', p.147.
5   Matabele Wilson diary, quoted in Cary, *A Time to Die*, p.49.

Raaff strayed a long way from the camp while he was searching and took so long to return that it was too late to continue the march, which caused further friction between the two. The weather continued to deteriorate and there were heavy storms.

The next morning, Captain Alan Finch, one of Forbes' staff officers who had gone to GuBulawayo to see a dentist before the second patrol left Shiloh, returned with a trooper and the two horses that had strayed back to Shiloh. Finch also brought a letter from Jameson carrying the news that Lobengula, who was in a bad way, had repeated his request that Usher and Fairburn be sent to speak with him. Forbes' party continued their search at 0630 hours the next day, but such was the difficulty of moving over the waterlogged ground that they were forced to camp in a spot without a water supply in middle of the day. The terrain was so difficult that the patrol could only travel eight miles during the day.

The next day Raaff sought permission to ride two or three miles ahead of the main body of the patrol in order to search for water which was now badly needed. Forbes complained that Raaff and his party of 25 including the scout Burnham actually went eight miles ahead and were fortunate not to have been cut off from the patrol by AmaNdebele warriors, especially since few of Raaff's party were experience soldiers.

Three AmaNdebele were captured by Raaff's men who all told the same story. Lobengula's party was getting smaller as his followers were deserting him. He had reached the Shangani and intended to stay there for some time. Forbes realised that this was an opportunity to complete his task but in order to catch up with the King it was necessary to leave the waggons behind, especially since the rain was continuous and the going increasingly muddy. He probably felt justified in doing this as he had only taken them along because several his officers had advised him to do so. In any case the oxen were 'knocked up'. The horses were also suffering and if the patrol was to catch up with Lobengula, its size must be reduced again. Checking the horses, Forbes decided that there were only 160 fit enough to continue. Most of these belonged to members of Wilson's original Victoria Column. The Shangani Patrol was therefore reduced even further as these horses were shared out. The patrol finally consisted of 28 of Forbes' Salisbury Column, 46 from Wilson's Victoria Column, 24 from the Tuli Column and 60 BBP. The remaining men were ordered to return to Umhlangeni under the command of Captain Dallamore and wait for fresh horses. Lendy was placed in an invidious position as his Maxims were also to return. He managed to come to an unofficial agreement with Captain Tancred who controlled the two that were to be attached to the now reduced patrol that he should control one of them. Lendy, considered to be a brilliant artillery expert, was losing respect for Forbes, who had again showed that he lacked judgement when managing his officers.[6]

Leaving the next day Forbes and his patrol travelled a total of 17 miles; they crossed the Imbembezi River, which was only three feet deep, along

---

6   Cary *A Time to Die*, p.50.

the way. They laagered at a burnt-out kraal, as the rain continued. On the next day, 30 November, the column travelled a total of 16 miles and came within two miles of the Bubye River Valley before they were forced to laager. They were continuing to follow the spoor of the Kings' waggons and passed *scherms* that had only recently been abandoned. During the journey, riders on the flanks captured a few men and women who were brought into the camp for questioning. At nightfall, news was received of a very large *scherm*, which, when investigated by Colenbrander, was found to contain over 200 AmaNdebele. Forbes, Raaff, and Wilson had previously agreed that any groups of AmaNdebele they came across should be treated kindly as attacking them could cause casualties the patrol would find difficult to manage. Additionally, Lobengula would hear about the fighting and not believe he would be safe if he surrendered.

Colenbrander ordered the natives to bring wood and water to the laager and although they agreed that they would, they did not do so. Their *Induna*, when question gave the same information that had been heard before: Lobengula was at the Shangani River with only a few followers. There were also groups of warriors from several *Impis* concealed in the bush and acting as guards. The majority of AmaNdebele did not want to fight and many were returning to their home kraals. Smallpox and hunger were devastating the people and the *Induna* begged that his people allowed to return home to GuBulawayo. Forbes told him to take his people home and report to Jameson on their arrival. Somewhat naively, Forbes also ordered the *Induna* not to tell Lobengula that he was on his trail. Later, Forbes seemed surprised that the *Induna* had told Lobengula despite the threats that had been made if he did so. The next morning, Captain Fitzgerald was sent to confiscate the *Induna's* people's cattle in punishment for not bringing the wood but, unsurprisingly, the AmaNdebele were gone, and Fitzgerald returned with only 25 sheep and goats, which were all in poor shape.

With Burnham scouting ahead for water, Forbes' men moved off in the afternoon. They had to cross the Bubye River, which was a dry channel with steep banks and, through lack of care, one of the Maxims was overturned. It was quickly righted, and the column made eight miles before setting up camp in a large clearing. During its progress the patrol came across numerous *scherms* containing AmaNdebele and their cattle, which were in poor condition. They were, according to Forbes, relieved when they were told they could return home in safety.[7]

The patrol continued to follow the King's spoor, passing two burned-out waggons and, shortly afterwards, Lobengula's bath chair, which required 16 men to pull it. Forbes speculated, probably correctly, that it was this contraption that had given rise to the story that the King's waggons were being pulled by his followers and not by oxen. Lobengula's group was making too rapid progress for this to have been the case and the rumour probably led to Forbes feeling the King was just ahead of his column. Lobengula was obviously making haste as his men had done little clearing of the bush and

---

7   Forbes, 'In Pursuit of Lobengula', p.151.

only avoided the large trees – another reason to conclude that his waggons were being pulled by oxen. The weather continued to be challenging and there were constant heavy storms. Forbes thought that his patrol might be 15 miles further down the Bubye from the point where they had earlier turned back for Shiloh.

The three waggons with Lobengula had split up and the column was delayed while finding which was the correct spoor to follow. It turned out that they had simply divided to avoid a large muddy bog, going around each side rather than in single file which would have slowed them down. The spoor continued down the east bank of the Gwambo River and then turned due north through a wide, open valley at the edges of which were abandoned *scherms*. The pursuing patrol made six miles that day and Colenbrander was

Lobengula in his favourite chair. (*The Graphic*, 1893)

able to entice an AmaNdebele out of the bush who provided Forbes with some vital information.

The informant had been educated by the missionaries at Umhlangeni where his home kraal was situated. He said that on the previous day Lobengula had been around 15 miles ahead on the west bank of the Shangani. He had few warriors with him but there were a larger number of his followers herding his cattle. The King had been joined by a number of important *Indunas* including Ingubugubu, the King's brother. The AmaNdebele did not know the exact whereabouts of the *Induna* Gambo, who had led an attack on the Tuli Column, but suspected that he too had now joined Lobengula. It was also rumoured that Gambo believed that the only way out of the AmaNdebele's trouble was for them to make peace with the white men. Forbes must have realised that capturing such an important group of *Indunas* would be both a military coup and a political triumph. Lobengula's spoor turned into the bush around three miles ahead. The native warned Forbes that there was no water until they reached the Shangani.[8]

While he was digesting this news, Forbes decided to send Burnham, Ingram, and Bain with Grootbanum as their interpreter to scout ahead.[9] Having followed the King's spoor until it left the track and then turned into the bush, they decided to continue to move into this riskier area. On reaching a ridge of high ground, Ingram's horse broke down and could no longer bear his weight. This, as Burnham pointed out, was a very serious matter. All the horses were weak but for a man to be on foot in the dense bush was to put himself at serious risk.[10] Ingram resolved that he would lead

---

8   P.W. Forbes, 'The Loss of the Wilson Patrol', in Wills & Collingridge, *The Downfall of Lobengula*, p.153.
9   Forbes names the third scout as 'Mayne' and Burnham names him as 'Bain' who was a Canadian.
10   Burnham, *Scouting on Two Continents*, p.89.

his horse back towards the patrol, but Bain and Burnham decided they still needed to find out just how large was the *Impi* in front of them but, warned by the condition of Ingram's horse, found a safe place in long grass in order to give their mounts a rest. This seemed foolhardy, for as Burnham admits, they could see large numbers of warriors near to where they were trying to hide.

They unsaddled and Bain, instead of keeping his rifle within his grasp, foolishly placed it against a tree a few feet away. Suddenly, out of the long grass 15 or so AmaNdebele appeared with their rifles at the ready. They were very intimidating and said they were from Gambo's *Impi*. Grootbanum, without showing any fear, came to the rescue and being fluent in the warriors' language, interpreted Burnham's shouted command to put down their rifles. 'How dare you advance with weapons in the presence of the *Induna*? Put your guns down!' The AmaNdebele warriors may have been slightly nonplussed by the hauteur of the scouts who were, after all, in a vulnerable position, but their leader made a move towards Bain's rifle. Bain reacted with speed, grabbed the rifle and pointed it at the warrior's stomach. Both Burnham and Grootbanum also reacted quickly, and the situation appeared to be something of a stand-off. The AmaNdebele warriors could overpower the scouts, but it would be at the cost of three of their own lives to do so. Burnham and then Bain took turns to saddle their horses while the others covered the AmaNdebele leader, they then both covered him while Grootbanum saddled his horse. All that was left was for the three men to mount their horses. Slowly, step by step the scouts were able to withdraw, and the warriors disappeared into the bush, perhaps fooled by Burnham's suggestion that there was a large group of white men nearby who would appear very quickly if they heard shots. With exhausted horses, the three men slowly moved back to the patrol and were very relieved when they overtook Ingram leading his horse, unaware of the danger he had escaped. All four safely returned to the patrol but were described as looking 'slightly pale'.[11]

It seems the experience was one of the very few times during the war when Burnham was frightened by events.[12] Forbes discussed Burnham's fears with Wilson and Finch but not with Raaff, whom Forbes saw as a gossip and doom monger. Forbes boasted that he and Wilson were aware that the patrol was liable to be attacked by between 2,000 and 3,000 warriors but both were confident that the Maxims would see them off as they had done in the two previous engagements. Forbes momentarily seems to have forgotten that he had far fewer men under his command, half the number of Maxims and no waggons behind which to take cover. An attack on the patrol in the middle of dense bush would be a very different affair from the Battle of Imbembezi, even if Wilson was keen to make sure that the patrol was ready to fight at a moment's notice.

On 3 December, the patrol started off again and followed the path Burnham had taken the previous day. They passed several *scherms*, and the scout estimated that they were following around 1,500 AmaNdebele men women and children.[13] The patrol ascended the ridge where Burnham had

11   Bulpin, *The White Whirlwind*, p.79.
12   O'Reilly, *Pursuit of the King*, pp.50–51.
13   Burnham used the ingenious method of counting the discarded blocks of wood which the AmaNdebele had used as pillows. Forbes, 'The Loss of the Wilson Patrol', p.155.

encountered the frightening warriors and on descending the other side into a wide valley suddenly came across a large pool with wild pigs grazing nearby. The water was unexpected as they had been told that they would not reach water until they arrived at the Shangani. The pigs were very nervous and easily frightened, and Forbes took this as a sign that there were no AmaNdebele in the area. The patrol continued to move forward with a Maxim placed at its front and rear. The men marched in close order remaining in their original sections: Salisbury, Victoria, Tuli and, finally, the BBP. Forbes had posted an advanced guard of four men rather than risk his scouts being caught unawares because they were too far in advance. Ascending a second ridge, the patrol received a warning from this advanced guard who reported that they had seen five or six warriors crossing the path and disappearing into the bush. Forbes decided that extra caution was needed and did not order a pursuit. He expected an attack as this was the last stretch of bush before they reached the Shangani.

Suddenly the patrol heard an unexpected and unexplained shot coming from their left flank. Raaff investigated and confirmed it had not been fired by any member of the column. Neither Forbes nor any member of the patrol had seen anything. Raaff sent his conclusions via an orderly who received a poor reception from Forbes, who either because the Major was slightly deaf or to rebuff Raaff, said it had actually been two shots. Those around Forbes soon put him right and he concluded that it must have been a signal from the enemy to either attack or retreat.[14] There were signs of a group of AmaNdebele moving in the opposite direction to the column, but none were seen.

The patrol then descended the ridge into a large open space. Burnham and Colenbrander had by now joined the advanced guard which had captured a young AmaNdebele. The boy quickly told Forbes that Lobengula was a little way ahead. The King had tried to move off the previous day, but his waggons had become stuck, forcing him to return and seek out enough men to extract the waggons from the mud. The fight had gone out of the King, the boy claimed, and he had sent one of his sons to tell Jameson that he was returning to GuBulawayo. Forbes formed the patrol into a marching square and broke through the bush into a clearing in which he found the King's camp. Many AmaNdebele fled into the bush unharmed as Forbes rode up to the huts, but they were all deserted except for a young boy who, when questioned, indicated that Lobengula had moved on and not returned.

With only two hours of daylight left, Forbes ordered Wilson to take his best 12 horses and follow the King's spoor towards the River Shangani where there was probably a drift over which Lobengula had crossed. Wilson was to try and find out how far the King's party was ahead and to gather any other useful information but, Forbes stressed, the Major must return by nightfall. Cary is correct in emphasising the important part of the instructions given to Wilson.[15] His obedience to them may have prevented the tragedy to come.

---

14 This shot was to figure in the trial of Daniel and Wilson. See Chapter 16.
15 Cary, *A Time to Die*, p.52.

11

Back to the Shangani River

Being given such an opportunity to distinguish himself must have appealed to Wilson. Here was a chance to complete the patrol's mission almost single-handed or a least with the aid of members of his own Victoria Column. Such was the enthusiasm to get the job done, that when Wilson and his 12 men rode off towards the river, they were joined by several officers, perhaps as many as eight, eager to share the glory.[1] This was a reconnaissance patrol whose objective was to find the whereabouts of the waggons and then return, but Wilson had other ideas.[2]

Wilson's Patrol had left without any help from the scouts, so Forbes sent Ingram and Burnham to follow Wilson's men, even giving Burnham his own horse as the scout's mount was very weak. The rest of the column laagered a short distance from the river and could hear natives building *scherms* on the other side of its banks. The issue of lack of supplies again became a factor. Forbes specifies that, in a conversation with Wilson the previous day, they had both agreed that the Shangani would be the limit of the patrol's range. They had been out nine days, were roughly 60 miles from Shiloh, and the return journey would need all the remaining food.

Forbes once again questioned the youth who had been found in the King's camp. He turned out to be someone of importance and very free with information. The youth was a son of the *Induna* of GuBulawayo and may have shocked Forbes when he told him that although Lobengula's gout meant the King could only move very slowly, he was accompanied by 3,000 warriors mainly from the Insukameni and Siseba *Impis*, both of which were still loyal to the King. Forbes, who believed most of these warriors were useless in a fight, and again believing what he had been told, made mental, if not actual preparation to take 50 men and a galloping Maxim across the river when Wilson's Patrol returned with the information they had gathered. Forbes

---

1   Glass, *The Matabele War*, p.228. Forbes names two of the officers as Captains Kirton and Greenfield and indicates that Kirton knew he was expected back shortly because he asked that his dinner be kept warm. Cary (*A Time to Die*, p.36) reminds his readers that this was a group of amateur, volunteer soldiers who might not regard orders in the same way as professionals. See also Forbes, 'The Loss of Wilson's Patrol', p.157.

2   In order to distinguish the Forbes' Shangani Patrol from the men with Wilson, the latter will be referred to as 'Wilson's Patrol'.

confided as much in confidence with Bugler Chappé.[3] After he returned, Wilson was to remain at the laager and take charge of the remaining sections of the Shangani Patrol that would be left behind while Forbes and his 50 troopers made a dash to capture the King. Cary suggests that the rumour of this plan reached the ears of Wilson and might have accounted for what he was about to do.[4] It is certainly true that he would not have enjoyed being side-lined.

In truth, Forbes acted with professionalism throughout the campaign as can be seen in his instructions to make sure the Combined Column's various contingent parts operated as discrete units, which meant that Wilson continued to make the decisions for the Victoria Column. Yet here was an opportunity for Wilson to gain all the glory and perhaps the authority resting on Forbes' shoulders. Wilson must have felt that if Lobengula could be captured, he was the man to do it. It is also possible that Wilson believed that to return to Forbes' laager would give Lobengula an opportunity to slip away into the bush and escape yet again. Since it had been agreed that the Shangani was the limit of the patrol's range, the King had to be taken quickly because of the food shortage.

As darkness fell, Chappé, who had further interrogated one of the captives, informed Forbes that the *Induna's* son had lied. There were only 100 men, mainly Maholi, with Lobengula and the rest had moved into the bush ready to attack the Shangani Patrol. Further information was obtained suggesting that the attack would be that night and so Forbes took great care arranging his laager and deploying his pickets. It became dark at around 1830 hours but there was still no sign of Wilson's return.

At 2100 hours, two members of Wilson's Patrol, Sergeant Major Judge and Corporal Ebbage, arrived back at the laager with news.[5] Wilson's party had crossed the river, the bed of which was some 100 yards across but virtually dry. Despite this, they passed one of the King's remaining waggons that had become trapped in the mud. Ascending the river's steep far bank which led into thick bush, Wilson ordered that Burnham and Bain should take the lead some 50 yards in front of his patrol. The bulk of the men should ride in a column of twos with Lieutenant Hofmeyer and two troopers acting as rear guard.[6] The patrol followed Lobengula's spoor for five miles. Judge and Ebbage were then sent back because their horses were 'knocked up'. They were instructed to tell Forbes that Wilson intended to continue following the spoor and to camp out that night. Forbes could, if he felt it necessary, send more men across the river to join him, but it was probably not necessary for the reinforcements to bring a Maxim, though the track was good enough for them to do so. The tone of this message is interesting and suggests a possible change in command. Wilson was disobeying Forbes' instruction to return

---

3   Cary, *A Time to Die*, p.54.
4   Cary, *A Time to Die*, p.54.
5   Cary follows Forbes in using the name 'Judge', while O'Reilly names him as 'Judd' and many have confused him with Commandant W.J. Judd who had been in command of the Victoria Burghers. Colvin, *The Life of Jameson*, Vol. I, p.253.
6   Arend Hofmeyer was the son of a Cape Town clergyman.

by nightfall and was almost casually suggesting how the Shangani Patrol's designated commander might act in such a way Wilson felt necessary.

John Wilcox, in his highly readable but fictitious account of the Shangani Patrol sums up Forbes' reaction to Wilson's message extremely well. 'I told the man to be back here before dark. Now he has set himself up right on the enemy's doorstep and as good as ordered me to come and rescue him. Bloody fool.'[7] Cary makes much of the fact that Wilson did not send a written message, which he deduced indicated that Wilson did not feel that he was in danger.[8] It is true that this might be a strange conclusion as Wilson had only a few men in his patrol and no Maxim and was therefore vulnerable to attack. However, Judge and Ebagge explained that it was still believed that there were only a few AmaNdebele attendants with the King and that the main *Impi* was behind Forbes' party. Perhaps because of this sobering news, Forbes recorded that no one got a good night's sleep as they were expecting a silent, surprise attack. He had magnesium flares and rockets at the ready to illuminate the area just in case. Whatever his previous reluctant attitude to taking precautions when laagered, which were probably because of his supreme confidence in the power of the Maxims, Forbes now became ultra-cautious. Pickets were doubled, the men's saddles and blankets were used to form a protective if small wall in place of the missing waggons and the rockets and flares were checked.

At around 2300 hours, Captain Napier and two troopers appeared and provided further news that the Wilson Patrol had come across a *scherm* on the other side of the Shangani where a native told them that Lobengula was a short distance ahead and confirmed that he had few followers and that the defending *Impi* was actually behind Forbes. The AmaNdebele volunteered to take them to the King and so Wilson and his men had travelled as fast as they could towards his supposed resting place. As they moved onwards, they passed an increasing number of *scherms*, containing men, women, children and cattle. About three miles from the river, Wilson's Patrol came to five more substantial *scherms* and called to each one in turn that they did not want to harm anyone but just wanted to speak with Lobengula. Whether caught by surprise at the sudden appearance of the patrol in their midst or uncertain as to what to do without orders, the AmaNdebele did nothing. Wilson's men could see at the end of the track a very large circular *scherm*, which loomed out of the darkness. It was surrounded by a palisade through which the shape of two waggons could be seen.[9] Further confirmation that this was Lobengula's *scherm*, if such was need, was provided by the presence of a small white horse. Horses were rare among the AmaNdebele and it clearly indicated the presence of someone of high status. Napier, who spoke excellent Zulu, called out to the *scherm*, using all Lobengula's flattering titles, that they were distinguished messengers spent by Dr Jameson to escort the King to GuBulawayo where he would be honoured, and peace be made. There was no response.

---

7   John Wilcox, *The Shangani Patrol* (London: Headline, 2010), p.310. Wilcox's novel centres around the fictional character, Simon Fonthill, who seems to have been present at many of the major events in Africa during the nineteenth century.

8   Cary, *A Time to Die*, p.63.

9   Burnham, *Scouting on Two Continents*, p.95.

By this time, those AmaNdebele in the *scherms,* which Wilson's men had previously passed, had recovered their composure and, realising that Wilson's Patrol was not the advanced guard of a much larger force, began to advance in numbers, armed with rifles, towards the patrol's rear. Hofmeyer and some troopers were sent to control one of the most belligerent-looking groups, much in the way that mounted policemen might do and this quietened things down. Wilson, realising that events were getting out of hand ordered his party to retreat into the bush, which was successfully done without a shot being fired. As his patrol did so, a heavy storm broke out and, together with the darkness, contributed to Lieutenant Hofmeyer and two troopers becoming detached from the group and unable to find their way through the bush to re-join the patrol. Wilson, uncertain what to do next, sent Napier and two troopers back to Forbes' laager to inform him what had happened. Napier also confirmed that they had not seen anyone during their return journey which seemed to suggest that the *Impi* really *was* behind Forbes' men.

Forbes was increasingly perplexed as to how to proceed. He asked Napier his opinion as to what he thought Wilson would expect him to do. Napier replied that Wilson would assume that Forbes would immediately cross the Shangani with the whole force and attack the King's kraal at daybreak. Forbes was shocked at this suggestion. The noise the Maxims would make while they went through the bush would cause the Shangani Patrol's movements to be heard and prevent them launching a surprise attack, which, given the likely numbers of AmaNdebele ahead, was essential to success. Forbes' belief was that his patrol was at that moment surrounded, and an attack that night was imminent. Dismantling the laager in the dark would be a certain invitation to the AmaNdebele to launch an attack while his men were very vulnerable. Although the river was low and a crossing was possible, Forbes had no idea how many warriors were hidden in the bush on its far bank waiting for him to begin the crossing. Either from lack of knowledge of the country or foolishness, Forbes was unaware despite the weather that there had been heavier rains further up the river that would play a decisive part in the fate of the patrol.

On the other hand, it seemed that Forbes had two alternative actions to crossing the river – both unsatisfactory. First, he could order Wilson to return. This would mean that the Shangani Patrol had failed at the point of success. Forbes appears to have had no doubt that Wilson was on the verge of completing the mission. Success would enhance the reputation of both men and boost the value of the BSAC's shares. Failure would mean that all Forbes' efforts had been for nothing and would undoubtedly bring criticism from Jameson and Rhodes. Perhaps if Forbes had been more willing to take a risk it would have saved Wilson from disaster and death. Such a gamble, however, would have been somewhat out of character.

Forbes second option was to detach men from his already depleted patrol and send them to assist Wilson at least until the rest of the Shangani Patrol was able to move towards him.[10] This would create three small groups of

---

10   It is unclear whether Wilson's definitely suggested he needed reinforcements. At the Court of Inquiry held as a result of the Patrol's failure, Forbes was unclear. Napier, one of Wilson's

troopers and would allow the AmaNdebele to attack each group individually, especially since two Maxims could not be divided three ways. Throughout the patrol, the value of the Maxims predominated. All the patrol's members believed that these weapons were the key to their success if attacked by thousands of AmaNdebele. An attempt to cross the Shangani at night might result in the guns becoming stuck in the mud, which would mean that the patrol would be at the mercy of an attack and almost certainly overwhelmed.

Both Forbes and Wilson were determined to catch the King and suspected that Lobengula was aware of how close they were to his camp and so would not hesitate to continue his escape as quickly as possible if he could. Since the Shangani River was the agreed limit for the patrol, it would not be able to follow him should Lobengula continue to flee. The patrol's efforts would be for nothing and Forbes, as commander, would be seen to have failed in fulfilling its objectives.

Forbes eventually decided in spite of the risks to send a group from his remaining patrol to support Wilson. He undoubtedly knew the maxim that a commander should not needlessly divide his forces and his education at Sandhurst Military College may well have provided him examples of disasters that had happened as a result of ignoring this rule.

Having decided to take the risk, the question that posed itself to Forbes was how many men should he send? Forbes' reluctant decision, given that Wilson only had 12 men in his party, or perhaps 15 if Hofmeyer and his two troopers had eventually returned, was to send Captain Borrow with 20 men of the Salisbury Column whose horses were still relatively sound. Again, following Jameson's orders, Forbes consulted Raaff who, having been assured that the Maxims would not be sent, appears to have agreed with the plan. Both men seemed, understandably, to want to ensure the survival of most of the patrol and this would be more likely to be achieved by sending Wilson only a few reinforcements while ensuring the patrol's most effective weapon, the Maxims, remained with the larger force.

Such was Forbes' version of events, and it included a quote from Raaff in which the Commandant said, somewhat ambiguously: 'This is the beginning of the end'.[11] Colenbrander, however, who had slept through Napier's arrival, questioned Raaff as to what was happening. Raaff is said to have told Colenbrander that Wilson's decision to divide his party was 'lunacy'. Wilson hadn't returned because he was not in danger, argued the Commandant, and he wanted the credit for capturing the King which would be one in the eye for Forbes.[12] Lendy and Francis heard the discussion between Raaff and Forbes and, once it was over, subjected Raaff to a tirade. They were concerned that sending so few men was courting disaster. The correct decision would have been to recall Wilson or for all the remaining group to move towards him in support. They begged Raaff to speak to Forbes in these terms. Raaff, however, would not be openly disloyal to Forbes and felt he must obey orders despite examples where he had not done so in the past.

---

senior officers, would almost certainly be aware of Wilson's wishes.

11   Forbes, 'The Loss of the Wilson Patrol', p.162.

12   Bulpin, *The White Whirlwind*, p.380.

In retrospect one must conclude that Lendy and Francis were correct in identifying the best strategies Forbes should have adopted. Giving Wilson a direct order to return would have extracted his patrol from immediate danger. The Shangani was still a fordable obstacle, and it would probably mean that Lobengula would escape but it would also save Wilson and his men. Advancing towards Wilson with the remainder of the patrol would provide positive support especially as the power of the Maxims would be available to keep off the attackers. It might also keep Lobengula in sight and enable Forbes to succeed in his objective.

Forbes eventually solved his dilemma by deciding to send Captain Henry Borrow with his detachment from the Salisbury Horse to support Wilson.[13] Borrow was very popular among the members of the patrol and was described as 'a thoroughly good, brave man … who we all knew and loved'.[14] Borrow was keen to go, but the disappointed Napier, believing that a mere 20 men would mean that Wilson could only act defensively and being very wet from his journey, declined the offer to return. Mayne, who had become feverish, also remained with Forbes' party. As Borrow was preparing to ride off into the semi-darkness, he asked that his men not be required to take the full ammunition allowance of 100 rounds for their Martini-Henrys as they were very heavy for the horses to carry and would slow his progress. Forbes said that they must do so and records that, in addition to the rifles, they each had a revolver with 20 rounds.[15] Robertson, perhaps because he had no choice being a mere trooper, was designated to guide Borrow to the place where Wilson's men were camped. Borrow was given a 'written' message to deliver to Wilson which said that Forbes party could not leave until daylight as he expected that they would be attacked that night. Wilson, being the man on the spot, should use his own judgement as to what to do. One might consider this to be sound practice or another example of Forbes lack of decisiveness.

Borrow and his 20 troopers left the camp between 1230 hours and 0100 hours and, as they left, having driven out the slaughter cattle, Forbes reorganised the camp's structure into that of a triangle. The two Maxims were place at two of its corners. They could not hear any sounds from any nearby AmaNdebele and the rain began to fall again. Forbes gave orders that reveille be sounded at 0300 hours and his party be ready to move off as soon as possible thereafter.

As Forbes had suspected, the AmaNdebele were close to his camp. Mjaan had guessed that the patrol would move at first light and had led part of his force towards the King's kraal close to which Wilson's men were sleeping. Mjaan's remaining men again divided, with half staying close to Forbes' Patrol and the rest, having skirted around it, crossing the Shangani and setting an ambush on the northern side of the drift over which they would cross.

---

13   Borrow was born in Cornwall, the son of a clergyman. After leaving school he went to South Africa as a farmer. In 1896 he joined Carrington's Horse and took part in the Warren Expedition. He then became a prospector and successful entrepreneur, taking part in the Pioneer Column.

14   Unknown trooper, quoted in Cary, *A Time to Die*, p.77.

15   Forbes, 'The Loss of the Wilson Patrol', p.162.

12

All are Lost!

Forbes and his party prepared to set off as soon as it was light, but the slaughter cattle had somehow strayed, in spite of his precautions, and the AmaNdebele, seeing these valuable animals apparently grazing unattended, herded them into one of their own kraals. Since these animals represented the patrol's main source of food, Forbes sent John Grootbanum to find them. This he successfully did and returned to report that the AmaNdebele had been very cooperative in releasing the cattle. Just as Forbes' party was ready to leave, they heard firing coming from what they assumed was Lobengula's camp. This surprised the local natives as they had expressly said that the King's escort did not want to fight and repeated that they certainly did not want to do so. It is likely that this firing was the sound of the AmaNdebele attacking Wilson's Patrol which, at that point, consisted of 37 men.

Forbes' Column of between 113 and 121 men began to advance down the riverbank towards the drift in close order with the Maxims on its left flank, which was bordered by bush and the river to its right. They saw three women carrying water pots cross in front of them and then, more significantly, a warrior on a white horse with 12 others on foot come out of the bush and move down the riverbank towards the drift. The Shangani Column approached the river, the banks of which were some ten feet high, and then entered an area of thinned-out brush. Suddenly they were attacked from the left flank where there was thicker bush shielding the attackers. Forbes found it difficult to estimate the size of the attacking force since only a few came into open view, but he guessed that it was around 300 AmaNdebele. The attackers' fire was, as usual, inaccurate, and mostly ineffective but the patrol could only return fire by aiming at the puffs of smoke of the AmaNdebele rifles. The attackers then turned their attention to firing at the Maxims and several of the draught horses were hit. The AmaNdebele were aware that the horses were vital to both the men and the Maxims, and 16 horses were killed, together with five mules.

The patrol had been caught in a tricky situation; it dared not move forwards or backwards since this would involve inspanning the Maxims, which meant that these essential weapons would be temporarily out of action, allowing the AmaNdebele to charge in large numbers.[1] Unexpectedly, two troopers from Borrow's party, Landsberg and Nesbitt, who, having crossed the Shangani behind the patrol, then joined Forbes' men. They had become separated from Wilson and thought the safest thing for them to do was to return to the main body of troops rather than blundering around in the bush. The troopers' ability to cross the river at this time further proved that Wilson could have returned to the safety of the main patrol if he had chosen to do so.

After about an hour, the AmaNdebele's fire began to slacken, and Forbes thought that it was safe for his column to proceed. Deciding to make sure that at least one Maxim was in action, he inspanned the horse Maxim ready for it to be moved. The enemy fire suddenly increased from the front right of the column and Forbes supposed that the AmaNdebele were attempted to outflank him. Reversing his decision, Forbes had the horse Maxim outspanned and its bursts of fire were directed to the column's right.[2] This had the desired effect on the AmaNdebele, and the firing ceased. Thinking once again that it was safe to proceed, both Maxims were inspanned and the Shangani Column began to move forward slowly with the dismounted men on its safer riverside flank. The column then moved into thicker bush and the enemy fire ceased altogether. At this point, the scouts Burnham and Ingram accompanied by Trooper Gooding, having crossed the Shangani, galloped up and joined the main body. According to Forbes, Burnham jumped off his horse and said: 'I think I may say that we are the sole survivors of that party!'[3] Forbes, not wishing to spread alarm among his men, ordered Burnham to say nothing else and tell no one, until his own current battle was over.

We have only two partial eyewitness accounts from members of the Shangani Patrol of what happened to Wilson's men: Napier, who had left Wilson to carry his message to Forbes but did not re-join Wilson and the others and Burnham's report as recorded by Forbes; and the scout's own account in *Scouting on Two Continents* which, has already been suggested, was an something of an exercise in self-publicity. Where they can be compared, Burnham's account is somewhat different from that of Forbes, possibly because the Shangani Patrol's overall leader wanted to preserve his reputation, which, by the time he contributed to the work of Wills and Collingridge, was under threat.

When describing Wilson's message to Forbes which Napier had carried, Burnham portrays a more concerned Wilson and suggests he was more insistent regarding how essential it was that Forbes send support, including the Maxims which Forbes should bring at all costs.[4] This is clearly different from Forbes' description of the content of the message. On the other hand, one might suggest that Napier's reluctance to return to Wilson's party could suggest that both Wilson and Napier felt things were still under control but, in the case of Napier, the opposite feeling could be the case and he might have thought that to return to Wilson's Patrol was courting certain death.

---

1   'Inspanning' means harnessing up.
2   'Outspanning' means unharnessing.
3   Burnham, *Scouting on Two Continents*, p.187.
4   Burnham, *Scouting on Two Continents*, p.96.

In support of the idea that Wilson really did want assistance and wanted it quickly, however, one should not forget that the message Ebbage and Judge brought, as recorded by Forbes, indicated that the Forbes' Patrol should set off as soon as possible and be at Lobengula's kraal by 0400 hours. Forbes would not do this as he expected to be attacked at any moment and the patrol was at its most vulnerable while it was decamping.

Having described delivering the message with Forbes, Burnham recorded a conversation he had previously with Wilson about disappearance of Hofmeyer and the two troopers, Cahoun and Bradbury, whom Wilson had ordered to act as rear guard. The Major argued that it was important that they were found and not left to be overwhelmed by the surrounding warriors. Burnham was consequently given the task of tracking back to where the three had been last seen and he then gives a graphic account of his tracking techniques, which he claimed, so interested Wilson, who leading the scout's horse, that the Major carefully watched how Burnham distinguished the horses' hoofprints from those of the cattle. Initially Burnham had difficulty finding the right spoor, especially as the night was cold and wet and the scout was only wearing a thin shirt. Wilson offered him his own large cape – a gesture which Burnham clearly remembered over 30 years later.

The scout eventually identified the hoofprints of the missing men's horses and Wilson decided that they should follow them to the edge of the AmaNdebele camp. There was still no sign of the three lost troopers, and Wilson and Burnham quietly worked their way further down the shallow valley but still saw nothing. At this point Wilson called out 'Coo-ee'.[5] This was somewhat extraordinary behaviour as the two men were alone and vulnerable, but it worked. Hofmeyer and his companions slowly made their way up the valley to join Wilson and Burnham. Not surprisingly, the AmaNdebele were also alerted by Wilson and Burnham's calls. It seems that some of the younger warriors thought the calls were a precursor to a night attack and were only quieted when their *Indunas* were able to persuade them that the strange noises were animal rather than human in nature.

The five men returned to their waiting companions and Wilson decided that since they had been in the saddle for 16 hours, they should all try to get some sleep 'before the Column and the Maxims arrived'. Clearly, Burnham is suggesting that Wilson expected Forbes' men to arrive before daylight as his message had requested. After about an hour, Wilson woke Burnham asking if he could hear anything. Taking a billy can, Burnham placed it on the ground and used it as an amplifier of sound by resting his ear on the can's base, but he could hear nothing.[6] The scout tried to fall asleep again, but a concerned Wilson asked him to go out into the bush to look if he could see anything. Having moved away from the distracting noises of heavy sleepers and their horses, Burnham was able to make out the noise of a great number of splashing feet moving slowly towards the Shangani, which would place them between Forbes' men and those with Wilson. The noises Burnham

---

5   Burnham, *Scouting on Two Continents*, p.96.
6   A 'billy can' or 'billy' is a lightweight cooking pot in the form of a metal bucket commonly used for boiling water over a campfire.

heard were probably made by the men Mjaan had sent to form an ambush for Forbes' Patrol to ride into as they attempted to cross the river.

Shortly before dawn, Wilson, who seems to have been becoming more anxious, asked Burnham to follow the trail left by the King's waggons where he should intercept Bain the scout to make sure that Forbes' Column did not go astray. If dawn arrived before the Maxims, it would 'be all up'.[7] Burnham records that his rest had improved his ability to concentrate, and he quickly found the waggons' spoor. As dawn broke, Burnham could hear the slight noise of heavy animals that he knew could not be AmaNdebele cattle. Much to his surprise and disappointment, it was Ingram – not Bain. Burnham told Ingram not to come any further and returned to report to Wilson as quickly as he could. Wilson's men speedily saddled up and went to meet Ingram fully expecting to see Forbes and the Maxims, but it was only Borrow and his 22 troopers.[8] Burnham claims that, at this point, 'all of us knew … then that the end had come'.[9] Although this turned out to be correct, the very presence of Borrow and his men indicated that it was still possible to cross the Shangani – at least at the time that B Troop had done so – but strangely Wilson did not attempt this method of escape.

Burnham then provided Wilson with an account of the exchange about the perilous situation that had taken place between Napier and Forbes. Napier had reported to Forbes the dangerous circumstances Wilson's Patrol was in, but Forbes was indecisive as to what to do next, even though Napier had urged Forbes to come to Wilson's aid at once as there were many AmaNdebele approaching Wilson and his patrol. Eventually, after much thought, Forbes sent Borrow and his troop as reinforcements, but in reality they had been sent to die with Wilson. Since Bain was ill with fever, Ingram was the only one who could guide Borrow and his men to Wilson's whereabouts.

A clearly disappointed and extremely concerned Wilson called a conference of his senior officers, Captains Judd, Kirton, Fitzgerald, Greenfield, and Brown. The Major then asked each one in turn what they considered to be the next best move. The most favoured suggestion was to try and cut their way through the intervening *Impis* to re-join Forbes' party but there was little belief that they would survive if they did so. Wilson decided that it would be better if they sold their lives dearly by attacking Lobengula's kraal and perhaps capturing him or, in the process, kill some of his most senior warriors in the Imbezu *Impi* and its *Indunas*. Thus resolved, the men formed up into sections and, with Wilson and Burnham leading, rode towards the King's camp.

They rode slowly and, in the increasing daylight, saw lines of armed AmaNdebele. Wilson's Patrol rode into a circle of warriors, who stood without firing. They came within sight of the King's palisade and Wilson called for Lobengula to surrender. The response was a shot and then a ragged volley that spooked Burnham's horse which carried him to the edge of the

---

7   Burnham, *Scouting on Two Continents*, p.97.
8   Forbes had instructed Borrow to take 20 men with him but 22 was the number of Salisbury Horse troopers under his command.
9   Burnham, *Scouting on Two Continents*, p.97.

forest. A large warrior burst out and fired at the scout but missed. Regaining control of his horse, Burnham charged at the warrior who was struggling to reload his rifle. The *Induna* reverted to his stabbing spear but was shot by Burnham before he could use it. The dismayed AmaNdebele accompanying him, stepped back into the forest. The fallen warrior was the son of Mjaan.

Gaining his composure, Burnham was now able to see what had happened to the rest of the patrol. Two horses had been killed and Ingram had picked up Fitzgerald and they were riding in tandem. The loss of the horses was significant since they each carried saddle bags or pockets with spare ammunition. These were saved at great risk and the men fell back to a large anthill which, was big enough for them to shelter behind. Burnham describes the dynamic Wilson standing on top of the heap directing his men. In response the AmaNdebele warriors charged the patrol but were carefully picked off one by one and their charge was broken. Warriors, whom the patrol had ridden past as it approached the King's palisade, now came into action, and approached the patrol from its left, firing their weapons. Once again, their fire was erratic and inaccurate but heavy enough that the patrol could no longer remain where it was. Wilson ordered his men to mount, and, at this point, a bullet knocked Burnham's rifle out of his grasp and, to demonstrate how cool members of the patrol remained, even in this threatening situation, he wrote that Captain Judd pointed out he had 'lost something'.[10]

While being covered by its sharpshooters, the patrol moved back towards the trees which forced the AmaNdebele to come out into the open in order to continue the attack. After several attempts to engage the patrol in hand-to-hand combat, the warriors fell back realising that it was only a matter of time before the patrol's ammunition ran out and it could be overwhelmed. Having reached the trees, Wilson reorganised his men with the wounded and those on foot in the centre. Wilson seems finally to have decided to make a dash towards Forbes' Patrol and Burnham and Judd were told to take the lead and head towards the river while Wilson, Ingram, and Borrow acted as rear guard. After about a mile, Wilson, again pinning his hope on the arrival of Forbes and the Maxims, asked Burnham to attempt to ride towards Forbes' Patrol. Wilson offered Trooper Gooding, an Australian, as companion. Burnham asked if he could take Ingram whom he knew well, presumably thinking that he would be reliable when danger arose. Wilson agreed but such was Gooding's desire to go and accompanied by the fact that his horse was in reasonable condition, all three men set off but without much hope. As Burnham wrote, he felt that 'it mattered little where we should fire the last shot'.[11]

The three men soon encountered a large group of AmaNdebele waiting to attack them. Burnham had a choice: he could try to avoid the group by heading for a nearby clearing, or ride to their left towards a thicket of young trees. He chose the dense thicket and, as his horse entered, it stumbled and fell to its knees knocking down some of the young tress but also clearing some space for Ingram's horse. The three horses continued to struggle to get

---

10   Burnham, *Scouting on Two Continents*, p.97.
11   Burnham, *Scouting on Two Continents*, p.99.

through the trees but, fortunately, after a short distance, the trees thinned out and they were able move more easily. The men were followed by a large group of warriors who were unable to catch up with the quicker moving trio. Leaving the AmaNdebele behind, Burnham, Ingram, and Gooding were able to let their horses slow down to a walk.

Eventually, their pursuers could be heard approaching and Burnham and his companions made a false trail to deceive them as to which direction they had fled. Hiding nearby, they could hear in the distance the firing and shouts from Wilson's men. The AmaNdebele in pursuit of Burnham's party were deceived and, after they passed them following the false trail, Burnham, Ingram, and Gooding were able to continue their journey towards the river from which the sound of the Maxims in action could be heard. Arriving at the Shangani they found that the river was now in flood and, although the sound of the Maxims had grown louder, they were unsure on which bank Forbes was fighting. Burnham, believing that Forbes would always take the cautious approach and was unlikely to have set off in the dark, gambled that his patrol was still be on the far bank. Taking the risk, the three men swam their horses across the river and were able to lead them up the bank about a mile upstream from Forbes' men. The three men arrived at Forbes' position and were able to help his men fight off the last AmaNdebele attack.

We would know nothing at all about the very last moments of Wilson's Patrol if it had not been for the diligence to discover the details of its fate by some newspaper reporters. One of the first published AmaNdebele interviews was with M'Kotchwana, who had fought at the Battle of Shangani; it was conducted by a reporter of the *Matabele Times* and later published in the *Sydney Mail* on 28 July 1898. There was also a series of accounts recorded by Foster Windram, a journalist on the staff of the *GuBulawayo Chronicle*, who, in November 1937, with the help of two interpreters, Peter Kumalo and J.P. Richardson, interviewed three AmaNdebele who were present at the death of Wilson and his patrol.[12] These four warriors provide us with an oral tradition of the events which, though requiring cautious use, since some were over 40 years old, offer an interesting insight into the events and the way Wilson and his patrol's death was regarded by their enemies.

The AmaNdebele warrior M'Kotchwana described how Mjaan, who was leading an amalgam of surviving *Impis* from the Battle of Imbembezi, led them to attack Wilson's Patrol early in the morning.[13] There were roughly 1,000 warriors involved, who were described as moving slowly and quietly through the bush in order to surround the patrol's camp which M'Kotchwana estimated contained a total of 30 men.[14] There were two men on watch and one of them heard a noise as the AmaNdebele approached and woke up a sleeping companion whom M'Kotchwana assumed was Allan Wilson.[15]

12 National Archives of Zimbabwe, CR: 2/1/1. The interviewees were Siatcha, Ginyalitsha, and Ntabeni Kumalo.
13 M'Kotchwana stated that the main *Impis* involved were the Imbizo and Insukamini, and the Nyamandhlovu.
14 *'Three times the fingers on my two hands'*.
15 Cary argues that the fight began at around daybreak and ended somewhere between 0930 and 1030 hours.

Having visually searched the bush Wilson woke up the rest of the patrol, who were wearing black capes against the rain. They began to prepare their ammunition and saddled their horses. The AmaNdebele started to fire at the patrol as dawn broke on a cloudy, rainy morning. The members of Wilson's Patrol mounted and tried to ride towards the Shangani but some of their horses were killed. Wilson and the others realised that they could go no further and shot their remaining horses to provide a defensive barrier behind which to fight. As the sun rose higher, the AmaNdebele could see that several of Wilson's men had been killed and Mjaan ordered a rush at the defenders who, using their revolvers, held the warriors at bay.[16]

The attackers withdrew to the shelter of the trees and sniped at the patrol until Mjaan again ordered an assault and they rushed the surviving white men. M'Kotchwana recollected that, at this point, some of the AmaNdebele were for sparing the survivors as they had fought so bravely with a display of courage the warriors could appreciate, but the members of the Imbezu *Impi*, who had suffered so many casualties at the Battle of Imbembezi, argued for killing them all. The AmaNdebele made a second rush during which M'Kotchwana heard the white men singing and loudly shouting three times.[17] During this second attack, M'Kotchwana was hit on the temple, possibly by a spent bullet, and was knocked unconscious. Two of his sons were killed and his brother received a stomach wound during the fighting. Wilson's Patrol, said the warrior, died fighting to the last man.

On the following day, the white men were stripped, and the face of the largest corpse was skinned in the belief that he was the patrol's commander. These prizes were taken to Lobengula, but he told his warriors that the skin was not that of the leader and they returned and brought another skin which satisfied the King. Lobengula asked if his royal regiment, the Imbezu, had done most of the killing and was disgusted when he was told that they had done no more than the rest of the *Impis* involved. 'Have I then all this time put my trust in a lump of dirt?,' he asked. M'Kotchwana's admiration for Wilson's men was obvious: 'The *amakiwa* were brave men; they were warriors.'[18]

In the accounts given by three other warriors, Siatcha, Ginyalitsh, and Ntabeni Kumalo, there is considerable agreement with M'Kotchwana's description of the Wilson's Patrol's last stand. When combined, these accounts describe how the patrol, which they believed consisted of 30 men, found Lobengula's waggons but the King had left on horseback earlier in the day. The patrol moved away and camped while the AmaNdebele surrounded them. The AmaNdebele attacked and suffered many casualties while the patrol used its dead horses as protection against the AmaNdebele's rifles and finally took to firing their revolvers when their rifle ammunition had been used up. When all their ammunition was exhausted, one member of the patrol is said to have asked the AmaNdebele to stop their attack and, in

---

16   The *Matabele Times* reporter asked M'Kotchwana how many AmaNdebele had been killed in this first rush and, using his hands, he indicated that the number was 60. Seeking clarification as to how many warriors had been killed outright, M'Kotchwana indicated 40.

17   The earliest suggestion that the men sang the National Anthem and gave three cheers.

18   '*amakiwa*' = Whites.

return, the whites would return to GuBulawayo and say what brave men the warriors were. Realising that this request was being ignored, Wilson and his men cheered and sang the National Anthem.[19] To Cary, this is a romantic fairy tale, for, while acknowledging that it was possible that Wilson's men did sing and it might have been the National Anthem, he suggests that it was just as likely to be a ribald soldiers' song set to a Victorian hymn tune. The AmaNdebele accounts do mention singing and that it sounded like a hymn. The Victorian newspapers were in no doubt that these men had been overcome at the moment of their death by patriotic fervour and sang the National Anthem as a natural display of these feelings. Again, we will never know.

Such was their fear of the accuracy of fire of the members of Wilson's Patrol, that there are reports that the AmaNdebele hesitated for some time before making the final attack. Ginyalitsha claimed that some of the patrol committed suicide when they were almost out of ammunition. Two of the warriors describe how there was one man surviving when the AmaNdebele made their final rush and that he was the same man who had not taken cover throughout the attack. The behaviour of this individual, a commanding figure, has been taken to be that of Wilson. Another AmaNdebele described him as 'the big, dark, bearded man who defied them to the last'. He is described as being extremely tall, but the various sources differ in suggesting who he might have been. Mjaan identified the last survivor as Allan Wilson, as did Burnham, but the scout was not present at the end. Others have suggested that it was Henry Borrow, Trooper John R. Robertson, Captain Harry Greenfield, or Trooper Tom Watson.[20] The man's real identity will never be known for sure. O'Reilly states that he examined all the photographs of the members of Wilson's Patrol in the Rhodesian, (now Zimbabwean) National Archives and he found it impossible to identify one with a moustache and a beard similar to the description of this last survivor.[21] How accurate are these accounts of the patrol's last hours? It is hard to decide, and various commentators differ in their views.

In conclusion, it seems clear that Wilson's Patrol was wiped out by overwhelming odds after putting up very stiff resistance during which they killed many of their AmaNdebele attackers. They were brave and often shouted insults at their attackers attempting to get them to come out of the trees. The *Impis*, who valued bravery, admired the way in which the white men died. One of the interviewees, Ginyalitsha, suggested that, if the patrol had not run out of ammunition, the AmaNdebele would have been defeated, possibly meaning if the attackers had suffered many more casualties they would have given up. Later, Mjaan is said to have reflected on the numerous

---

19   One account, that of Siatcha, records that Wilson's men did not sing, but prayed.
20   A.J. Smit, *The Shangani Story* (GuBulawayo: Allan Wilson Technical Boys High School, 1952), p.19.
21   O'Reilly, *Pursuit of the King*, p.112.

The Last Stand. (*London Illustrated London News*, July 14, 1894)

casualties the small patrol had caused and questioned how many warriors he would need to drive all the white men back across the mountains.[22]

The fate of Wilson's Patrol was uncertain for some time. Goold-Adams, leader of the Tuli Column, in a telegram sent to Sir Henry Loch on 6 January 1894, over a month after they had died, reported that, based on information brought in by the 'natives' things did not look good for Wilson and his men. Nothing had been heard of them, so Goold-Adams feared the worst. The rivers were in flood, and it was too dangerous to send a detachment to where it was thought that Wilson's final fight had taken place. Goold-Adams reported that he would send a search party when he considered it to be safe to do so. He acknowledged that it would be a case of interring the remains rather than a rescue mission since survivors would have made their way back by this time.[23]

In December 1893, a party of Cape Mounted Rifles commanded by Lieutenant Harry Woon was despatched to try to discover the remains of Wilson's Patrol, but the heavy rains made the going impossible and they were forced to return to GuBulawayo. In the middle of January 1894, Goold-Adams sent a second patrol with the intention of burying the bodies as well as making a military demonstration in the area in which Wilson's men had died. This again was forced to return because of the weather. In April a further patrol of 16 under the command of Captain Tancred journeyed down the Shangani River and recovered the Maxim gun carriages that Forbes' men had abandoned.[24]

---

22   O'Reilly (*Pursuit of the King*, p.101) estimates that the Wilson Patrol killed 300–400 AmaNdebele.
23   PA C 7290 Further Correspondence … Enclosure 1 in No. 86. Received 6 January 1894
24   ZNA HC 3/5/30/6 (Correspondence) Adams to Loch 12 April 1894, Adams to Loch, 21 April 1894.

Some two months after the last stand, James Dawson, the interpreter, together with another European, James Reilley, and five AmaNdebele, were sent by Jameson to discover the patrol's remains. Dawson crossed the Shangani on 23 February 1894, and, in his diary, he described what they found at the site of the last stand.

> [It] was a small space of about 15 yards in diameter, literally covered with bones; men and horses mingled ... all the heads were in this space except one which was about 10 yards off. This was the man who was so hard to kill that they [the AmaNdebele] were almost going to leave alone because he was a wizard. This we determined to bring back for recognition – a strong built dark man with clipped beard and moustache.[25]

They collected all of the bones and 33 skulls but, in Dawson's words, 'could not find the others [sic]'.[26] All the remains, save one, were lying inside a circle close to a pile of horses' bones. There was one exception, whose remains were on an anthill 20 yards away from the rest. Dawson states that they were of the man who was the last defender to be killed and described them as having been of an individual who was dark, not very tall with a long moustache and close-cut beard. However, since Dawson had only found a skull, this physical description could not be verified. There was a peculiarity in the set of the teeth in the skull and Dawson decided to return with it to see if anyone of the Shangani Patrol could recognise to whom it belonged.[27] The rest of the

The popular image of Wilson's last stand. (*Illustrated London News*, 1894)

---

25 Glass, 'James Dawson, Rhodesian Pioneer', p.74.
26 As O'Reilly (*Pursuit of the King*, p.110) states, it is possible that Dawson thought there had been more than 34 on the patrol. *The Times* of 9 January 1894 reports that there were 38 in the patrol. It is likely that, if there were 34 as is usually accepted, the missing skull was either taken by a scavenger or an AmaNdebele as a souvenir.
27 O'Reilly (*Pursuit of the King*, p.112) suggests that this skull has, unsurprisingly, since disappeared.

remains were buried together with a marker which read: 'To Brave Men'. The bones were later moved and transferred to Fort Victoria, but finally found a resting place in the Matopos Hills close to the graves of Rhodes and Jameson.

There was a rumour resulting from a supposed deathbed confession of Gooding that he, Burnham, and Ingram had not been sent to ask Forbes for help but had in fact deserted.[28] Since the three were the only survivors, one cannot be definite as to this confession's veracity. Cary's work is perhaps the most thorough examination of the Wilson Patrol, and he dismissed this accusation almost out of hand. Although Burnham was, as always, capable of exaggerating his part in events, there is no real reason not to believe that the three had been ordered by Wilson to find Forbes. Their accounts continued to be consistent over time and there is no evidence to conclude that all three, especially Ingram and Burnham, who were courageous men and had repeatedly put their lives on the line, would have deserted Wilson.[29]

---

28   O'Reilly, *Pursuit of the King*, p.77.
29   Cary, *A Time to Die*, p.103; Ash, *Matabele*, p.160.

13

Retreat

Forbes must have suspected the worst when he heard Burnham's account. His patrol had driven off the attackers and things were now quiet. Five men of the BBP, including Captain Napier and a mule driver, had been wounded and were being treated by Surgeon Captain Hogg, the patrol's medical officer, who had previously been asked by Captain Kirton to keep his dinner warm before he had left with Wilson.[1] A small incident suggesting that some of Wilson's Patrol had heard Forbes' instructions and expected them to be carried out.

The question which one must ask is: Was the flooding of the Shangani the major reason for the loss of Wilson and his men? Certainly, Forbes would like to have his contemporaries believe this was the case.[2] It was a more reasonable explanation for the Shangani Patrol's failure to help Wilson than that a few AmaNdebele had been able to halt the pursuit of Lobengula after a short skirmish on the opposite side of the river from the King's camp.

The fact that the river did rise is undeniable. Borrow and the reinforcements, however, found no difficulty in crossing what was, in fact, a relatively small stream, when they went to join Wilson at 0100 hours. By the time Forbes' Patrol had reach its banks, the river had been transformed into a ranging torrent because of heavy rains further upstream. Perhaps if Forbes' men had not been delayed by the AmaNdebele attack, which lasted about half an hour, his patrol would have still been able to cross the Shangani and join up with Wilson. The AmaNdebele strategy was such that Forbes could only concentrate on preserving his own force, which was undoubtedly a genuine reason for delay and at least as much of an impediment as the rise of the river. Once they had entered the denser bush, Forbes, probably expecting an attack from the far side of the river, ordered his men to dig rifle pits along its banks.[3] He clearly expected further attacks from the far side of

---

1   Arthur William Hogg was born in London in 1862 and qualified as a surgeon in Scotland in November 1887. He is listed as a qualified doctor, resident at Huddersfield in the 1891 Census, but shortly thereafter he made his way to South Africa and was appointed a Surgeon Captain to the Victoria Column.

2   Cary, *A Time to Die*, p.113.

3   Forbes, 'The Loss of the Wilson Patrol', p.166.

the Shangani where Wilson's Patrol was fighting. Even if Forbes' men could cross the Shangani, getting the Maxims across would not have been so easily accomplished and leaving them behind was unthinkable.

After a quiet hour, Forbes tried to persuade a reluctant Raaff to take a patrol into the clearing where the initial fighting had taken place to determine whether the AmaNdebele were still waiting in ambush. Again Raaff, who was clearly depressed, persuaded Forbes to wait longer arguing that it was premature and dangerous to explore the clearing. Raaff pointed out that this would split the patrol again, the dangers of which have already been discussed. It was not until 1000 hours that a few troopers began to move forward in order to see if they were fired upon. They were not challenged and saw only a few natives moving towards the river.

The unfortunately tasked Forbes seems to have thought of little else other than defence and retreat since the fighting had begun that morning. Given the situation in which he found himself this is not surprising. He had been put in charge of a poorly equipped and provisioned patrol with a divided command structure which was by then in an even poorer state. Even the Maxim's superior firepower was limited by the AmaNdebele tactics of surprising the patrol while remaining hidden in the dense bush. Given the circumstances it is hard to lay the blame entirely on Forbes but, as we shall see, Sir Henry Loch did not hesitate to do so.

Once the laager had been made safe, Forbes met with Raaff and Napier. The Shangani had continued to rise and could not now be crossed but they still hoped that some or even all of Wilson's party had escaped. Since it was now impossible to cross the river, the only action that appeared open to Forbes was to return to GuBulawayo. Raaff agreed and wanted the patrol to leave at nightfall, but Forbes decided against this as he believed that such haste would lead the AmaNdebele to believe that they had beaten him. This was one of a number of occasions when Forbes' decisions were based on what the enemy might think rather than what was actually the best action for the patrol. It is possible he thought that continuing to make a show of strength might dissuaded the AmaNdebele from launching an all-out attack.

Forbes also wanted to give Wilson's men time to re-join the main patrol if they were able to do so. Delaying his departure might infer that Forbes was not entirely convinced that Burnham had not exaggerated Wilson's plight and decided that the patrol would not leave until the following morning.[4] Meanwhile, one of Forbes' pickets reported seeing a group of AmaNdebele bringing four white men to the riverbank and dancing round them. Since no one else saw this, Forbes dismissed it as a mistake.[5] There is no evidence that this event actually occurred, and all the accounts of Wilson's death suggest that there were no survivors.

It was time for Forbes to begin to prepare to face the music for his failure to capture Lobengula and his apparent loss of a significant number

---

4   Interestingly, Forbes ('The Loss of the Wilson Patrol', p.167) describes the return to GuBulawayo as 'a retreat'.

5   Forbes, 'The Loss of the Wilson Patrol', p.169. Few authorities believe that this actually occurred and the AmaNdebele accounts do not mention it.

of his men, so he intended to send a letter by two gallopers to Jameson at GuBulawayo. His report contained information as to what had happened and stated that the patrol was alright and that he intended to move up the river. They had sufficient ammunition left, Forbes reported, to endure a major attack but, if this happened, he would have to laager and await new supplies and reinforcements. Forbes also wrote to Captain Dallamore, who was at Umhlangeni with the remainder of the original flying column, instructing him to rendezvous with him on the west bank of the Shangani. Having completed his letters, but before he could hand them over, he was approached by Raaff and Francis who argued against putting anything in writing. It is difficult to know why they were so resistant. As Forbes pointed out to them, the only natives who could read were attached to the patrol, which implied that if the letters were to fall into the hands of the AmaNdebele, they would be useless as a source of information.[6] This did not satisfy Raaff and Francis and they suggested that perhaps the word 'ammunition', could be substitute by a codeword.[7] Such was the pressure Raaff and Napier were able to put on Forbes, that he partially gave in and only sent the letter to Dallamore which the Major claimed 'did not refer to our position at all'.[8]

Assuming that Forbes was correct about the AmaNdebele illiteracy, why did he back down in the face of Raaff and Francis and not send a written report to Jameson? Forbes was clearly sensitive about his failure to complete his mission, particularly the loss of Wilson's Patrol, and knew he would almost certainly have to face a court of inquiry into his actions. His contributions to Wills and Collingridge's *The Downfall of Lobengula*, are often critical of Raaff and others including Francis and were probably meant to explain and excuse the failure of both the flying column and the Shangani Patrol. He had been hamstrung by Jameson's instruction to consult the ailing Raaff at every turn. In a disparaging letter in the *GuBulawayo Chronicle* of 5 December 1958, Llewellyn Raaff, Commandant Raaff's eldest son, criticised Forbes' character assassination of his father. Forbes was not a military genius and had ignored Raaff's advice, Llewellyn claimed. The discussion around sending the letter to Jameson could not be true, argued the son, as Raaff did not tell his wife or family that it happened. It is difficult for an outsider to know how valid Llewellyn Raaff's evidence is. It is true that Forbes' is the only source of information regarding Raaff and Francis 'protest'. However, in constantly referring to Raaff's ability to influence him, Forbes does not advance a positive view of his own leadership qualities.

One suggestion, which has not been made, is that Raaff, who had considerable military experience and knew how colonial administration worked, was personally apprehensive that Forbes, with whom he was on less than good terms, was prepared to put in writing an account of the

---

6   When Dawson searched the place of Wilson's last stand, he found notebooks and papers which the AmaNdebele had ignored. Unfortunately for the historian, and more importantly General Money whose son, Harold was a member of Wilson's Patrol, the rain had made these documents illegible. Cary, *A Time to Die*, p.111.

7   Cary, *A Time to Die*, p.118.

8   Forbes, 'The Loss of the Wilson Patrol', p.169.

Shangani Patrol's actions and in particular the loss of Wilson's Patrol. Such a document would likely be considered an official report written by the patrol's commanding officer. It would be an important document in the inquiry that was bound to follow, and such a significant account might best be written when things were not so perilous and calmer minds would carefully be able to consider what to put down on paper. This may be an elaborate way of saying that Raaff was worried about what Forbes would write about him, especially the way in which the Major could report that Raaff had been able to change his mind on a number of occasions. The patrol had ended in failure and disaster, and Forbes might blame the advice Raaff had given him, and Jameson had instructed him to seek. All the officers of the flying squad would be conscious that their actions would come under great scrutiny and the loss of Wilson's Patrol and the failure to capture Lobengula would decrease any credit that might have accrued from the earlier capture of GuBulawayo.

In the end, the letter to Jameson was not sent, but Ingram was instructed to carry a verbal message to GuBulawayo.[9] It seems that this was acceptable to Raaff and Francis, who must therefore have thought it unlikely that the scout might be caught and tortured by the AmaNdebele and his verbal report would not mention individuals by name. If the suggestion that a written document could be held against the officers is correct, a verbal message could always be discounted as inaccurate because the messenger either got its tone or its contents wrong. It would also rely on the memory of the recipient about which there could be debate. A written document could not be dismissed so easily. Ironically, some of Raaff's men gave letters to Ingram to take to GuBulawayo so the rumour mill would begin to work even before the patrol could return. Naturally Forbes was not pleased when he learned of Raaff men's behaviour and his apparent inability to prevent them doing so. The fact that they were Raaff's supporters was also a worry for Forbes as he might have suspected that they would favour Raaff's contribution at the expense of his own.

The two horses the scouts used, which were in better condition than most of the rest of mounts available, belonged to Captains Coventry and Tancred and were called 'Brandy' and 'Soda'.[10] Ingram left the laager heading to GuBulawayo and was helped to elude the AmaNdebele by the heaviest thunderstorm yet experienced by the patrol. He arrived so exhausted that he had to be helped off his horse but went straight to Jameson and delivered his report. Jones, however, claims that the messengers' journey to GuBulawayo was so hazardous and exhausting that they were initially unable to deliver a coherent message to Jameson.[11]

On the 5 December the remains of Forbes' Shangani Patrol began their return journey to GuBulawayo. The horses were weak and could only walk or be led. Food was in short supply and the troopers were forced to eat horsemeat. The weather was very wet and the strain on the men

---

9   Ironically, Forbes was to discover that some members of his flying squad did send letters full of doom and gloom to friends in GuBulawayo.

10   Burnham, *Scouting on Two Continents*, p.100.

11   Jones, *Rhodesian Genesis*, p.99.

Members of the retreating Shangani Patrol killing horses for food. (Open source)

considerable.[12] The AmaNdebele continued to harass them and sniped whenever possible. Colenbrander, who was riding point, had a lucky escape during such an attack when his horse was killed.[13] The rest of the day was without incident and Forbes' party travelled 14 miles before laagering in a strongly constructed *scherm*. Still hopeful of discovering the fate of Wilson's Patrol, Forbes asked Burnham if he thought he could swim his horse across the Shangani and try to find their spoor. The scout declined to volunteer but offered to do so if it was Forbes' order. It was too dangerous, argued Burnham, but Walter Howard, a trooper in Raaff's Rangers, volunteered to go. Forbes refused the offer for, although Howard was personally willing to go alone, no one was willing to accompany him.[14] This, Forbes, concluded was too great a risk to take and might incur additional criticism.

On 6 December Forbes' men made another 14 miles but the condition of the horses continued to deteriorate. Forbes was now reduced to walking as Burnham had borrowed his first horse and the Major had given his second mount to a wounded man. Raaff's pony, on the other hand was still quite fit as were the horses of some of his men which might suggest they were better horsemen than many in the patrol. The Commandant was suffering from sore feet and could only walk with considerable pain. Consequently, Forbes decided to put Raaff in charge of the mounted men who rode at the front and flanks of the march while Forbes ensured that the men on foot kept

---

12 Jones, *Rhodesian Genesis*, p.100.
13 P.W. Forbes, 'Retreat from the Shangani River,' in Wills & Collingridge, *The Downfall of Lobengula*, pp.173–174.
14 Forbes, 'Retreat from the Shangani River,' p.174. (Thomas) Walter (John Wright) Howard was born in Sheen, Surrey, in 1865, and educated at Winchester and Middle Temple. He emigrated to South Africa in 1891. He was to have a distinguished career in the Second Boer War. He left accounts of his experiences of the flying squad.

together. They laagered that night and had to kill one of the two remaining pack oxen for meat having failed to capture some cattle they had seen during their journey.

One wonders whether Forbes' arrangement, which seems a reasonable one, was actual handing over the command of the column to Raaff. O'Reilly had no doubt that Forbes had done so as, during his research he had received two letters from Raaf's great nephew, Hugh Gorringe, who argued that the column was not retreating but simply withdrawing from an untenable situation.[15] 'Any commander who did not hand over the withdrawal to the best man would be guilty of criminal negligence.'[16] Sir Henry Loch's comments on the Report of the Inquiry into the patrol were less complimentary. Loch wrote that the retreat of the demoralised force 'degenerated into a complete rout'.[17] Burnham also alleged that Forbes appeared to have lost the confidence of his men and it was Raaff who saved the day: 'He [Raaff] led us back: had Forbes continued in command probably not a single man would have escaped.'[18] This view was confirmed by P.B. Clements who served as a trooper under Forbes and described him as being 'entirely passive during the retreat'.[19] Burnham, in his account, began to refer to Raaff as 'Colonel' during the retreat but continues to describe Forbes as 'Major'.

Having shared a hunted waterbuck for breakfast, the patrol started off early the next morning and saw smoke from fires and heard cattle. Raaff was sent to try and catch some but failed as the ground was too broken for the horses to pursue them. Captain Lendy, who described himself at this stage of the patrol as a 'simple volunteer' as he no longer had any guns to control, was alarmed that Forbes should create a potential conflict with the owners of the cattle. Lendy believed that the patrol could not stand another full-scale attack and seizing AmaNdebele cattle was a sure way of encouraging one. Forbes, who was very unhappy with Lendy's interference in his organisation, was very dismissive of Lendy's over-cautious attitude.[20] It is clear these two senior men had a very tenuous relationship during this perilous time. Later, the patrol came across some calves which Captain Francis was able to capture. The food situation was also improved when some fish were caught by the patrol's native bearers.

The patrol recommenced its march on 8 December and Colenbrander was able to shoot an antelope after it had only gone three miles. As his men were extremely hungry, Forbes ordered a halt but, as they were cutting up the animal, they saw some cattle around 500–600 yards ahead and Raaff was sent to bring them in. Interestingly, Forbes says he suggested Raaff do so rather

15   A non-military expert might regard this as mere sophistry.

16   Gorringe, quoted in O'Reilly, *Pursuit of the King*, p.129.

17   ZNA HC 3/5/30/6 Sir Henry Loch's Memorandum on the Report of the Inquiry into the Patrol under Forbes, 12 March 1895.

18   Burnham, quoted in Gustav Preller, *Lobengula: The Tragedy of a Matabele King* (Johannesburg: Afrikaanse Pero-Boekhandel, 1963), p.233; Stephanus Jacobus Du Toit, *Rhodesia: Past and Present* (London: Heinemann, 1897), p.147.

19   *The Star*, 5 June 1923.

20   Lendy had previously interfered with the way in which Forbes had place the pickets around the laager.

than having to order him to act.[21] The Commandant brought back 100 cattle, together with their young herdsman who claimed that they were royal cattle and he was on his way to join the King. Since such a large number of cattle was difficult for his men to manage, so Forbes decided that only 20 should be taken and the rest left with the herder together with the calves they had taken the previous day. It is claimed that Forbes originally suggested that only ten cattle should be taken but it was Raaff, who could not understand why Forbes was reluctant to take them all given the starvation rations upon which the patrol existed, who increased the number to 20.[22]

Forbes' Patrol continued for a few more miles and he then decided to laager in a partially clear space where the men were able to eat. Suddenly, just as they were about to saddle-up they were attacked. It appeared that the attacking AmaNdebele had almost completely caught one of Forbes' pickets napping. The man had heard a strange sound from one of the grazing horses and, on going to investigate, was surprised by the attackers. It was with difficulty that the patrol drove the AmaNdebele off, but they lost the cattle they had taken, and the one remaining pack ox was capture by the AmaNdebele. Fortunately, only one of the patrol's vital horses, the safety of which had been the focus of the patrol's defensive action, was slightly injured. Lendy had proved correct in suggesting that taking the King's cattle would result in retaliation. 'The action would not have taken place had not the cattle taken by us for meat been the private property of the King,' he claimed.[23]

Raaff again expressed his annoyance at Forbes' command decisions claiming that he had placed the pickets badly, having ignored his own suggestions as to where to do so. The Commandant claimed this was why the AmaNdebele had almost taken the column by surprise. Forbes, who was forced to finally acknowledge his ignorance of fighting in the bush, agreed that Raaff should have the responsibility of placing the pickets in future. It is clear Raaff's greater experience meant that he was gradually taking over command of the column from Forbes as was to be suggested later.

On 9 December, the patrol endured two tremendous thunderstorms as they tried to continue their retreat. Forbes comments on the fact that their two maps were old and inaccurate, but they indicated that that they still had between 60 and 100 miles to go before they would cross the Shangani at the chosen drift and some of the men were becoming depressed by their conditions and the constant fear of assault. AmaNdebele were often seen in the distance but did not attack and the patrol skirted a high ridge because the horses were too weak to ascend it and their lack of strength meant that the Maxims were now having to be manhandled when the going became difficult. Without warning, Forbes' men suddenly came to a *scherm* in which women, children and a few men were sheltering, together with, more importantly, some sheep and goats. These AmaNdebele were opponents of Lobengula and were in the process of returning to their home kraals having previously fled the King's vengeance. They claimed they were strangers in that part of

21   Forbes, 'Retreat from the Shangani River', p.175.
22   Cary, *A Time to Die*, p.123.
23   Captain William Napier, quoted in Cary, *A Time to Die*, p.127.

Matabeleland and could not help Forbes with directions. They were, however, friendly and provided the patrol with sheep and some cattle. Forbes describe these friendly AmaNdebele as part of the following of Mlangabesa, a brother of Lobengula, whom the King had killed out of jealousy.[24]

The patrol continued as did the rain and the land next to the Shangani became difficult to travel over and it was impossible to remain close to the river. The ground became so uneven that it was difficult to move the Maxims, and the horses pulling them were quickly becoming exhausted. Thus, only five miles were covered that day. During the night the cattle they had obtained from the friendly natives strayed off into the bush.

On 10 December, the patrol had a late start as the men tried to get their clothes and equipment dry. The track they were following became even worse, putting more strain on the remaining horses. It led to a deep, dry gully the men would have to traverse and which was too deep for the weak gun horses to pull the Maxims across. Raaff was sent (or decided) to scout ahead and found that the land beyond the gully was just as bad as that over which they had just travelled so it was decided to laager on the near side of the gully. One Maxim was taken over by hand under the supervision of Napier and his men who sheltered their horses at the bottom of the deep gully. The other Maxim was kept on the approach side since Forbes felt it necessary to keep a part of the patrol on either side for mutual support in case of an unexpected attack.

Forbes' intention was to have short break before pressing on but having unsaddled the horses his patrol was suddenly surprised by an attack by AmaNdebele who had crept towards them through the long grass. It is clear that on this and other occasions, the AmaNdebele were cunning in choosing the moment to launch their attacks and chose a time when the whites were vulnerable. The troopers were alarmed by rifle shots, and Forbes and Captain Finch hurriedly drove the rest of the horses into the gully but some of the animals were killed by the attackers in the ensuing mayhem. If the AmaNdebele had made a sudden rush at this moment and decimated its mounts the patrol would have been in very serious peril but, surprisingly, the natives did not attempt to do so. Perhaps they reasoned that there was no need for them to take risks as they were winning this battle of attrition.

Forbes, having saved most of the horses, then turned his attention to his men and found that they had all taken cover. He warned them to be careful not to waste ammunition as the AmaNdebele were not in clear sight but content to fire at any trooper who revealed himself. Two of the troopers began to panic as they could hear nearby AmaNdebele talking among themselves but did not understand what was being said. The troopers believed that the attackers were planning to surround the patrol and attack it after dark.

The firing died away but, because of the dense bush, Forbes was unsure whether the attackers had left or were just waiting until dark before they attacked again. Eventually, taking the risk that the AmaNdebele were gone, Forbes ordered the horses to be saddled and the men on the approach side of the gully began gradually to cross it, two at a time. The remaining Maxim was

---

24   Forbes, 'Retreat from the Shangani River', p.177.

then taken across the gully as were the rest of the horses. During the attack, Sergeant D.W. Gibson of the BBP, who was in charge of one of the Maxims, was shot through the head and eight precious horses were killed.

The men continued to retreat. The horses were now led by natives accompanying the patrol, either because Forbes knew the animals would be a target for any attackers and native lives were not considered to be as valuable as those of the troopers, or because this freed the troopers to better handle their weapons if attacked. A Maxim was placed in the lead and one in the rear and Forbes encouraged the men not to bunch up in order to reduce the chance of them becoming an easy target even for the inaccurate shots of the AmaNdebele. Having advanced roughly two miles, they came to a small valley that had many loose stones on the side they had to descend. These stones prevented the very weak horses from pulling the Maxims. It was necessary for the men to manhandle one gun down the slope while they were covered by the other which was stationed at its summit. Once again, the AmaNdebele showed their skill in guerrilla warfare and attacked but were fired at by Raaff and his men who were on the right flank. While this was happening, the Maxim was pulled back to the top of the valley and the two guns engaged the enemy

There was a heavy exchange of fire, but the troopers suffered no casualties. As the shooting died away, the weather broke, and Forbes decided that his men should laager for the night so he and Raaff found a suitable place that would offer some protection from future attacks. According to Forbes, Napier suggested that the Maxim carriages should be abandoned as the horses were becoming too weak to pull them.[25] Forbes was in two minds as to whether this was a good idea. He could appreciate that leaving the carriages would speed the patrol's progress but felt that it would give the wrong message to the attackers, indicating that the patrol was in some way defeated or, in Forbes' words 'inconvenienced'.[26] Either Forbes was retrospectively putting a brave face on the situation for his audience, or he had lost a grip on reality. As usual, Forbes discussed the matter with Commandant Raaff who agreed that the carriages should be abandoned. All of the wounded were able to ride, and Tancred discovered that the guns could be put in blankets and carried by six men.

It was at this point that it seems that Raaff made the crucial suggestion that the patrol make a 'silent escape' from the AmaNdebele whose threatening voices could be heard from the bush nearby. This would mean abandoning the Maxim carriage and the lame horses. The remaining horses' hooves would be muffled and the various dogs which had accompanied the patrol killed to prevent their barking and alerting the enemy.[27] The men were to carry either only one blanket or a cape and move as silently as possible. No smoking was to be allowed. Burnham suggests that because things were so precarious

---

25 Cary (*A Time to Die*, p.129), using evidence from the Court of Inquiry, says that the idea may have come from Lendy rather than Napier.
26 Forbes, 'Retreat from the Shangani River', p.180.
27 They included Captain Lendy's white bulldog, which had a habit of trying to chase the Maxims' bullets.

Forbes 'reluctantly allowed Colonel Raff [sic] to arrange the full disposition of our force'.[28] Whether or not this was actually Forbes' intention he certainly asked Raaff to let his men know what these arrangements were.[29] Whether Raaff took these instructions more seriously than intended or Forbes told Raaff to take command, it seems that the Commandant decided to do so.

Having spoken to Napier, Forbes returned to find Captain Francis and Lieutenant Farley, Raaff's staff officer, shouting 'Order!' to the assembled men and then Raaff addressing them as if he were in full command. Raaff pointed out that the patrol was in a tricky spot that they had to get out of in any way possible. He then described the preparations necessary for them to make a 'silent escape'. Apparently, Raaff omitted the necessity of killing the dogs and Forbes added this information when Raaff had finished.[30] Forbes puts Raaff's actions in speaking to the men down to a lack of knowledge of military etiquette. 'The little man looked as he had taken charge,' muttered Forbes to Napier but he did not stop Raaff from doing so.[31] For those officers who had doubts about Forbes' ability, this was a turning point. Raaff was now the de facto commander of the Shangani Patrol. It seems unlikely that Forbes did not realise this, and it was not just a lapse in etiquette on Raaff's part. To many of the men, Raaff had always been a significant figure in the patrol and, as the situation had deteriorated, they gradually looked to him for direction. Given his much greater experience of this type of fighting this is not surprising. Burnham was full of praise for Raaff but had one reservation, although Raaff was both brave and stoical he did not have sufficient control of his mind 'to be able to sleep when under great responsibility'.[32] Clearly, writing in retrospect, Forbes conveyed the impression he was still in charge and that Raaff continued to report to him. One suspects that Raaff was merely keeping the Major informed and was genuinely aware of military etiquette. Sir Henry Loch was singularly unimpressed by this turn of events and wrote that 'the retreat reflected no credit on whoever was in command'.[33] He was appalled at this cavalier abandoning of government property and sent out a search party to recover it. He presumably thought that the AmaNdebele would not have had the same thought and taken any useful equipment the patrol had abandoned.

The men made careful preparations before they left to make the AmaNdebele think they were still in the laager. They placed the lame horses in its centre where they would be clearly visible and arranged the Maxim carriages in observable spots with pieces of wood resembling the missing guns. They slowly left the laager at 2200 hours in single file, making several

---

28   Burnham, *Scouting on Two Continents*, p.103.

29   Forbes, 'Retreat from the Shangani River', p.181.

30   The sentimental Burnham (*Scouting on Two Continents*, p.103) wrote: 'That to kill such friends is one of the most trying ordeals a soldier can experience.'

31   Forbes, 'Retreat from the Shangani River', p.181. Raaff was 5 feet 4 inches tall and, according to Burnham (*Scouting on Two Continents*, p.103), weighed 120 pounds.

32   Burnham, *Scouting on Two Continents*, p.103. Burnham put Raaff's death down to lack of sleep rather than the exertion of the retreat.

33   ZNA HC 3/5/30/6 Sir Henry Loch's Memorandum on the Report of the Inquiry into the Patrol under Forbes.

stops to ensure that there were no gaps in the line. Forbes and Burnham were in the lead and the horses were led in fours with one man attending them. The only unwounded mounted man was Raaff because of his sore feet. The Maxims proved extremely heavy, and it was necessary to frequently change the men who were designated to carry it. Eventually it was found that much faster progress could be made by placing the gun on the back of a horse and supporting it with a man on either side. The men were so exhausted that when the patrol stopped, they immediately fell asleep, and Forbes was worried that because of this one would be left behind when they started off again. Forbes fears were realised when, after moving off after the first halt, they discovered that Trooper Sheldrake, originally of the Victoria Column, was missing but knew it was too dangerous to send anyone back to find him.

By 0500 hours the patrol had travelled 12 miles and reached an open space close to the Shangani and laagered on its banks. Having constructed some simple fortifications and posted pickets, those men who were not needed were allowed to sleep. The next day the patrol continued knowing they were gradually approaching the waggon drift over which they could cross. Four natives including John Grootbanum were sent ahead to see if the expected waggons were there. If not, two were instructed to return to the patrol with news of what they found and if the waggons were not there, two others were told to go to Umhlangeni and ask Captain Dallamore to bring his men and waggons to meet the column.

Food was now in even shorter supply than before with little bread or coffee available.[34] The men were forced to kill a horse, which was not to the taste of some of the troopers, but it was improved when wild garlic, growing nearby, was used to improve its flavour. Many of the men's riding boots had worn out and some were using leather bags as substitutes. The grass was too sparse to feed the horses and Forbes decided to move on but to everyone's surprise, the missing trooper, Shelldrake, suddenly appeared. He had returned to the laager after the silent escape to collect something he had left behind but lost the patrol's tracks when he tried to catch up with it. Forbes, in something of an understatement, describes Shelldrake as being very tired and hungry but glad to get back safe. Temptingly, they saw a number of cattle in the near distance but, in spite of their hunger, Forbes having learned his lesson decided not to attempt to take some as they had too few spare horses to do so, and previous experience suggested that this would result in an attack by the cattle's owners.

As the patrol approached the river they were again fired at from the nearby bush. The wounded and the horses took cover under the river's bank and the rest of the men sheltered near the Maxims which had been quickly brought into action and kept the attackers at bay. The AmaNdebele rifle fire was unusually accurate. Sergeant Pyke, commanding a Maxim, was shot through the arm and Trooper Nesbitt, who was feeding the gun, was hit in

---

34   Forbes ('Retreat from the Shangani River', p.183) suggests that each man was responsible for hoarding his own rations.

the wrist.[35] The men gradually were able to withdraw to the river and, using its high bank as a protection, then moved alongside the river for two miles until they came to a rocky outcrop offering further protection. Raaff had already reached these rocks and was able to provide them with covering fire as they withdrew, and this kept the attackers at a distance. The skirmish continued until dark when there was another thunderstorm.

The patrol marched off again at 2300 hours and travelled through dense bush and small *kopjes*. They halted at daylight and, after a rest, continued to move alongside the river until they could see a large range of hills running down to the river's edge that were impossible to go around without going into the river. The patrol could see tracks in the grass indicating that a large number of AmaNdebele had recently made their way towards the *kopjes* ahead of the patrol. Forbes assumed that they would be lying in ambush and attack the patrol when it reached the *kopjes*. He decided that it was time to cross the river, which was now shallow and, sheltering under its banks, re-cross when they had passed the *kopjes*.

The patrol continued to move towards the drift where they hoped to meet Captain Dallamore, crossing and re-crossing the Shangani until it came to the conjunction with the Longwe River. Here they came across Maholi kraals in which there were cattle. Forbes wanted to approach the Maholi and steal their beasts, if necessary, but Raaff was vehemently against it and the patrol had to continue to eat horsemeat flavoured with wild garlic. Forbes was piqued when he discovered that Raaff, perhaps because he had been more careful than the majority of Forbes' men, still had some cookies and coffee left. According to O'Reilly, Gorringe, Raaff's nephew, believed that Raaff had shared his food with his men arguing that they had bigger bodies and needed more food than he.[36]

However, shortly after passing the kraals, a Maholi approached with good news. There were no AmaNdebele in the area but numbers of them were returning with their cattle to their home kraals. Forbes was able to obtain two cows which were immediately slaughtered, and the patrol ate one and carried the carcass of the other. While this was happening, the two natives Forbes had sent to the waggon drift returned and reported that there were no waggons waiting for them. John Grootbanum had, as instructed, carried on to Umhlangeni where Captain Dallamore was meant to be waiting.

Having eaten the improvised meal, the patrol set off again, this time with the native guides, and travelled five miles They arrived at a wide, open valley and began to make camp when, almost out of nowhere, Frederick Courtenay Selous and Charles Acutt rode towards the laager. They were the advanced guides for a relief column of 150 men led by Captain Heany which, they reported, was only a mile and a half away. Rhodes, Jameson, and Willoughby had accompanied Heany as had Major Sawyer, Sir Henry Loch's military

---

35   PA C 7290, Enclosure in No 91 Telegram, Lieutenant Colonel Goold-Adams, Buluwayo [sic], to His Excellency the High Commissioner, Cape Town. (Received 12th January 1894) Report by Captain Coventry. Pyke had originally been a member of the Salisbury Column, while Nesbitt had been part of the Victoria Column.

36   O'Reilly, *Pursuit of the King*, p.138.

Frederick Selous (seated centre) with H Troop in Bulawayo. (Selous, *Travels and Adventure in South East Africa*)

secretary, who had been sent to report and investigate events. Until this point, the relief column had almost no information as to how the patrol had fared. Some natives, following those examples that have already been described, told Rhodes and Jameson what they hoped to hear, claiming that Wilson and his party had beaten Lobengula and were driving him towards the Zambesi. The two BSAC representatives decided not to do anything and wait until Forbes' men arrived or, at least, reliable information became available about their situation.

One can imagine the joy of the patrol when they heard the news that relief was so close. Interestingly, Forbes, reasserting his command, instructed Raaff to follow on with the patrol while he and Selous rode forward to the relief column, where they arrived at 1815 hours. Forbes was greeted by Jameson who was accompanied by Rhodes, with the latter being described by the interpreter Colenbrander as riding his horse like a sack of potatoes.[37] Both men shook Forbes and Selous by the hand but when Forbes tried to engage Rhodes in conversation he was ominously virtually ignored. Jameson did, however, speak to Forbes and held a lengthy conversation, but Forbes was not to reveal what was said.

Two hours later, in contrast to Forbes' somewhat cool reception, the arrival of Raaff and the rest of the patrol was greeted by the men of the relief column with three cheers. The survivors of the Shangani Patrol were bowed down and unkempt; their appearance shocked those who greeted them, who felt it was hard to believe that they were the same men as the band of proud soldiers who had set off in pursuit of Lobengula. Trooper Bottomley and Corporal Campbell of the relief party who witnessed their arrival described them as looking miserable and weak with some using their saddle bags as boots.[38]

---

37   Bulpin, *The White Whirlwind*, p.292.
38   Cary, *A Time to Die*, p.138.

One can only guess how Forbes felt at that moment. Neville Jones, who was a witness to the events expressed a feeling of sorrow for Forbes who had endured the same trials as the patrol and was just as dishevelled as the rest of his men.[39] Gustave Preller states that Rhodes publicly thanked Raaff for his efforts in saving the column.[40] This view of Raaff's conduct was not shared by all, however, since Preller also asserts that Jameson and his biographer, Ian Colvin, were not above showering 'unmerited blame' upon Raaff: 'The terror of the threatening bush and the constant forebodings of Captain Raaff almost overwhelmed [the patrol].'[41] In an article in *The Star* mentioned previously, Clements was quoted as saying that he was sure that 'every officer and man who served with the Shangani Patrol will agree … that Commandant Raaff was actually the man the survivors had to thank for being led out of a dangerous and almost hopeless situation.'[42] Clements continued that it was 'undoubtedly with the general approval of the column that Raaff, in this dire predicament, assumed command on his own initiative'. Clements went on to refute the suggestion that Raaff was 'sick unto death' and the accusation that this had affected his courage and determination was not true; Clements was adamant that the survivors of the Shangani Patrol, including himself, owed their lives 'to the brave Dutchman'.[43]

Gorringe argues that the accusation that Raaff's death was a result of the arduous campaign was false; the cause he states was ptomaine poisoning – a catch-all phrase for food poisoning.[44] O'Reilly believes that the cause of Raaff's death was the result of circumstances that occurred in GuBulawayo rather than during the patrol. This might be hair-splitting since members of the patrol were forced to eat very unhealthy food during their retreat from the Shangani. The patrol was met by the relief force on 14 December and Raaff died on 26 December. Without knowing Raaff's actual symptoms it is difficult at this distance in time to be certain as to the actual cause of his death. It appears that Raaff had suffered for some years from Bright's Disease and a liver complaint.[45] However, neither of these would explain the symptoms Raaff displayed at the time of his death, but they would seem to suggest that he was far from in the best of health and makes it difficult to know whether these symptoms or the perilous situation in which the patrol found itself had the greater influence on his psychological and physical health. Clements suggests that it was the sumptuous meal to which Raaff was treated on his return to GuBulawayo after living on garlic and roots during the patrol because he would not eat horsemeat that caused his stomach inflammation. Whatever the cause, Commandant Raaff was given a funeral with full military honours.

---

39   Jones, *Rhodesian Genesis*, p.103.
40   Preller, *Lobengula*, p.234.
41   Colvin, *Life of Jameson*, Vol. 1, p.291.
42   *The Star*, 5 June 1923.
43   Preller, *Lobengula*, p.234.
44   O'Reilly (*Pursuit of a King*, p.142) quoting from a letter from Hugh Gorringe dated 11 September 1969
45   PA C 7290, Enclosure 3 in No. 83. From Lieutenant-Colonel Goold-Adams, Buluwayo [sic] to His Excellency the High Commissioner, Cape Town. Telegram. Received 2 January 1894.

It seems that Forbes was very aware of the part Raaff had played during the retreat and sought out Jameson in order to pay wholesome tribute to Raaff's contribution. He was also clearly aware of its cost to the Commandant's health. He asked the doctor to go to Raaff and officially thank him for his efforts which Jameson, accompanied by Rhodes, duly did. Forbes' attempt at a reconciliation or to restore his own reputation was too late, however, since Raaff's officers had already dripped poison into Jameson's ear about Forbes' apparent lethargy during the latter part of the patrol. Their intervention seems to have been effective, as Jameson changed his mind about confirming Forbes as the Resident Magistrate in GuBulawayo – a position the Major had occupied in a temporary capacity since the middle of November.

The Shangani Patrol was over and after a good night's rest and a good meal, escorted by the relief column, which provided waggons for the wounded and horses for those on foot, set off for Umhlangeni. They reached it by dark after travelling the 22 miles.

The following day Forbes and the BSAC men set off for GuBulawayo and arrived after a very wet journey of three days. The BBP and the Cape Mounted Rifles were left at Umhlangeni. On 19 December Rhodes ordered a general assembly of the patrol's members. He thanked the men, especially those of the Salisbury and Victoria Columns who were volunteers, for their efforts in defeating a hostile chief 'without the aid of the Imperial Government'. This was somewhat ironic since Jameson had done his best to make sure that Goold-Adams's Column was delayed in setting off to capture GuBulawayo and therefore had a smaller part to play in the war. In truth Goold-Adams's men had engaged with a large *Impi* which, had they not been travelling to GuBulawayo, would have posed a considerable threat to the Combined Column's progress. Loch, in his correspondence with Lord Ripon, believed that Gambo's men, who had been involved in attacking Goold-Adams's Column, represented as many as half of the AmaNdebele's military strength. It also should not be forgotten that the BBP, commanded by seconded imperial officers, was also involved in the Shangani Patrol.[46] Although the speech was well received by most, others such as Bottomley and Tyndale-Briscoe were much less appreciative, feeling 'it was not worth listening to'.

Jameson, ever practical and frugal, began to organise the disbanding of the BSAC's volunteer troops. On 20 December the men handed in their horses and equipment and on the following day the Salisbury Horse, Victoria Rangers, and Raaff's Rangers were disbanded. Those who wished to return to Salisbury or Victoria left with a month's rations and those who had come from Johannesburg left the following day. However, after risking so much it is not surprising that a large number decided to remain in Matabeleland, and many became eager to make their fortune and set off to do so. The BSAC created a 150-strong police force from members of the Combined Column under the command of Lieutenant William Bodle of the Salisbury Horse.[47] On Christmas Day 1893, Matabeleland was opened for prospecting and farming.

---

46   PA C 7290, No 82, Loch to Ripon, No 82 Received 12 January 1894.
47   Bodle was to play an important part in the Jameson Raid.

Although Lobengula had escaped capture, the main purpose of the invasion had been achieved. The AmaNdebele surrendered *en masse* and offered to hand in their arms. Jameson thought this was an important way to show the AmaNdebele that they had been defeated.[48] Sir Henry Loch felt, on the other hand, that this would be too humiliating for such proud warriors and directed that they should keep their rifles but return to their kraals and plough and raise grain.[49] The issue of the King's herds seemed more important than the warriors' rifles and steps were taken to identify which cattle belonged to Lobengula and which did not. This became an issue during the Matabele Rising in 1896 when many beasts suffered from Rinderpest and the AmaNdebele went hungry, claiming that many cattle which had been confiscated were theirs' and that Jameson had given away too many to his cronies.

Cecil Rhodes, the driving force of the British South Africa Company, had achieved his aim. He had successfully conquered a large area of Southern Africa at minimum expense in money and lives with the reluctant support of the British government, which had seen the Empire expand still further. Even the missionaries who had protested at the BSAC's schemes were pleased to have the AmaNdebele to proselytise. Only a small section of the press, in particular Henry Labouchère's *Truth*, protested that Rhodes had supported Jameson's plans because it would save the BSAC from bankruptcy.[50]

---

48 PA C 7290, Enclosure No 2 in 83. Telegram from Jameson to Sir Henry Loch. Received 9 January 1984.

49 PA C 7290. No. 47. This leniency proved to be a mistake for when the AmaNdebele rose in rebellion in 1896, there was no shortage of weapons available to them.

50 Thomas Pakenham, *The Scramble for Africa* (London: Abacus, 1992), p.495.

14

'I'm afraid that there was a little error of judgement'[1]

So wrote Dr Jameson to his brother Sam who was in business in Johannesburg. Jameson felt that the relatives of those who had died during the Shangani Patrol's pursuit of Lobengula deserved to know whether anyone was to blame for their deaths. Forbes also wanted an inquiry in order to exonerate him from any blame. It seems that at the celebratory dinner given for the officers of the patrol, Raaff had spoken critically about Forbes' part in the venture and Forbes was aware that his position with the BSAC was in jeopardy.

So it proved, for the Court of Inquiry was assembled on 20 December 1893 at GuBulawayo with Goold-Adams as President, together with Major Sir John Willoughby and Captain Herman Melville Heyman, an experienced member of the British South Africa Police who had been a member of the Tuli Column.[2] Jameson believed that the Inquiry would result in 'washing dirty linen in public but it couldn't be helped'.[3] Raaff was too ill to appear before the inquiry and the written evidence he provided only covered events up until 3 December. He was to die shortly afterwards on 26 December 1893 and buried the same day with full military honours. His family believed that his death was caused by sharing most of his food with his men. There is also a suggestion that sumptuous banquet which attended after the return of the patrol overwhelmed his digestive system. He was suffering with 'Bright's' disease throughout the Patrol.[4]

Napier also did not give evidence, and this would have been useful in the inquiry's investigation as to why Borrow and his men were sent to join Wilson. Forbes, however, was both present and systematically prepared when the inquiry opened its first session.[5]

---

1   Jameson to his brother Sam, 24 December 1893, quoted in Preller, *Lobengula*, p.235.
2   Heyman had been selected to replace Forbes as the Resident Magistrate in GuBulawayo.
3   Jameson to his brother Sam, 24 December 1893, quoted in Preller, *Lobengula*, p.235.
4   O'Reilly, *Pursuit of the King*. p.142 Bright's Disease is classified as chronic nephritis today.
5   The record of the inquiry can be found as part of TNA CO 119/514 Administration of Oaths to Judges; Basutoland Affairs; Enquiry into Loss of a Military Patrol on Shangani River; Native Regulations; Private Conversation with President Kruger (April 1893); The Tati Concession

At the inquiry's first sitting, Forbes presented a 20,000-word, handwritten statement detailing each step he had taken and every decision he made from the Shangani Patrol's departure from GuBulawayo on 14 December. Throughout the document there was no admission on Forbes' part that any of his decisions were faulty. His statements reveal an arrogance that is hard to reconcile with the events of the patrol, especially during its retreat when Raaff seems to have taken over command even if only unofficially. Statements such as 'All that was told to us by natives turned out correct' seem somewhat hollow when, as we have seen, Forbes was gullible enough to believe almost anything he was told by AmaNdebele and which subsequently turned out to be false. Similarly, the claims that 'we found precisely what we expected to find' and 'I do not consider that the expedition failed' are remarkable when one considers that the object of the Shangani Patrol was to capture Lobengula, and 34 men were lost in the attempt. The secondary objective of the patrol, Forbes stated, was that if the King could not be captured, he was to be driven out of Matabeleland. This, claimed the Major, had been carried out 'most effectively'. One might consider this to be something of an exaggeration. It is true that Lobengula had rapidly moved ahead of the patrol, but at the time of the patrol's retreat the King's whereabouts were still unknown.

Forbes' own account of the patrol in Wills and Collingridge mentions that on a number of occasions he did defer to advice, particularly that given by Raaff. It is true that Forbes' authority had been somewhat hamstrung by Jameson, who had insisted that he consult with Raaff on every important issue. Speed was of the essence in attempting to prevent Lobengula from escaping and, consequently, the BSAC drastically under-provisioned the patrol to improve its speed, which meant that its members spent a considerable time with meagre supplies of food.

Until the events of the patrol, Forbes had been a diligent and successful officer of the BSAC. He had been Magistrate at Salisbury for two years and handled difficult situations with skill and diplomacy. His regular army experience and his status in the community made him an obvious choice for command of the volunteers of the Salisbury Column, which had successfully advanced to Bulawayo. His weaknesses became apparent when Jameson decided to launch the Shangani Patrol with limited resources and deliberately chose to split the command structure. Not only the authority given to Raaff, but the presence of Lendy were obstacles to success. Human nature suggests that Forbes felt not just the pressure of leading the patrol but also that there were serious critics among his senior staff who questioned many of his decisions.

When these critics, including Captains Francis and Lendy, Colenbrander the scout, and Lieutenant Farley, Raaff's staff officer, were called to give evidence, they did not hesitate to blacken Forbes's reputation. They criticised the careless manner in which the patrol was conducted and quoted examples of the delay in posting pickets and the lack of sufficient protection when the column was laagered for the night. Perhaps the most significant criticism

Company. NZA, Cape Town Office of BSAC. CT 1/14/3 Court of Inquiry; Pursuit of Lobengula by Forbes, December 20–27, 1893.

they made was 'the continual splitting up of the column' the result of which meant that a small force was overwhelmed by a much larger AmaNdebele *Impi*.[6] Francis bore witness that when he had begged Forbes not to send Borrow and his men to support Wilson, he was ignored.[7] Even the dying Raaff's written evidence was critical of Forbes' conduct, pointing out that when he had objected to Forbes' original plan to send both a Maxim as well as troopers to support Wilson, Forbes had replied that he would send the men but not the gun. Whether this was Forbes' military assessment of the situation or simply his determination to ensure that at least a part of his order as the commanding officer was executed is hard to tell. It certainly was an extraordinary compromise. It was the Maxim that had been at the heart of the column's victories at the battles of Shangani and Imbembezi. Without them the column might well have been overwhelmed on a number of occasions. If Borrow had taken one of the two Maxims with him, the story of Wilson's Patrol might have had a different ending. It was Forbes' decisions immediately before the disaster that were the most questionable and the blame for these could not be levelled on Raaff, even though there were other earlier occasions when Raaff had changed Forbes' mind. Captain Finch, late of the Lifeguards and one of Forbes' staff officers, spoke in Forbes' defence, but he was the only witness to do so.

The inquiry did not come to a formal conclusion but forwarded the cumulative evidence to Jameson, which indicates that it was acting on behalf of the BSAC and not the British government or the High Commissioner. Jameson, perhaps sensitive to the implied criticism of the BSAC's inadequate preparations for the Shangani Patrol, wished to send the evidence to Sir William Cameron who was the General Officer Commanding, South Africa, and hoped he would decide responsibility or blame without the need for the witness' statements being published. Sir Henry Loch refused to agree to this subterfuge since he felt that the inquiry was not an official one. The doctor may have hoped that the BSAC would be exonerated from culpability for the disaster and Loch would blame individuals for Wilson's death rather than the Company as a whole. Sir Henry, who had considerable military experience of his own, considered the testimony of the witnesses and observed that Forbes had failed to follow the 'invariable practice' of laagering on the far side of the Shangani rather than the near side before attempting a crossing. Had he had done so he would have been closer to Wilson's Patrol and able to offer it support.[8] When Forbes laagered on the banks of the Shangani on 3 December there was no reason why he couldn't have crossed the river and laagered instead on its north bank – the side where Wilson's Patrol was operating. It would certainly not have split the patrol into three parts and thus would have reduced the risk of being overwhelmed. It was this fear of being swamped by the AmaNdebele that Forbes claimed had prevented him from doing so.

---

6   Cary, *A Time to Die*, p.140.

7   Glass, *The Matabele War*, p.231.

8   ZNA HC 3/5/30/6 Loch's Memorandum on the Report of the Inquiry.

Loch was also critical of the BSAC's original organisation of the patrol based on the supposition the Lobengula had been deserted by his people. The patrol's experiences of attacks and the massacre of Wilson's men demonstrated that this was far from the case. This assumption meant that the Shangani Patrol was too weak for its professed purpose and the need for safety was sacrificed for the need for speed. There was also the constant fear that the patrol would run out of ammunition because insufficient amounts had been allocated to its various armaments. Forbes may not have been a brilliant commander but even so it was hard for him the be an effective one when there was so much friction between the leaders of the patrol. He was not confident of their ability, and they lacked loyalty to their commanding officer. This was essential to good discipline, argued Loch, and this faulty relationship meant that if the patrol ever came under real pressure there was likely be a disaster. Hindsight is a wonderful thing.

Despite these stinging criticisms, Loch did not take any formal action since he regarded the inquiry has having no official status. It was the responsibility of Jameson and the BSAC, argued Sir Henry, to deal with any member of the patrol who was in the BSAC's employ if they wished to do so. Loch would confine his attention to the BBP who were officially under his authority. The BBP proved to be safe from official sanction since Loch, having examined the BBP's part in the patrol, concluded that they had been heavily involved in the various actions and, as such, had played a considerable part in its safety. The High Commissioner argued that the number of casualties the BBP had experienced was evidence of this. Perhaps this is a rather exaggerated view.

Willoughby was angered by the lack of a formal conclusion and launched a vitriolic attack against Forbes' conduct during the patrol. Frederick Rutherfoord Harris, the BSAC's Secretary in Cape Town, informed Jameson that it was likely that Forbes, stung by the outcome of the inquiry, would either demand a second hearing or that the proceedings of the recent inquiry be published. Jameson and Loch agreed that this would be dangerous for both the BSAC and the British government. On reflection, Willoughby also agreed, since after all, Forbes was a 'gentleman of no importance'.[9] This was a final insult to Forbes who felt he had done his best in very difficult circumstances.

The lack of an official report contributed to the mystery of Wilson's Patrol and made Forbes' position untenable. He was an obvious scapegoat and had no influential friends who could argue in his defence. In February 1894, he went on six months leave and returned to England. As early as December, Tyne-Briscoe had noted in his diary that Forbes was going on six months' leave and he doubted that the Major would return.[10] Bottomley, who had witnessed the return of the patrol to GuBulawayo, rejoiced that Forbes was no longer going to be the magistrate of the town.[11] Norris Newman also links Forbes' removal from the post of Resident Magistrate to evidence given to

---

9 Jameson to Harris, quoted in Norris Newman, *Matabeleland and How We Got It*, p.151.
10 Tyne-Briscoe, quoted in Cary, *A Time to Die*, p.139.
11 Bottomley, quoted in Cary, *A Time to Die*, p.139.

the inquiry despite its lack of conclusions.[12] The mystery of the Shangani Patrol continues as important records of the BSAC were destroyed in the London Blitz in 1941.

Forbes arrived in Plymouth in February and was quickly interviewed by the press, which saw him as something of a hero. Afterall, the Matabele War was a victory for the British Empire and such triumphant events were very popular with the general public. Not all the English newspapers supported Forbes' actions or those of the BSAC. In particular, *Truth*, edited by Labouchère, who had made his attacks on the BSAC something of a passion, had seized upon an article in a Pretoria newspaper written by Captain Francis of Raaff's Rangers in which he claimed that he had been ordered to shoot AmaNdebele prisoners. Francis also claimed that there had been a number of other atrocities perpetrated by employees of the BSAC. Norris Newman sarcastically described Francis as having 'distinguished himself' by his action of shooting the prisoners as well as his garbled description of it but goes on to point out that this was the only occasion when such an event occurred, thus laying the blame at Francis's feet rather than the BSAC.[13] It should be noted, however, that Norris Newman leans towards the BSAC throughout his version of events. On the other hand, one must also remember that Francis had already been accused of being unreliable by Forbes, perhaps because he was an unreliable witness at the inquiry. Labouchère accepted Francis's version of events and accused the BSAC of 'unbridled ruffianism' and then described its officials as being involved in 'hideous scenes of drunken behaviour'.[14] Labouchère's article was attacked as being untrue by Frederick Selous and the prickly MP replied with a letter in *The Times*.[15]

Labouchère despised the members of the Shangani Patrol as mercenaries fighting for the BSAC, a company with the objective of improving its finances by looting and taking over land and mines. The vast majority of the members of the patrol were motivated by repugnant self-interest. Although Labouchère was sorry for the fate of Wilson and his patrol, this sorrow was because they had died in a base cause and so they should not be regarded as noble heroes.

In taking this extreme view regarding the gallantry of Wilson and his men, Labouchère destroyed his own argument. Many regarded the BSAC as fair game for criticism and even thought its practices might be questionable. To attack men whom most thought had died bravely fighting for Queen and Country, however, meant that the accusations about the practices of the BSAC were mostly overlooked. Public focus was directed towards the comments of others such as the author Henry Rider Haggard, who had turned his experiences in South Africa into successful adventure novels. Rider Haggard asked people to sympathise with the 'gallant dead' and to ignore those who did 'not scruple to spit upon their bones'.[16]

---

12   Norris Newman, *Matabeleland and How We Got It*, p.145.
13   Norris Newman, *Matabeleland and How We Got It*, p.193.
14   *The Truth*, 8 February 1894.
15   *The Times*, 10 February 1894.
16   Rider Haggard in an address given to the Anglo African Writers' Club, 23 April 1894.

British South Africa Company Medal, obverse. (Author's collection)

Rider Haggard was not the only public figure to defend both the war and Wilson's Patrol. General Digby Willoughby, who was as much a self-publicist as an African adventurer, arrived in GuBulawayo at the close of the campaign. Later, in a public lecture at St James Hall, London, Digby Willoughby reminded his audience that Wilson's men were Englishmen, who had been all alone facing a foe that thirsted for their blood. They stood shoulder to shoulder as they had done on the football fields of their youth.[17] Even more dramatically, a tableau at the Empire Theatre entitled *British Pluck* showed its audience how Englishmen could fight and bravely die in the cause of duty.

Such was the significance of the war that in 1896 Queen Victoria sanctioned the BSAC to issue a medal to commemorate the victory. It was awarded to the troops who had been engaged in the war and later to those who took part in the Matabele Rising of 1896. The obverse depicts a left-facing effigy of Queen Victoria wearing a diadem and veil. Around the edge is the inscription '*Victoria Regina*'. The reverse, designed by Richard Caton Woodville Jr, depicts a charging lion, wounded in the chest with an *assegai*. In the foreground are native weapons and a shield, in the background is a mimosa bush, and below the scene the inscription: '*BRITISH SOUTH AFRICA COMPANY*'. Most of the medals were awarded to locally raised troops rather than imperial soldiers. The original medal had three clasps: Matabeleland 1893, Rhodesia 1896, and Mashonaland 1897. In 1927, the Southern Rhodesian government reissued the medal with a fourth clasp, Mashonaland 1890, to commemorate the Pioneer Column.

---

17   Digby Willoughby, quoted in Cary, *A Time to Die*, p.144.

15

The Last King of the AmaNdebele

What became of Lobengula after the defeat of Wilson's Patrol? Rumours abounded. Some believed that the King had been buried under a baobab tree near the town of Lindazi in northeast Rhodesia as late as 1922. Another version is that his body was placed in a cave at Pupu – the site of the defeat of Wilson's Patrol.[1] Equally disputed were the circumstances of Lobengula's death. Was the cause dysentery, smallpox, food poisoning, or even suicide? Princess Catherine Radziwill, the self-proclaimed fiancée of Cecil Rhodes and convicted fraudster, claimed that Rhodes killed the King.[2] The princess's record of deceit, however, suggests that this claim may be as unreliable as many of her others.

In January 1944, *Time Magazine* reported that Lobengula's remains had been found in a cave close to the banks of the Manyanda River, north of GuBulawayo.[3] The *Time* article describes how Arthur Huxtable, District Commissioner for Native Affairs, was guided to the spot by a native prospector named Ginyilitshe. There Huxtable found a cave from the entrance of which a stone had been rolled away and there was evidence of previous intruders. Huxtable questioned the AmaNdebele elders who had accompanied him as to what had happened to Lobengula in his final days.

King Lobengula of the Matabele; by Ralph Peacock, based on a sketch by E. A. Maund. (Open Source)

---

1   *The Zambia Sunday Mail*, 15 December 2013.

2   Catherine Radziwill, *Cecil Rhodes, Man and Empire-Maker* (London, Cassell & Co., 1918), p.37.

3   Anon, 'The Skull of Lobengula', *Time Magazine*, 10 January 1944.

Reluctantly, they explained that the King had fled when he knew that the war was lost.

In despair, Lobengula burned the trappings of his office, his leather head-ring, his famous monkey-skin sporran, and his girdles. The elders reported that the defeated monarch then declared he was an outcast and no longer their king. They should return to Rhodes, who would be both chief and friend among them. Lobengula and his heir, Magwegwe, then drank poison. On inspection of the cave, Huxtable is said to have found some old rifles, a skull with some human bones and the chair that had been presented to Lobengula by Queen Victoria.[4] There have been suggestions that the grave was a decoy to divert attention from the real place of burial but, whether true or not, the site has been acknowledged as the grave of Lobengula by both Europeans and the AmaNdebele down to the present day.

Another legend is that Lobengula found refuge with the Ngoni people whose land was also being threatened by the BSAC. The truth will probably be never known, but there is a long history of unscrupulous, as well as genuine, treasure seekers who have spent years attempting to discover the whereabouts of Lobengula's 'treasure', which is an interesting story in itself.[5] What is certain is that one of Lobengula's sons, Nyamanda, led a rebellion known as the 'Rising' against the BSAC administration in 1896. It was a bloody affair and put down only after the intervention of imperial troops.

---

4   Anon, 'The Skull of Lobengula'.
5   R.S. Roberts, 'The Treasure and Grave of Lobengula: Yarns and Reflections' *Heritage of Zimbabwe*, 23, 2004. See also Hedley A. Chilvers, *The Seven Lost Trails of Africa* (London: Cassell & Co., 1930), pp.101–116.

16

Regina v. Daniel and Wilson

Life is full of 'What ifs?' and history is no exception. In Chapter 9 it was explained that Jameson sent out the Shangani Patrol because he was not prepared to wait any longer for a positive reply from Lobengula saying that he would return to GuBulawayo. This apparent lack of response led to both the Shangani Patrol and, subsequently, the loss of Wilson and his men. The truth was that Lobengula had sent such a letter, but it had been intercepted by two troopers from the BBP, James Wilson and William Daniel, and the reason they had not forwarded it was because it was accompanied by gold, which they pocketed. The circumstances leading to the loss of the gold are worth examining since, had Daniel and Wilson not acted as they did then Major Wilson and his men might not have perished.[1]

The story seems to have been as follows: Lobengula, having reached the Shangani, was exhausted; his oxen were worn out and his accompanying followers extremely dispirited. The King decided to surrender and summoned Mjaan to whom he gave a letter and a bag of sovereigns as a peace offering with instruction to deliver these to the leader of the Shangani Patrol. Mjaan selected two reliable messengers, Sehulohulu and Impala, who were given the bag of sovereigns, together with the message to the leader of the patrol asking him to stop the pursuit in order to meet Lobengula.[2]

Mjaan was to give evidence at the trial of Wilson and Daniel at which the two BBP troopers were accused of becoming the 'moral murderers of Wilson and his men'.[3] Sehulohulu's evidence delivered at the trial and the preliminary investigation held in front of Magistrate Heyman when the story came to light was used to construct the meeting between him and the two BBP troopers.[4] Sehulohulu claimed that he and Impala had tried to move round the patrol which had, unknowingly, passed the place where Lobengula was camped. They hoped to reach the head of the patrol where they expected

---

1   For a fuller version of the Wilson and Daniel affair, see Glass, *The Matabele War*, pp.241–264; Cary, *A Time to Die*, pp.152–162; O'Reilly, *Pursuit of the King*, pp.149 & 151.

2   Glass, *The Matabele War*, pp.249–250.

3   Jameson in a telegram to Rutherfoord Harris, quoted in Cary, *A Time to Die*, pp.152. A record of the trial can be found in *Regina v. Daniel and Wilson*, High Court of Matabeleland Civil Records, Case No. 275.

4   It appears that Impala had died of smallpox shortly after delivering the gold.

its leader to be. Their plan went awry and instead of the reaching the head of the patrol, they came upon its rear where they found the two troopers, both of whom were officers' batmen and engaged in clearing up the camp.[5] Sehulohulu and Impala handed over the bag of gold sovereigns, saying that it was from Lobengula, and conveyed the message that the King was beaten.

Having delivered the King's message, the two AmaNdebele vanished into the bush. Perhaps believing that the possible witnesses (that is, the AmaNdebele) would never be identified, Daniel and Wilson decided to pocket the sovereigns and 'forget' the message. As Stafford Glass remarks, it is because of their actions that 'Lobengula's last overtures [of peace] remained undisclosed'.[6] However, rumours about what had happened began to circulate and William Usher, the trader whose store had been spared when much of GuBulawayo had been destroyed after Lobengula fled, heard the story from a pair of AmaNdebele. Usher was one of the few white men who was fluent in the native language but when he heard the story in January 1894, he was extremely doubtful of its veracity. Surely if Forbes had received the gold and the message he would have attempted to negotiate with the King. Similarly, specie was in very short supply in Matabeleland and had someone intercepted the messengers, they would have been unable to take advantage of their good fortune as their sudden wealth in gold sovereigns would have become obvious. Usher felt, however, that, no matter how unlikely it was that there was any truth behind the rumour, he ought to pass it on to Dr Jameson when he returned to GuBulawayo.

Jameson was not convinced either. He had received a number of messages from Lobengula claiming that the King wanted to return to GuBulawayo but there were always conditions attached which the doctor felt were simply attempts to delay Forbes' advance and thus enable the King to retreat further away from his former capital. It was also possible that the story was an attempt to put the blame for the continued war at the feet of the BSAC. Despite his doubts, Jameson could not totally ignore the rumour. Lobengula was known to have considerable treasure, and little had been found in GuBulawayo. He had received the £100 gold payments from the BSAC for agreeing to the Rudd Concession on several occasions. Such was Jameson's unease that he felt the rumours needed investigating, if only to maintain the good reputation of the Company.

James Dawson, when sent in February 1894 to discover what had happened to Wilson's Patrol, was also charged with finding out whether the story of the stolen sovereigns was true. Dawson sent his conclusions regarding the gold as part of his letter of March 1894 in which he described finding the remains of Wilson's men. He had been told that gold had been sent and intercepted by two white men. His account was very similar to the rumour Usher had heard.

---

5   It seems that the 31-year-old William Charles Daniel, who had been born in Cape Colony, was the leader of the two batmen, and is described in the *Rhodesia Herald* as a 'short man apparently with a tinge of black blood in his veins'. James Wilson, a groom from Dartmouth, on the other hand, was described as 'a taller man of unmistakable English features, but not such as one would expect to find in a man prepared to do anything desperate'. *Rhodesia Herald*, June 1894. The racist hint in these descriptions is obvious.

6   Glass, *The Matabele War*, p.243.

Since it appeared that the culprits were men from the BBP, Jameson notified Goold-Adams and they agreed that a tactful investigation should be made of those troopers of the BBP who were stationed at Inyati. These men were the only ones in the area since the other volunteers had been disbanded and returned to their homes or gone prospecting.

The investigation quickly identified Daniel and Wilson as possible culprits. Both had been on a brief leave to GuBulawayo during which they had each bought the rights to farms valued at £70. They were also known to have gold in their possession. Goold-Adams personally interviewed the two batmen, and Daniel claimed to have won his gold gambling whereas Wilson asserted that it was the result of him saving money in order to buy gold claims or farms in the future. When Goold-Adams told Jameson of his findings, the doctor felt it necessary to warn Rutherfoord Harris, the BSAC Secretary at Cape Town, that he thought the story was true – Lobengula had sent messengers offering to treat with Forbes on 3 December, the day on which Forbes had sent Wilson and his men across the Shangani. The blame for this, argued Jameson, must be placed firmly on the shoulders of Daniel and Wilson and the BSAC's reputation must be preserved at all costs.

Ironically, the story of the stolen sovereigns was something of a boon to the Company. Opponents such as Labouchère had placed the blame for the loss of Wilson's Patrol at its door, but the BSAC had subtly done its best to pass the responsibility for their deaths onto Major Forbes. If the blame for the fatalities was really the fault of two unknown troopers in the BBP then the company's culpability would be significantly diminished.

The two men were arrested on a warrant issued by Magistrate Heyman. Such was the importance attached to the story that Goold-Adams travelled the 100 miles to Tati, which remained the nearest telegraph line to GuBulawayo, in order to communicate with Sir Henry Loch. On 25 March, Loch was told that Goold-Adams had arrested the two troopers on suspicion of theft since they had more money in their possession than they could reasonably account for. A somewhat incredulous Sir Henry enquired how much gold the men had on them and was surprised to be told that none had actually been found. The High Commissioner asked that if such was the case, why had the men been arrested. It was well known, explained Goold-Adams, that they had bought the rights to farms paying in cash.

Perhaps, because he was still full of doubt or because he wanted the imperial government to be kept out of the limelight, Loch, on the advice of William Philip Schreiner, acting as his legal adviser, resisted the idea that the troopers should be tried by general courts martial since a guilty verdict would incur a sentence of death.[7] This was an outcome which many, including Forbes, hoped for since if the men were tried in this way it meant that the two men had jeopardised the lives of members of 'Her Majesty's Forces.' Schreiner counselled that Daniel and Wilson were essentially policemen and unaware that they were subject to military discipline; for some inexplicable reason, the BBP had not been told that it was on active service. Any verdict of a court

---

7   Schreiner was to become Attorney General for the Cape Colony and later its Prime Minister.

martial could easily be overturned on this important technicality. Therefore, Schreiner advised that it would be more appropriate to try the men before the Administrator (Jameson) who was able to sentence thieves to indefinite periods of imprisonment as well as corporal punishment.

Schreiner's advice was not well received in GuBulawayo. Dawson had, by this time, confirmed that all Major Wilson's men had perished and the link between the gold thieves and their death was obvious to many. They were not just thieves of Lobengula's gold, but vicarious murderers of Wilson's Patrol. The pair were in danger of being strung up and even Heyman, somewhat injudiciously, proclaimed that he would hang the men if it were in his power. At the preliminary hearing, presided over by Heyman, Daniel and Wilson were charged with embezzling £1,000 which had endangered the lives of the Shangani Patrol and caused the death of Wilson and his men. They both pleaded not guilty, but Heyman was persuaded by Jameson's claim that if Lobengula's messengers had got through to Forbes, he would have halted his patrol and Wilson would never have been sent forward. They were remanded for trial on the basis of the theft, but with the unwritten charge of murder. The men were released on bail, together with additional securities paid by Captain Coventry and James Dawson.

Their liberty was short-lived, the BBP contingent was ordered to return to its base at Macloutsie as the formation of the new police force in Matabeleland meant that it was no longer required in GuBulawayo. Daniel and Wilson were also due to leave with their colleagues. Heyman contacted Coventry and Dawson seeking further securities as the two accused would be quite a distance from GuBulawayo and might desert, but both men refused. They also requested the return of their original security, which meant that Daniel and Wilson were taken into custody.

Jameson travelled to Fort Salisbury to confer with Arthur Edward Caldecott, the Crown Prosecutor, who had to decide whether the evidence collected by Heyman was strong enough to bring the men to trial. The delay and the uncertainty this caused frustrated Loch, who thought that it wasn't fair to Daniel and Wilson or the Administration. Jameson decided that it would be better if the two alleged thieves were tried by the resident magistrate rather than himself, but Heyman was to be the assisted by four assessors. The first group of names suggested for this role was criticised by the accused's lawyers, Messrs Hoyle and Hovell, who argued that three of them were 'government' men and so would be biased against the troopers.[8] Consequently, the approved assessors were Lord Henry Paulet, James Dawson, C.P. Clerk (an American mining engineer) and F.J. Newton of the Newton Commission.[9]

8　The original Assessors were: The Honourable Maurice Gifford, a British officer; Charles Vigers, the Resident Mining Engineer at Victoria (see Chapter 4); and Captain Henry Scott Turner, who was to be Adjutant and Paymaster of the Matabele Relief Force during the Matabele Uprising.

9　'A Report from Bulawayo', *Cape Times*, 1 June 1894. Until that point, Paulet had spent his life travelling and hunting.

The trial of Daniel and Wilson.
(*The Graphic*, 1894)

In opening its case, the prosecution attempted to prove what had actually happened. There were no white witnesses it could call and so it had to rely on the evidence of three of the AmaNdebele who had been involved, but Impala, who had been present when the gold was alleged to have been given to Daniel and Wilson could not be found. The three AmaNdebele witnesses were: Betchane, who had carried the message with the bag of gold from Lobengula to Mjaan; Mjaan, the *Induna*; and Sehulohulu, who had allegedly given the bag of sovereigns and the message to Daniel and Wilson. Only the last two AmaNdebele were present at the trial, but Mjaan's evidence given at the preliminary hearing was available. Their combined evidence was that Lobengula had sent sovereigns and a message to the leader of the Shangani Patrol and both money and words had been given to Daniel and Wilson who were not with the patrol at that time. None of the AmaNdebele could identify the two white men concerned. They all looked very similar as the common custom of the whites was to have heavy moustaches, which made it difficult for the AmaNdebele to distinguish between them. The court accepted this as a reasonable explanation.

The prosecution then attempted to prove that the bag contained 1,000 gold sovereigns. Neither Mjaan nor Betchane were able to confirm this important fact. The former testified that there were only a few coins and the latter had said that he did not know how many coins there were but that he had been able to carry the bag in one hand but not for long. A similar bag was produced but Sehulohulu believed that it was slightly bigger than the one he had been given. Having discussed the size and weight of the actual bag with local bank officials, Stafford Glass was convinced that Lobengula's bag had contained roughly 1,000 sovereigns.[10]

---

10   Glass, *The Matabele War*.

It was then necessary for the prosecution to establish when the meeting between the AmaNdebele and the troopers had taken place. The fact enabling it to do so was the mysterious shot mentioned in Chapter 10. Initially, Sehulohulu said that he had heard the shot just before he came across the troopers. Later he said that he had heard it at the end of his meeting with them. Although inconsistent, Sehulohulu's evidence was good enough to confirm that he had met Daniel and Wilson and it was to them that he had given the bag of sovereigns. This was partially confirmed by the evidence of Trooper William Henry Marx, who stated that just before the mysterious shot he had seen Daniel and another trooper, whom he could not identify as Wilson, some 30 yards to the rear of the patrol. Shortly afterwards, he had seen two natives, also at the rear of the patrol but they had quickly disappeared into the dense bush. Commandant Raaff, who noted the stragglers, sent Captain Alfred Ernest Wilson, a member of his staff, to chivvy them along. Wilson identified one of the men as Daniel, who was leading a packhorse covered by a large white, waterproof sheet just as Sehulohulu had described. Alfred Wilson could not remember who Trooper Wilson's companion had been. Sub-Inspector Martin Straker of the BSAC Police, however, confirmed that the pack horse of which Daniel had been in charge belonged to Captain Coventry and was easily distinguished by its distinctive waterproof.[11] Straker also confirmed that, to the best of his knowledge, there was no other packhorse in the patrol covered by a similar waterproof.

The prosecution's case against Wilson was, however, somewhat weaker. Neither Marx nor Captain Wilson could confirm that Trooper Daniel's companion was Wilson. Marx went so far as to say that he did not actually think it was Wilson. While the evidence against Daniel, though mainly circumstantial, was looking convincing, that against Wilson was looking somewhat flimsy. It seems, however, that because the two men were often in each other's company, both being batmen, it was thought that the second man was very likely to be Wilson. Both Coventry and Sergeant Major Willows had confirmed at the preliminary inquiry that the two men were often to be seen loitering at the rear of the column and they had been reprimanded for this which had improved their behaviour. No such evidence was presented at the trial, but it was accepted that batmen were always the last to leave a camp and the two accused were often seen riding together.

Having covered the incident on 3 December, the prosecution then had to address the issue of how the stolen gold had been used. At the preliminary hearing, Willows had confirmed that the two men had a reputation for being heavy gamblers. When the Shangani Patrol returned, another witness, Corporal S.M. Burrows, had seen them gambling with large quantities of gold. He stated that it was common knowledge that Daniel had sent £200 home to his wife. A Commission Agent, Frank Alexander Purdon confirmed that he had been given £70 in gold, presumably to buy the rights to a farm. Coventry also told the court that Daniel had given him a total of £212, partly in gold and partly in cheques, won at the gambling table, for safekeeping.

---

11   Daniel was Captain Coventry's batman.

However, if Daniel had bought a farm, the money for the purchase had come from elsewhere. Wilfred Honey, who was responsible for recording farm purchases, confirmed that Daniel had bought a farm in in January but there was no record of Wilson having done so.[12]

Wilson was not totally in the clear as Coventry reported that during the interview of the trooper conducted by Goold-Adams, Wilson had claimed that he had brought with him to GuBulawayo money he had saved. Coventry had asked Wilson to name from whom he had originally obtained the gold so that his story could be verified. Wilson had either been unable or refused to do so. Coventry confirmed that when they returned to Inyati he was informed that Wilson had a lot of gold in his possession. This was damming evidence since Coventry was prepared to swear that the BBP did not bring any gold into Matabeleland. They were paid with cheques or cash and not in sovereigns, which, according to Commission Agent Purdon, were very scarce in the country. Coventry had also expressed surprise as to the amount of gold Wilson had given him for safekeeping.

The court concluded that there was sufficient evidence to identify both Daniel and Wilson as the two men at the rear of the patrol and that they had met Sehulohulu. It also determined that the evidence about their gambling and possession of gold proved that they had been given Lobengula's gold and nothing that a somewhat incompetent defence could do would persuade them otherwise. The fact that there was no member of the BBP present during the trial who could advise the two was also greatly to their disadvantage. They were not called to appear in the witness box. Witnesses were called in their defence but their testimony as to their whereabouts and their inability to disguise a bag of gold crumbled during cross examination. One ray of comfort might have arisen when Sehulohulu was asked to inspect an identity parade of six or eight men to confirm that Daniel and Wilson were the culprits. The AmaNdebele was unable to do so and even picked out an innocent man, Corporal Burrows, as a culprit. Sehulohulu's inability to identify Daniel and Wilson was, he said, because he had spent so little time with them.

The court was convinced of Daniel and Wilson's guilt. They were the two men who had received the gold, having means, motive, and opportunity. There was one more important factor which weighed upon the court when considering its sentence. Jameson had argued at the preliminary hearing that sending the gold meant that Lobengula wanted to sue for peace. Had Forbes received the gold and the King's message he would have halted his advance, negotiations would have taken place and Allan Wilson and his men would not have been sent to their deaths. In making this link between the theft and the massacre, Jameson was clearly indicating that Heyman and the assessors must impose a heavy sentence.

They did not disappoint and decided that Daniel and Wilson had stolen the gold and, as a result, Wilson and his men had been slaughtered. On

---

12   Honey was to become the accountant of the first Standard Bank of South Africa in Salisbury which was established to provide currency to cover BSAC cheques. 'History of Banking in Zimbabwe', *The African Spectator*, 3 February 2015. https://africanspectator.blogspot.com

29 May the court sentenced the two troopers to 14 year's hard labour and ordered that all their property in Matabeleland be confiscated. It seemed that the case was closed to everyone's but Daniel's and Wilson's satisfaction.

Unfortunately for those who believed that Daniel and Wilson were 'moral murderers', Jameson's actions had been a mistake. His powers as Administrator could not be delegated to Heyman and a mere magistrate did not have the authority to dispense such a heavy sentence. On 2 June, Sir William Cameron, who was Acting High Commissioner in Loch's absence, was informed of the verdict.[13] Cameron took legal advice which confirmed his own opinion that only Jameson had the power to impose such a heavy sentence. One wonders why 'action man' Jameson had not conducted the trial himself. His statements about 'moral murder' indicated his real opinion but perhaps by letting Heyman preside, the doctor was attempting to distance the BSAC from the fate of Wilson's Patrol and place the blame on two unimportant troopers. It was the court that had condemned them as thieves rather than acting as servants of the company. Cameron informed Lord Ripon, the Colonial Secretary, that the convicted men had a good reason to appeal the sentence if they wished to do so. However, Cameron decided not to interfere as this discrepancy had not been 'officially' brought to his notice – a case of official ignorance outweighing unofficial knowledge. No one was sufficiently sympathetic enough to Daniel and Wilson to bring the error to the fore. Cameron believed that justice had been done, if by a roundabout way, and the ends justified the means.[14]

Was it true that the men were 'moral murderers'? Could they have reasonably anticipated that Wilson and his men would die or even that the Shangani Patrol would have been halted and the war ended? Was Jameson being blessed with the gift of hindsight when he claimed that the theft of the gold led to Major Wilson's death? The doctor had received at least two previous messages from Lobengula but had dismissed them as delaying tactics. A charge that Jameson's dismissive attitude was equally responsible for sending the Shangani Patrol that ended in disaster was never considered. Similarly, Jameson's instructions to Forbes to do his utmost to capture the King did not suggest that the Major's task was to negotiate with Lobengula if the opportunity arose.

Some six months later, Goold-Adams, probably after much reflection, remembered that Daniel and Wilson had been under his command, which meant he had a responsibility towards them. He wrote to Sir Graham Bower, the Imperial Secretary, suggesting that the trial had some irregularities – not least that Heyman had exceeded his powers in delivering such a harsh sentence. The men had not appeared in the witness box on the advice of their legal advisers who had told them that there was no way they would be convicted on such flimsy evidence. Bower was asked to bring these facts to the attention of Cameron in order that the Acting High Commissioner might investigate these irregularities if he saw fit. Bower did not approach

---

13   Cameron had a long military career that included service in the Crimean War, and he had been Governor of Hong Kong in 1887.

14   O'Reilly, *A Time to Die*, p.159.

his chief but contacted Francis Newton who had been one of the assessors. Newton naturally defended the court's proceedings and even claimed that it had bent over backwards to ensure that the accused had a fair trial when they felt their legal representation had been inadequate. Despite Heyman's limited powers, Newton was in no doubt of the men's guilt. Satisfied with these claims, Goold-Adams lost interest.

For 18 months the convicted pair continued their imprisonment until suddenly ex-trooper Wilson hired a Salisbury lawyer, William Patterson Grimmer from the firm of Frames and Grimmer, to organise a review of his conviction. Having looked at the evidence, Grimmer argued that there were five reasons why Wilson's conviction should be reviewed: (1) there was insufficient evidence for Heyman to have convicted him; (2) the sentence was beyond the magistrate's power to impose; (3) Heyman had not forwarded the record of the case to the appropriate authorities as he was legally required to do; (4) illegal or inept evidence had been permitted at the trial; and (5) the entire proceedings of the trial were illegal. Grimmer's application for the review accused Percy George Smith, the then Resident Magistrate at GuBulawayo, and Sir Thomas Scanlen, the Public Prosecutor at Salisbury, of being responsible for these legal errors. When these officials studied Grimmer's application, they realised that there were genuine grounds to review Wilson's conviction. The question of the magistrate's authority lay at the heart of the matter. Scanlen felt that this was such an important error that it provided grounds to set aside Wilson's conviction. Somehow, when Rutherfoord Harris had sent Schreiner's legal opinion to Heyman he had forgotten to indicate that a heavy sentence, such as the one which had been laid upon Wilson and Daniel, could only be given by Jameson, the Administrator. Since Jameson did not preside at the trial, Heyman had exceed his authority as a mere magistrate.

Once Scanlen identified this error, he went on to consider Grimmer's other points. Failure to send the records of the trial to a higher court also meant that it could not reconsider the case. Perhaps most damning of all was, after reviewing the evidence of the witnesses, Scanlen was of the opinion they did not prove the guilt of Wilson and Daniel 'beyond reasonable doubt', but merely made their behaviour seem suspicious. Scanlen discussed his findings with Mr Justice Joseph Vintcent, the Chief Judge of the High Court of Matabeleland, who agreed with his conclusions. Since Wilson had served a much longer sentence than that to which Heyman had the power to sentence him, Vintcent decreed that both the conviction and the sentence should be set aside.

Daniel was not so fortunate, for when Scalen and Vintcent took it upon themselves to review his conviction, they both felt that the evidence merited a guilty verdict. However, there was also the same issue of that of the severity of Daniel's sentence. At a sitting of the High Court on 4 August 1896, the two men's release was ordered. The court further ruled that the order for confiscation of the men's property was also contrary to law, and it should be restored.

The two men returned to the BBP in Salisbury, but it seems they were quickly dismissed from the force. Daniel then disappeared from history, but Wilson kept bobbing up to its surface from time to time. It appears he successfully sued for the back-pay owing to him while in prison. Shortly afterwards, he emigrated to New Zealand, but Wilson was not yet done. His conviction had deprived him of his entitlement to the medal for the Matabele War and he applied to Scanlen and Percy Temple Rivett Carnac, the Chief Staff Officer at Salisbury, for his name be reinstated on the medal roll and be sent the medal.[15] On the face of it, this seemed a reasonable request, but Wilson had gone a step too far. Since his was a letter sent from Napier, New Zealand, it had to be established that it was the same James Wilson who had been wrongly convicted that had written it. Investigations were to prove, however, that Trooper James Wilson's real name was Clifton and he had been a groom, who enlisted and then deserted from the 11th (Prince Albert's Own) Hussars on two occasions while the regiment was in South Africa. After being imprisoned for this offence, Frederick Clifton deserted a third time before joining the BBP. Such significance was attached to establishing Wilson's bona fides for being awarded the medal that this request passed over the desk of Joseph Chamberlain, the Colonial Secretary, who informed the High Commissioner for Southern Africa, Viscount Alfred Millner, that Wilson's request could not be considered unless he could produce a discharge certificate for the 11th Hussar. Wilson did not reply and, as Stafford Glass remarks about Wilson and Daniel, no more was heard from these 'two unlovely persons'.[16]

Norris Newman is probably correct in claiming that speculation as to what might have happened if Daniel and Wilson supposed actions had not been part of the patrol's story is a fruitless exercise.[17] As far as he is concerned as well as those he consulted, Forbes should have sent a larger party of reinforcements to save Wilson's Patrol while leaving 30 or 40 men with a Maxim to guard the river crossing so the whole party could return. He suggests that there might have been a loss of life as a result of this action, but not so great as that of the loss of all of Wilson's men. In doing so Norris Newman, despite his warning against speculation, engaged in it himself.

---

15   Lieutenant-Colonel Rivett-Carnac had fought in the AmaNdebele Uprising and was to be mentioned in despatches in the Second Boer War.

16   Glass, *The Matabele War*, p.262.

17   Norris Newman, *Matabeleland and How We Got It*, p.218.

17

To Brave Men

So who were the men of Wilson's Patrol that died on the banks of the Shangani? The following exposition has been compiled from various sources to try to put flesh on their bones which now lie in the Matopo Hills, Zimbabwe.[1] Death is the great leveller, and the names of Wilson's Patrol are listed below in alphabetical order.

Trooper William Abbott, B Troop, Salisbury Horse

Abbot was born in Thornthwaite, Cumberland, the son of Joseph and Dinah Abbot of Keswick. He was baptised on Christmas Day, 1863. He emigrated to South Africa in 1889 and entered Mashonaland in 1892. Before joining the Salisbury Horse, he was an employee of the Bechuanaland Trading Association for three years and then became a miner at Mazowe. His brother, Alan, a private in the Middlesex Regiment, was killed on 27 November 1917.[2]

Trooper William Bath, B Troop, Salisbury Horse

Bath was born in Middlesex in November 1856 and educated in the Commercial School in Clapham. He emigrated to South Africa in 1876 and, shortly afterwards, joined the Cape Mounted Rifles and served in the Basuto Campaign. He was promoted to the rank of Sergeant in 1881 but, shortly afterwards, left the Mounted Rifles to become overseer at a Kimberley diamond mine.

"TO BRAVE MEN": THE CROSS CARVED ON A TREE BY THE STOREKEEPER WHO FOUND THE BODIES. NOW PRESERVED IN THE NATIONAL MUSEUM AT BULAWAYO.

Epitaph to Wilson's men carved at the site where their bodies were found. (*Illustrated London News*, 2 January 1954)

---

1   Willis & Collingridge, *The Downfall of Lobengula*, pp.234–300; Norris Newman, *Matabeleland and How We Got It*, pp.114–139; O'Reilly, *Pursuit of the King*, pp.184–188; Cary, *A Time to Die*, pp.169–171.
2   *Penrith Herald*, 29 December 1917.

Obviously missing the military life, he went on to join the BBP but, in 1889 he returned to England for two years. He returned to South African in 1891 and worked for a mining company, entering Mashonaland in 1893. When the AmaNdebele War broke out, he volunteered to join the Salisbury Horse.

Sergeant Trooper William Henry Birkley, B Troop, Salisbury Horse

Birkley was born in London in 1862 and educated at Reading Grammar School. He emigrated to South Africa in 1884 and spent some time as a trooper in the Cape Mounted Rifles, later joining Carrington's Horse. He had been articled to a solicitor in England and established a practice in Salisbury. Like many others, he volunteered at the outbreak of the war.

Captain Henry John Borrow, OC. B Troop, Salisbury Horse

Born in 1865, Borrow, the son of a clergyman, was educated at Tavistock Grammar School and Sherborne College. Father and son emigrated to South Africa in 1882 where Borrow became an ostrich farmer, satisfying the demand for ostrich feathers among the fashionable ladies of Britain. Seeking a change of 'excitement', he joined Carrington's Horse and served in Sir Charles Warren's expedition. He was adjutant of the Pioneer Column in 1890 and then went into business as part of Messrs Johnson, Heany and Borrow in Salisbury. The three men had benefited from payments from Cecil Rhodes for their efforts in guiding the column and had the advantage of keeping the waggons and oxen the column had discarded. The three were extremely ambitious, as well as avaricious, and Borrow wrote in a letter to his parents: 'We ought to be the principal men in Mashonaland, with our claims, land, shares, transport, plant, salted horse etc.'[3] The partners concentrated on buying land and offered Frederick Selous £5,000 for his 20,000 acres. Borrow gave his name to Borrowdale, which is now a suburb of Harare in Zimbabwe. Borrow volunteered for the Salisbury Horse when the war broke out. A man to spot opportunities, he was undoubtedly brave and, with Willoughby, saved the horses at Battle of Imbembezi.[4]

Sergeant Clifford Bradburn, Victoria Rangers

Bradburn was born in December 1868 in Mosely, Birmingham. Educated at Queen's College, he worked at a Birmingham bank before emigrating to South Africa in 1890 and served in the Cape Mounted Rifles. He returned to England on the news that his mother was dying but, sadly arrived too late. After the formation of the BSAC, Bradburn was one of the first to join the Pioneer Column. When war broke out, he volunteered and was appointed a Sergeant in the Victoria Rangers.

Trooper William Henry Britton, B Troop, Salisbury Horse

Britton was born in 1870 in Halstead, Essex, and emigrated to South Africa in 1889.

---

3   Cary, *Charter Royal*, p.153.
4   See Chapter 8.

Trooper Edward Brock, B Troop, Salisbury Horse
Nothing is known about Brock other than that he was part of Wilson's Patrol.

Sergeant Harold Alexander Brown, Victoria Rangers
Brown was educated at Harrow School and Exeter College, Oxford. Widely travelled in countries such as Albania, Morocco, and Egypt, he was a member of the Pioneer Column. His anonymous letter to the *Pall Mall Gazette* about the column so interested Rhodes that he asked the editor to give him the writer's name.[5]

Corporal Frederick Crossley Colquhoun, Victoria Rangers
Colquhoun was born in Edinburgh in 1867, where his father served as Assistant Commissary General. The family later moved to Bedford, and Colquhoun was educated at Bedford Modern School where he had a reputation as a gifted sportsman. He emigrated to South Africa in 1887 and became a member of the Pioneer Column. His memory was commemorated at the school for some years after his death.

Trooper Philip Wouter De Vos, N Troop, Salisbury Horse
De Vos was of Dutch origin and born in Cape Colony on 14 June 1866.

Trooper L. Dewis, B Troop, Salisbury Horse
No details known.

Trooper Dennis Michael Cronly Dillon. Victoria Rangers
Dillon was born in April 1868 in Burdwan, India, where his father was Postmaster General. He was educated at St Edwards College Hertfordshire, London University and Stonyhurst College. Although a gifted scholar, he failed the entrance examination for the Ceylon Civil Service. He went to Africa in October 1888 and later joined the Pioneer Column. An athlete and very popular with his comrades, Dillon joined the Victoria Rangers at the outbreak of the war and acted as 'signaller' for the Victoria Column.

Captain Frederick Fitzgerald, OC. No. 1 Troop, Victoria Rangers
An Irishman, Fitzgerald had been a sub-inspector for the BSAC's police before joining the Victoria Rangers. He was responsible for selecting the volunteers from the Victoria Rangers who were to be part of the Shangani Patrol.

Captain Harry Moxon Greenfield, Quartermaster, Victorian Rangers
Greenfield was born in Tavistock, Devon, in 1861 and was educated at Tavistock Grammar School and Taunton Independent School. Greenfield, at 34, was a little older than many of his companions and left a wife and two children in Salisbury. He had begun his career working in a bank and went to the Orange Free State to work for its national bank. He later became an overseer

---

5   *Pall Mall Gazette*, July 1890.

at a Kimberley mine and went to Mashonaland to supervise the stores of a major South African company. A frequent letter writer, Greenfield, described his adventures and these were published in many British newspapers. His last letter to his father, T.W. Greenfield, written before the Shangani Patrol set off, is full of bravado but there is also a hint of apprehension for he warns his father that when he reads the letter it may have been written by the 'touches of a vanished hand' – perhaps anticipating his death.[6]

Troop Sergeant Major Sidney Charles Harding, Victoria Rangers

Harding was born in Kensington, London, in 1861, the son of Colonel Charles Harding, Honorary Colonel of the 4th (Volunteer Battalion), Queen's Royal West Surrey Regiment. Harding was educated at Felsted School in Essex and then went to St John's College, Cambridge. He served as a Lieutenant in the 2nd Cambridge (University) Rifle Volunteers but resigned for a more adventurous life in Cape Colony where he accepted a commission in Dyme's Mounted Rifles and took part in the Basuto War in 1881. He then journeyed to Natal and joined its Mounted Police. This fine 'young English man' returned home in 1885 but this stay did not last long, and he returned to policing in Natal. In 1889 Harding joined the BBP.

Trooper Harold John Hellet, Victoria Rangers

No details known.

Lieutenant Arend Hermanus Hofmeyr, No. 1 Troop, Victoria Rangers

Hofmeyr was born in Cape Town in 1873. He was an Afrikaner, and his father was a pastor in the Dutch Reformed Church and fathered 14 children. He was related to Jan Hendrik Hofmeyr who controlled the Afrikaner Bond and was an ally of Cecil Rhodes in the Cape parliament.

Lieutenant George Hughes, No. 1 Troop, Victoria Rangers

Hughes was an Irishman, the son of a Methodist minister. He was educated at the Methodist College, Belfast, and won a scholarship to the Royal University of Ireland but left before he completed his degree in order to emigrate to America. He later went to South Africa and joined the BSAC Pioneer Force. After the Force had been disbanded, he joined the Bechuanaland Exploration Company as a gold prospector. On the outbreak of the Matabele War, he volunteered and was commissioned in the Victorian Rangers.

Captain William Joseph Judd, OC. No. 4 Troop, Victoria Rangers

Judd was a farmer from Cape Colony who gave up farming to join the Pioneer Column as a trooper. Once discharged, he set up a transport business with riding horses based at Victoria. He obviously was well thought of by the locals as they elected him Commandant, a military role in charge of organising the local burghers if there was a threat. It was this confidence which saw

---

6   Wills & Collingridge, *The Downfall of Lobengula*, p.249.

him given command of a troop of the Victoria Rangers which many other burghers had also joined.

Corporal Harry Graham Kinloch, B Troop, Salisbury Horse7
Kinloch was born in Norwood, Surrey, in 1863 and attended Harrow and Trinity College, Cambridge, where he read law. He arrived in Mashonaland in 1891 and set up a successful practice in Salisbury. Described as having a quiet and unassuming manner, Kinloch was a useful cricketer and a champion lightweight boxer.

Captain Argent Blundell Kirton, Transport Officer, Victoria Rangers
Kirton was born in Portsmouth, Hampshire, in 1857, the ninth child of a Major attached to the Royal Engineers' Department at the War Office, and, at 36, another older member of Wilson's Patrol. Kirton emigrated to South Africa in 1873 at the age of 16 in order to join his two older brothers; one of whom was to die of fever and the other as a result of a fall from a horse. Kirton saw action in the First Boer War and carried despatches through Boer lines. He worked as a trader and had a farm near Zeerust. In 1887 Argent married, and he and his wife Caroline had three children. Kirton is said to have known Mashonaland and Matabeleland extremely well and to have been 'on terms of intimacy with Lobengula'.[8] Kirton was acting in Victoria on behalf of Sir John Willoughby and a syndicate that had bought several farms in Mashonaland.

Trooper George Sawyers Mackenzie, B Troop, Salisbury Horse
Mackenzie was born in Muree in India in 1860. He entered Mashonaland in 1889 with the Pioneer Column and when this was disbanded, he was employed as an assayer for the Zambesia Exploration Company until volunteering to join the Salisbury Column.

Trooper Mathew Meiklejohn, B Troop, Salisbury Horse
Meiklejohn, originally from Cape Town and a resident of the Transvaal, was an employee of Frank Johnson, who was to command the Pioneer Column.

Trooper Harold Dalton Watson Moore Money, B Troop, Salisbury Horse
Money was born in Bengal on 17 June 1872, one of six children of Major General Robert Cotton Money. Educated at Wellington College, he failed the entry examination for Sandhurst Military College and went to South Africa in 1893.[9] He had journeyed to Salisbury with Captain Borrow. Having missed out on a British commission he was keen to volunteer when the Matabele War broke out. He was one of the seven members of the 'Public School Mess' in Borrow's Troop.[10]

---

7   O'Reilly (*Pursuit of the King*, p.186) spells his name 'Kinlock'.
8   O'Reilly, *Pursuit of the King*, pp.186–187.
9   *South Africa Magazine*, 5 May 1894.
10   Many of the members of the patrol had attended public school in England and did not consider themselves to be of the lower classes.

Trooper Percy Crampton Nunn, B Troop, Salisbury Horse

Nunn was the son of Robert Nunn, a music professor who was also the organist of St Mary's Church, Bury St Edmunds. Born in in 1855 he was the oldest member of Wilson's Patrol. Percy arrived in Cape Colony in 1881, joined the Cape Mounted Rifles and, later the BBP. He volunteered for the Salisbury Horse and, while part of the Shangani Patrol, had letters publish in *The Graphic*.

Trooper Alexander Hay Robertson, B Troop Salisbury Horse

No details kmown.

Trooper John (Jack) Robertson, Victoria Rangers

Jack Robertson, another Scot, was born in Pitlochry in 1867. On the death of his father in the early 1880s Jack decided to seek his fortune in South Africa. Described as six feet tall and handsome and 'just the sort to volunteer for any hazardous undertaking', his letters home were full of AmaNdebele massacres, and his decision to volunteer for the Victoria Rangers came as no surprise.

Trooper William Alexander Thomson, B Troop, Salisbury

Thomson was a Scot born in Aberdeen in 1871 and educated at Elgin College as his parents had moved to Elgin when their son was only a few months old. At 15 Thomson moved to back to Aberdeen and 2½ years later left for Cape Colony. He was employed by J. Forrest & Co. and arrived in 1891 in Rondebosch, Mashonaland, where he seems to have gained knowledge of medicines. In an attempt to reconcile Boers and Britons by colonising north of the Limpopo, Thomson responded to an advertisement in *The Cape Times* of June 1891 for 'men of good parentage, a knowledge of riding and shooting and practically acquainted with agriculture' to form a trek led by Pieter Lourens van der Byl, an MP in the Cape Colony parliament. Thomson was offered a place on the trek along with 25 others and, because of his knowledge of drugs was placed in charge of the medicine chest and referred by his companions as the 'Doctor'. The object of the trek, which was financed by Cecil Rhodes, was to set up an agricultural settlement in Mashonaland.[11] The expedition initially settled at Inyatsitzi, north of Fort Victoria, but was quickly moved on by Dr Jameson to the Headlands/Rusape area, where the BSAC wished them to be a stabilising factor. In November 1891 they set up their settlement Laurencedale. The project was not a success; despite the extensive goods they carried, the party had insufficient resources and lacked cohesion. The young men also suffered severe attacks of malaria and blackwater fever. Tragedy struck when, after five month's struggle, Van der Byl died. Most of the young

---

11   Thomson, along with his companions, was required to take extensive supplies on the trek such as a stretcher bed, blankets, kettle, grid iron, 1 pan, tin mugs, cups, enamel plates, 3 knives, 3 forks, 3 spoons, tobacco, matches, 6 trousers, 2 jackets, 12 shirts, (6 flannel, 6 cotton), 4 pairs of boots, 2 pairs of *veldskoens* (leather walking shoes), 2 pairs of garters, 12 pairs of socks, 2 felt hats, 1 straw hat, musical, instruments, 2 caps, 3 bars of soap needles, pins, needles, thread, buttons, linen and cloth for patching, vegetable seeds, books and a camp chair. Cricket and football were to be encouraged and pet dogs allowed.

men quickly lost their enthusiasm for Mashonaland, but Thomson seems to have been one of the few determined to stick to it 'through thick and thin'. He was 23 when he died on the banks of the Shangani.[12]

Trooper Henry St John Tuck, B Troop, Salisbury Horse

Tuck was born in Bath in August 1868 and, like Wilson, was 37 years old when he died. His father, William Henry Tuck is described as a gentleman and a painter on the Lancing College War Memorial.[13] Trooper Tuck had a varied education; he was home tutored and then attended Lancing College before continuing his studies in Germany. Having served in the Royal Naval Volunteer Reserve,[14] he emigrated to South Africa in 1889, joined the Cape Mounted Rifles and took part in the Pioneer Column. After the Cape Rifles were discharged in 1891, he accepted the grant of land that had been part of his fee and set up as a farmer. When the AmaNdebele War broke out he volunteered for the Salisbury Horse.

Trooper Francis (Frank) Leon Vogel, B Troop, Salisbury Horse

Vogel was a New Zealander and born in Auckland in 1870. His father, Sir Julius Vogel, was the eighth Premier and first Jewish Prime Minister of New Zealand. Frank, his second son, was educated at Charter House and from 1890 worked in the London Office of the BSAC. The following year he left for South Africa and joined the Mashona Mounted Police as a trooper. The police were disbanded in 1892 and Vogel joined the BSAC Survey Department in Salisbury. He was Administrator Jameson's Acting Assistant Secretary. On the outbreak of the war, he volunteered for the Salisbury Horse and served under Captain Borrow, operating one of the Maxims at the battles of Shangani and Imbembezi during which he had a lucky escape. He appears to have been irrepressible as he volunteered for a number of scouting expeditions such as the search for Captain Williams, and he was involved in the expedition when Captain Campbell was killed. His luck was to run out when he volunteered to accompany Borrows as part of the relief party. The is a tablet in the cloisters at Charter House to the memory of Vogel, which bears the following inscription:

This tablet was placed by the Charter House Rifle Corps:

In memory of Frank Leon Vogel, of the Cape Mounted Rifles,
once a beloved member of the school corps.
He died, with all his comrades, near the Shangani River, Matabeleland,
December 4, 1893, aged 23, in a noble struggle against an
overwhelming force of enemies.
Sunt hic etiam sua praemia laudi.[15]

---

12 Details of the Van der Byl Trek based on a lecture given at the Mashonaland Branch of the History Society in September 1989 by J.W. Bousfield.

13 Lancing College War Memorial (www.hambo.org) Suffolk Artists – TUCK, William Henry.

14 Wills and Collingridge (*The Downfall of Lobengula*) say he was in the Royal Naval Artillery Volunteers. See Thomas Brassey, *The Royal Naval Artillery Volunteers* (London: Longmans, Green & Co., 1874).

15 A quote from Virgil Book 1: 'Here, too, the praiseworthy has its rewards.'

Trooper Henry George Watson, B Troop, Salisbury Horse
No details known.

Trooper Thomas Colclough Watson, B Troop, Salisbury Horse
Thomas Watson came from a military family, the son, grandson, and great grandson of colonels. Born in Bengal, India, in April 1866, he was educated at Wellington College and then left to join his father who was still serving in India. Shortly afterwards, the Watson family left for Tasmania where Thomas remained for a few years before returning to England. He emigrated to South Africa, arriving in Matabeleland in 1891.

Trooper Edward Earle Welby, Victoria Rangers
Despite Welby's distinguished surname nothing is known about him.

Major Allan Wilson, OC. Victoria Column
Much has already been written about Wilson, who was born in 1856 in Glen Urquhart, Scotland. His father Robert was a contractor for roads, bridges, and railways which meant that the family travelled extensively in Scotland as Robert pursued his work. Consequently, Wilson attended several schools, but the largest part of his education was carried out at Kirkwall Grammar School in Orkney and Milne's Institute at Fochabers in Morayshire.[16] A friend described Wilson as having 'a rough boyhood'.[17] It seems he was a popular pupil and, although only a poor cricketer, was made captain of the school eleven because of his ability to lead his fellows. After leaving school, Allan was apprenticed to the bank in Fochabers. In order to obtain such a respectable position Wilson had to be of good character and high moral habits; characteristics which were more important than mathematical competence.[18] Drunkenness was particularly disliked and, has already been noted, Wilson, unlike many of his peers, did not drink.[19] A bank clerk was a much sort after and fortunate position, offering better working conditions than many clerical jobs, and recruitment was mainly from the middle classes. Wilson is described as having an 'herculean' build, excelling in feats of strength and able to inspire others less well endowed. Apprenticeships at the bank usually lasted five years but Wilson left after

---

16 The Institute took its name from a benefactor of the town, Alexander Milne, who had originally been a footman to the Duke of Richmond and Gordon but found it hard to follow the duke's commands. Milne then emigrated to the United States where he grew to own the largest brickmaking company in New Orleans in which much of the work was done by slaves. When Milne died in 1838, he bequeathed $30,000 dollars (£6,000) to his relatives in Fochabers. In addition, he left $100,000 (£20,000) to provide a 'free' school for boys and girls in the town and surrounding areas. It was this school that Allan Wilson attended and indicates that his education was very different from many of those under his command. (There are still two schools named after Milne in Fochabers, and the modern primary school was formerly Milne's Institution. The secondary school is situated in Milne Street.)

17 Letter to the *Westminster Budget Magazine*, 1894, quoted in Wills & Collingridge, *The Downfall of Lobengula*, p.240.

18 Ingrid Jeacle, 'The Bank Clerk in Victorian Society: The Case of Hoare and Company', *Journal of Management History*, 16, 2010.

19 Wills & Collingridge, *The Downfall of Lobengula*, p.43.

three, seeking a more adventuress life and went to South Africa in 1878 in spite of being engaged to a girl from a neighbouring town.[20] Wilson joined the Cape Mounted Rifles in which he was described as having the ability to lead and command, but not always one to obey orders.[21] He certainly learned from his experience in the Rifles and having left the regiment and pursuing a period of trading and gold prospecting, he joined the Basuto Mounted Police with a lieutenant's commission. Wilson left the Basuto's to work for the Bechuanaland Exploration Company as a Chief Inspector at Fort Victoria where he was active in training the Victoria Rangers, especially at the outbreak of the war. Together with Captain Lendy and others, Wilson was a member of a lay committee that organized a mission to the Mashona and was much praised by Bishop Knight-Bruce.[22] Wilson became a Victorian hero, and it is not surprising that his hometown, Fochabers, was keen to commemorate its famous adopted son. In March 1895 a hexagonal fountain in red granite, commissioned by the Duke of Richmond and Gordon, was unveiled which bore tribute to Wilson as follows:

> Memory of Major Allan Wilson of Fochabers [and inscribed:] 1893. Erected by the natives of Fochabers to commemorate the heroic stand made against the forces of the King of Matebeleland by Major Allan Wilson of this town who with a small band of comrades fell bravely fighting against overwhelming odds near the Shangani River in South Africa on the 4th of December 1893.

The fountain still stands today and is in fairly good condition, but the fountain fittings are badly damaged.[23]

Such were the men of Wilson's Patrol. There are many common features that unite them other than a shared fate near the banks of the Shangani. It may surprise the reader that many were from wealthy middle-class homes and, like Troopers Money and Tuck, educated at the finest public schools of their day. Their portraits all show well-dressed young man with a proud bearing. Some like Sergeant Brown and Corporal Kinlock were Oxbridge graduates. Others such as Troopers Mackenzie and Colquhoun were the sons of colonial servants or military officers. Few if any could be described as professional soldiers, but all died bravely.

The bodies of the members of Wilsons Patrol were initially buried where they had died and Dawson had carved their epitaph on a nearby tree:

---

20   The lady, Mary Thompson, married James Dawson three years after Wilson's death. O'Reilly, *Pursuit of the King*, p.168.
21   Letter to *Westminster Budget Magazine*. The extremely flattering letter was probably written in retrospect before the details of the Wilson's Patrol were completely known.
22   Knight-Bruce, *Memories of Mashonaland*, p.205.
23   Aberdeenshire Council Historic Environment Record – Moray – NJ35NW0061 – WILSON MEMORIAL, FOCHABERS.

To Brave Men

Although initially appropriate such was the respect which the Settlers had for these fallen heroes that it was considered to be too remote for them to be given the honour they reserved. Cecil Rhodes decided that a more appropriate spot would be within the ancient ruins of medieval Zimbabwe which were close to Victoria. Between 18 July and 9 August, the bones were transported through the bush on ox wagons to Victoria. After a service was held on 13 August 1894 in the local church, St Michael and All Angels, the remains, escorted by six mounted representatives of the various units which had taken part in the fighting, were taken in procession to the Ruins and place in a communal grave, which was later surrounded by a stone enclosure.

This was not to be their final resting place, however, for Rhodes intervened again. Towards the end of the second AmaNdebele War, Rhodes discovered a site in the Motopo Hills which appealed to his sensitivities. He called it 'World's View' and he decided that he would be buried there. He also decided that Rhodesian heroes, 'those who deserved well of their country' should also be interred in the area. Clearly Wilson's men fitted the description of men who deserved well and in 1903 the Rhodesian Government decided that the bones should be removed from the Ruins and interred in a suitable memorial.

The inhabitants of Victoria resented the idea that 'their' heroes were going to be removed and held vocal protest meetings in order to make their feelings known. They claimed that the Government was acting in a high handed and illegal manner, Such was strength of their feeling that many of the military Volunteers in Victoria resigned. The *Bulawayo Chronicle* attempted to remind the local that the idea was to play great honour to Wilson's men and that they were national heroes not ones belonging to Victoria. The paper did, however, ask the Government to explain why its was ignoring the feelings of the people of Victoria. The Government remained silent.

Slowly the anger subsided and people began to understand that the protest was unseemly and did little to enhance the reputation of Wilson's men. In July 1904 the remains were buried in a vault in the centre of the monument which was to be their final resting place.

The Prince of Wales visits the grave of Cecil Rhodes in 1925. The bodies of Wilson's Patrol were buried nearby. (*Illustrated London News*, 1 August 1925)

A Panel from the Shangani
Memorial: Matopos Hills.
(Open source)

Wilson's Patrol Memorial
photograph taken in 1925
when visited by Prince of
Wales. (*Illustrated London
News*, 1 August 1925)

18

The Survivors

The Matabele War had consequences for many who took part other than the Shangani Patrol. It was the first of a two-part drama that ended with the Inquiry into the Jameson Raid in 1897, which saw some of the participants in the war imprisoned, such as Willoughby and Jameson, or ruined, such as Cecil Rhodes. Some of the participants' subsequent activities are described below.

Major Patrick William Forbes
Forbes was born in 1861 at Whitchurch-on-Thames, Oxfordshire. His grandfather, John Forbes, was a distinguished Scottish physician who was famous for his translation of the classic French medical text *De L'Auscultation Mediate* by René Laennec, the inventor of the stethoscope. He was also physician to Queen Victoria for twenty years. Patrick, who was educated at Rugby School and Sandhurst, was commissioned in the 6th Inniskilling Dragoons in 1881 and joined his regiment at Fort Napier in Natal. In 1889 he was seconded to the British South Africa Company Police in Cape Colony as second in command and promoted to the rank of Major in 1891. His actives during the Matabele War have already been described. When he arrived back in England on leave after the end of the war, he was well received in some quarters and invited to a number of formal dinners in the City. He was given an audience by the Duke of Cambridge, Commander in Chief of the Forces, who made some complimentary noises about Forbes' activities but explained that, since no British regular troops had been involved in the patrol, there could be no official recognition for his endeavours. Cary speculates whether this was because the duke was a stickler in doing things by the book or a subtle way of pointing towards the fact that Forbes was going to be blamed for the loss of Wilson and his men.[1] Jameson, on the other hand, received many plaudits and was made a Commander of the Order of the Bath. Cambridge had great influence and could have ensured that Forbes was rewarded in some way if he had chosen to do so. After return from leave in England in 1895, Jameson appointed him Administrator of

---

1   Cary, *A Time to Die*, p.163.

the BSAC's territories north of the Zambesi. The post was something of a sinecure as he received no funding and Jameson was really in charge. Forbes main task was to ensure that the African Transcontinental Telegraph Line was erected as quickly as possible. In 1897 Forbes was invalided home on leave suffering from a complaint which made riding a horse impossible. The following year Forbes returned to Salisbury and became Staff Officer to the Eastern Division of Southern Rhodesian Volunteers which was a mounted corps supported by cyclists, engineers, and signallers. The Volunteers served during the Second Boer War, but Forbes resigned shortly before its end and returned to England in 1902. In January 1903 Forbes married Beatrice Grey, whose father was the treasurer of the London Foundling Hospital. The happy couple received gifts from Forbes' colleagues which included a motorcar and an illuminated address praising his services in the development of Rhodesia. Shortly afterwards he became Governor of the Foundling Hospital.

Forbes continued as Governor until the outbreak of the First World War when he applied to the War Office for more active employment. He was appointed a staff officer in charge of prisoner of war camps in Wiltshire including the Eden Vale Camp in Westbury and the Stratton Factory Camp at Swindon. Forbes retired from the Army in 1916 at the age of 55, and he and his wife set up home in Salisbury, Wiltshire. Forbes died in 1922.

Eustace Macleod Forbes

Forbes brother, Eustace, served as a trooper in the Salisbury Horse and was badly wounded in the arm at the Battle of Shangani. Another public school and Cambridge graduate, he trained as an electrical engineer but, unable to find work in Britain, emigrated to Mashonaland and joined his brother. He worked as a clerk in the BSAC's Public Prosecutor's Office and the Mines Office. After the war was over, while returning home, Eustace was drowned attempting to find a suitable drift for waggons on the Umsingwani River in February 1894.

Leander Starr Jameson

Jameson's career after the conquest of Matabeleland needs little exposition. His influence in the BSAC continued to grow and his partnership with Cecil Rhodes became even stronger. The raid in 1895 was a significant but temporary setback and, after his release from prison for contravention of the Foreign Enlistment Act 1870, Jameson lived in Ladysmith throughout the siege during the Second Boer War. He was then elected to the Cape parliament as the Member for Kimberley – his disgrace forgotten. In February 1904, as Leader of the Progressive Party, he became Prime Minister and remained in office until he resigned in January 1908. In 1909, now completely reintegrated into respectable society, he was knighted and two years later became President of the BSAC. Jameson died in London in 1917 and his memorial service was attended by the King and Queen, Prime Minister David Lloyd George, General Smuts, and soldiers from the Rhodesia Regiment. It was recorded by

Pathé News. After the end of the war Jameson's body was carried to Rhodesia and laid beside his friend at World's View.[2]

Captain William Napier

Napier was extremely active in the subsequent AmaNdebele uprising which occurred partly because Jameson had withdrawn the police force to join his raid. He was to command all the local forces, which he did so successfully that he was created a Commander of the Order of St Michael and St George. During the Second Boer War, he commanded a squadron of the Southern Rhodesia Reserve Force. On his retirement, he became General Manager of the Estates Company in Umvuma which still exists today. Napier died in 1920.

Frederick Russell Burnham

Burnham, whose self-promotion obscured some of the realities of the Shangani Patrol, continued to have adventures. Having done a little prospecting, he became a scout for the Bulawayo Field Force during the AmaNdebele uprising and claimed to have killed the Mlimo, the mysterious spiritual leader of the AmaNdebele – a claim about which many, such as Marshal Hole, were sceptical. During the Second Boer War, Lord Roberts appointed Major Burnham chief scout, and Burnham took part in several dangerous expeditions and was captured twice by the Boers. During one expedition he was severely wounded and invalided back to England in 1901. Never one to miss an opportunity to blow his own trumpet, Burnham recounted the thanks given to him by Lord Roberts in which the Field Marshal said that he doubted that any other man in his force could have carried out the perilous enterprises Burnham had undertaken. Burnham was awarded the DSO.[3] Having recovered from his wounds, Burnham continued to explore the remoter parts of West and East Africa before retiring to become a cattle rancher in the United States. After trying to raise a battalion as part of Teddy Roosevelt's failed attempt to raise a Roosevelt Division for the First World War, Burnham went prospecting for tungsten and manganese. He died at the age of 86 in 1947 at his home in Santa Barbara, California.

Cecil Rhodes

Rhodes had three objectives in life: he wanted to expand the British Empire, become rich and powerful, and expand the influence of the British South Africa Company. It is difficult to know which of these was his prime ambition. The conquest of Mashonaland and Matabeleland were examples of all three. His final throw of the dice was the Jameson Raid, during which his friend launched an incursion into the South African Republic that ended in disaster. It cost Rhodes his position of Prime Minister of Cape Colony and, temporarily at least, his seat on the BSAC's Board. Although he did bounce back, surviving the inquiry into the raid and attempts to remove him from the list of Privy Councillors, he was no longer the Colossus he

---

2   Colvin, *Life of Jameson*, p.320.
3   Burnham, *Scouting on Two Continents*, p.18.

had been before Jameson's Raid. He played a significant and uncharacteristically active part in the AmaNdebele Uprising and spent the rest of his life befriending unsuitable men and women who were keen to get their hands on his wealth. Always active in many fields, he was constantly afflicted by poor health and died in 1902 at the age of 42. He was buried at World's View in the Matopo Hills. His friend, confidant, and *eminence gris*, Jameson, was buried close by. In July 1904 Wilson and his comrades were buried in a large granite tomb close to the graves of Rhodes and Jameson. The tomb bore the inscription 'There were no Survivors'.

An AmaNdebele warrior as depicted in Baden Powell's account of the Amandebele Uprising. (Robert Baden Powell, *The Matabele Campaign*)

19

'A House Divided against itself.'

It is clear, from the evidence already presented, that Forbes was given the lion's share of the blame for the Patrol's failure.[1] However, one could argue that he was a victim of circumstances rather than solely responsible for the failure of the Patrol. As we have seen Jameson considered him as a man of no importance and yet it seems that Forbes had done well whilst commanding the Combined Column on its way to GuBulawayo. Forbes was undoubtedly lacking the experience of Raaff and the self-assurance of Wilson. He admitted as much when, after the Battle of Shangani, he wrote 'it was the first time that I and the majority of those who were there had been under fire.'[2] As we have seen, Wilson had gained experience in the Zulu War and the First Boer War and Raaff had been decorated for his work in the Zulu War and had almost been executed because of his support for the British in the First Boer War. It seems that Forbes' self-confidence was further damaged during the retreat from the Shangani when Raaff's greater experience came to the fore and the men tended to look to the Afrikaner for guidance. Major P B Clements, who had served as a trooper under Forbes, writing in *the Star* in June 1923, described Forbes as a passive commander during the retreat and many insisted that Raaff taker over command.[3] Wilson, however, was seen by many as a hero but it is necessary to examine how far he was responsible for his own death and those of his patrol.

First, he seems to have disobeyed a direct order from Forbes to conduct a simple scouting expedition on the far side of the Shangani and return by nightfall. Had Wilson obeyed, his men would have returned to the main body of the Patrol which was in a less vulnerable position.

Secondly, was Wilson justified, as the officer on the spot, in disobeying this direct order? There can be no definitive answer to this question as most, if not all, who could answer it died as a result of Wilson's decision.

Thirdly, did the discovery of what was presumed to be Lobengula's kraal offer Wilson the opportunity of fulfilling the Patrol's objective single handed? He had been a subordinate to Forbes throughout the Patrol and, although

---

1   Cary, *A Time to Die*, p.163
2   Forbes quoted in O'Reilly, *Pursuit of the King*, p.11.
3   Clements, *The Star*, 5 June 1923, quoted in O'Reilly, *Pursuit of the King*, pp.130, 140.

Forbes had respected Wilson's position as commander of the Victoria Column, there had been occasions when he had given orders to Wilson's men to ensure that the two sections of the Column acted coherently especially in times of danger.[4] There seems to have been a role reversal when Wilson sent a request for the rest of the Patrol to join him across the Shangani. Forbes was tempted to see this as an order and a threat to his status as commander, which by the instructions of Jameson to always consult Raaff, had already been damaged.

The Shangani River was the limit of the Patrol's range, but it was very close to fulfilling its objective in capturing Lobengula whom it was believed to be a few miles on the far side. Forbes' dilemma was whether to break the agreement, cross the river and possibly capture the King or remain on the nearside and let Lobengula escape. Forbes was cautious and Wilson possibly did not appreciate the danger in which his men had placed themselves especially since they did not have the firepower of the maxim which had proved so effective in previous encounters with the enemy. Similarly, Wilson's men did not have waggons or sandbags behind which to shelter if attacked. His men were forced to kill their horses to provide a defensive barrier behind which to fight, but in doing so reduced their ability to escape.

There is also the suggestion that Wilson knew if he returned to the larger group, Forbes was planning to marginalise him and claim the glory for himself. [5]This might explain why Wilson wanted Forbes and his men to join his company which would guarantee that they both would share in the glory.

It is also worth speculating how much Commandant Raaff contributed to the Patrol's overall failure. Forbes depicts him as a pessimist and something of a law unto himself. He often placed his own interpretation on Forbes' orders. It is true that the Commandant had much more experience in carrying out such missions as the Shangani Patrol. He did claim that Forbes' decision to send Wilson a few reinforcements without the maxims was folly He was able to ensure his horses did not lose fitness at the same rate as other groups and that food was used judiciously. Claims that Raaff was very ill during the patrol are unproven. If he had been very ill it is unlikely that he could have held the respect of the men and conducted the retreat from the Shangani in such a professional manner. Raaff's death shortly after the patrol's return was not just a tragedy but also convenient for Forbes. Both of his rivals for command were dead and his version was prime.

Similarly, the version of events provided in Wills and Collingridge was largely dictated by Forbes, who clearly wanted to place the blame on Wilson and clear himself of blame for the Patrol's failure. Forbes was the senior officer of the patrol with ultimate responsibility, but Wilson and Raaff's greater experience, individual personalities, and considerable confidence in their own abilities, also contributed to the failure of the Patrol. It is probable that all three men, as well as Jameson's instruction to Forbes to consult Raaf on all things, contributed in different ways to the Patrol's failure.

---

4   Forbes, The Occupation of Bulawayo. In Wills and Collingridge, *The Downfall of Lobengula*, pp.119, 121.

5   Cary, *A Time to Die*, p.54.

Jameson was too senior to blame and was lauded as a hero for the War's conclusion. Wilson and Raaff died regarded as a hero by most of the survivors and only Forbes remained to be held responsible for the failure. As we have seen Loch told Rutherfoord Harris not to publish the Inquiry's findings. Willoughby was furious that the Court of Inquiry's findings were not made more publicly available and demanded a second Inquiry which would expose Forbes inadequacies during the Patrol. Willoughby was satisfied when he discovered that the official report of the War would be edited by Rutherfoord Harris in order to remove any damaging incidents including those about the Patrol. [6] Forbes' whose statement to the Board, showed that he felt that he had not made any errors of judgement during the Patrol but went on to criticise Wilson and Raaff whom others thought them to be the heroes of the venture and unable to defend themselves. Forbes was considered, in the eyes of officialdom, to the obvious culprit, or perhaps an obvious scapegoat, and to place the blame on his shoulders protected both the BSAC and the Colonial Office.

---

6   Loch quoted in O'Reilly, *Pursuit of the King*, pp.150-151.

Appendix I

The Moffat Treaty 1888

The Chief Lobengula, ruler of the tribe known as the Amandebele, together with the Mashuna and Makakalaka tributaries of the same, hereby agrees to the following articles and conditions:

That peace and amity shall continue forever between Her Britannic Majesty, Her subjects, and the Amandabele people; and the contracting Chief Lobengula engages to use his utmost endeavours to prevent any rupture of the same, to cause the strict observance of this treaty, and so to carry out the spirit of the treaty of friendship which was entered into by his late father the Chief Umziligaas [Mzilikazi] with the then Governor of the Cape of Good Hope in the year of Our Lord 1836.

It is hereby further agreed by Lobengula, Chief in and over the Amandebele country with its dependencies as aforesaid, on behalf of himself and people, that he will refrain from entering into any correspondence or Treaty with any foreign State or Power to sell, alienate or cede or permit or countenance any sale, alienation or cession of the whole or any part of the said Amandebele country under his Chieftainship, or upon any other subject, without the previous knowledge and sanction of Her Majesty's High Commissioner for South Africa.

In faith of which I Lobengula on my part have hereunto set my hand at Gubulawayo, Amandabeleland this eleventh day of February and of Her Majesty's reign the Fifty first.

Lobengula his mark
Before me   Witnesses
Feb. 11. 1888   J.S. Moffatt, W. Graham
Assist. Commissioner. G.B. van Wyk

Appendix II

The Leask Concession

GuBulawayo, AmaNdebele Land
25 January 1884

I Lo bengula, King of the AmaNdebele nation have this day granted to Messrs Thomas Leask, George A. Phillips, George Westbeech and James Fairbairn permission to dig and mine for gold and other minerals in my country between the Gwaie [Gwaai] and Hunyani [Manyame] rivers and to remove the product. Also I have given them permission to have a few white men to work and prospect for them. By this grant I cancel all former grants and concessions and this is the only one valid. I give the said company power to add to their number and I also promise to protect them.

    Lo Bengula Xhis mark
    As Witness
    Elephant Seal Embossed
    T. Halyet
    John H. Whitaker

Appendix III

The Rudd Concession

Know all men by these presents, that whereas Charles Dunnell Rudd, of Kimberley; Rochfort Maguire, of London; and Francis Robert Thompson, of Kimberley, hereinafter called the grantees, have covenanted and agreed, and do hereby covenant and agree, to pay to me, my heirs and successors, the sum of one hundred pounds sterling, British currency, on the first day of every lunar month; and further, to deliver at my royal kraal one thousand Martini-Henry breech-loading rifles, together with one hundred thousand rounds of suitable ball cartridge, five hundred of the said rifles and fifty thousand of the said cartridges to be ordered from England forthwith and delivered with reasonable despatch, and the remainder of the said rifles and cartridges to be delivered as soon as the said grantees shall have commenced to work mining machinery within my territory; and further, to deliver on the Zambesi River a steamboat with guns suitable for defensive purposes upon the said river, or in lieu of the said steamboat, should I so elect, to pay to me the sum of five hundred pounds sterling, British currency. On the execution of these presents, I, Lobengula, King of Matabeleland, Mashonaland, and other adjoining territories, in exercise of my sovereign powers, and in the presence and with the consent of my council of *Indunas*, do hereby grant and assign unto the said grantees, their heirs, representatives, and assigns, jointly and severally, the complete and exclusive charge over all metals and minerals situated and contained in my kingdoms, principalities, and dominions, together with full power to do all things that they may deem necessary to win and procure the same, and to hold, collect, and enjoy the profits and revenues, if any, derivable from the said metals and minerals, subject to the aforesaid payment; and whereas I have been much molested of late by divers persons seeking and desiring to obtain grants and concessions of land and mining rights in my territories, I do hereby authorise the said grantees, their heirs, representatives and assigns, to take all necessary and lawful steps to exclude from my kingdom, principalities, and dominions all persons seeking land, metals, minerals, or mining rights therein, and I do hereby undertake to render them all such needful assistance as they may from time to time require for the exclusion of such persons, and to grant no concessions of land or mining rights from and after this date without their consent and concurrence; provided that, if at any time the said monthly payment of one hundred pounds shall be in arrear for a period of three months, then this grant shall cease and determine from the date of the last-made payment; and further provided that nothing contained in these presents shall extend to or affect a grant made by me of certain mining rights in a portion of my territory south of the Ramaquaban River, which grant is commonly known as the Tati Concession.

(signed by Lobengula, Rudd, Maguire, Thompson, Helm and Dreyer)

I hereby certify that the accompanying document has been fully interpreted and explained by me to the Chief Lobengula and his full Council of Indunas and that all the Constitutional usages of the Matabele Nation had been complied with prior to his executing the same.

(signed by Helm)

[Author's note: Notice that the Concession is all one sentence.]

Appendix IV

Lobengula's announcement in the *Cape Times*, 26 November 1888

All the mining rights in Matabeleland, Mashonaland and adjoining territories of the Matabele Chief have been already disposed of, and all concession-seekers and speculators are hereby warned that their presence in Matabeleland is obnoxious to the chief and people. Lobengula.

Appendix V

Notice in the *Bechuanaland News and Malmani Chronicle* suspending the Concession[1]

Notice:
I hear that is published in the newspapers that I have granted a concession in all my country to Charles Dunnell Rudd, Rochford [sic] Maguire and Francis Robert Thompson. As there is a great misunderstanding about this, all action in respect of the said concession is hereby suspended, pending an investigation to be made by me in my country.

    Lobengula
    Royal Kraal
    Matabeleland
    18th January 1889

---

1   The original document is countersigned by Phillips, Riley and Usher.

Appendix VI

Lobengula's letter to Queen Victoria

Some time ago, a party of men came into my country, the principal one appearing to be a man called Rudd. They asked me for a place to dig for gold and said they would give me certain things for the right to do so. I told them to bring what they could give and I would show them what I would give. A document was written and presented to me for signature. I asked what it contained, and was told that in it were my words and the words of those men. I put my hand on it. About three months afterwards I heard from other sources that I had given by that document the right to all the minerals of my country. I called a meeting of my *Induna*s and also of the white men and demanded a copy of the document. It was proved to me that I had signed away the mineral rights of my whole country to Rudd and his friends. I have since had a meeting of my *Induna*s and they will not recognize the paper, as it contains neither my words nor the words of those who got it. After the meeting, I demanded that the original document be returned to me. It has not come yet, although it is two months since and they promised to bring it back soon. The men of the party who were in my country at the time were told to remain till the document was brought back. One of them, Maguire, has now left, without my knowledge and against my orders. I write to you, that you may know the truth about this thing and may not be deceived.

With renewed and cordial greetings,
I am your friend,
LOBENGULA.

Norris Newman provided an additional version of the letter which attempted to establish whether Queen Victoria actually existed as follows:

Lobengula desires to know that there is a Queen. Some of the people who come into this land tell him there is a Queen, some tell him there is not.

Lobengula can only find out the truth by sending eyes to see whether there is a Queen. The *Induna*s are his eyes.

Lobengula desires, if there is a Queen, to ask her to advise and help him, as he is much troubled by white men who come into his country and ask to dig gold.

There is no one with him upon whom he can trust, and he asks that the Queen will send someone from herself.[1]

---

1   Norris Newman, *Matabeleland and How We Got It*, fn. pp.22–23. Perhaps the two versions represent the complete letter?

Queen Victoria's reply to Lobengula

The Queen has heard the words of Lobengula. They say that Lobengula is much troubled by white men who come into his country and ask to dig gold, and that he begs for advice and help. Lobengula is the ruler of his country, and the Queen does not interfere in the government of that country; but as he desires advice, Her Majesty is ready to give it, and, having consulted Her Principal Secretary of State holding the Seals of Office for the Colonial Department, now replies as follows:—In the first place, the Queen wishes Lobengula to understand distinctly that Englishmen who have gone out to Matabeleland to ask leave to dig for stones have not gone with the Queen's authority, and that he should not believe any statements made by them to that effect. The Queen advises Lobengula not to grant hastily concessions of land, or leave to dig, but to consider all applications very carefully. It is not wise to put too much power into the hands of the men who come first, and to exclude other deserving men. A King gives a stranger an ox, not a whole herd of cattle.

Appendix VIII

The Foreign Office view of the Concession and the BSAC[1]

It is understood that the concession from Lo Bengula never actually passed, in full propriety right, to the Chartered Company, but is leased by 'The United Concessions Company'[2] to the Chartered Company for a payment of one half on the net profits of all their present and prospective undertakings, which, however, have to be conducted entirely at the expense of the Chartered Company ...

... It may be safely stated that no persons concerned with Her Majesty's Government had any idea that such a scheme was in contemplation when the Charter was being considered and settled. If it had been disclosed the Charter would certainly have been refused. It may even be a question whether the announcement of it now does not render it necessary to consider whether the Charter should be revoked. This would be a very objectionable course, because it would involve the establishment of an administrative protectorate over all the Company's territories ...

---

1 TNA: Colonial Office. 879/37. Memorandum on the Origin and Operations of the British South Africa Chartered Company, 13 October 1892.
2 Another of Rhodes' companies.

Appendix IX

Composition of the Flying Squad (Wilson's Patrol)

Overall Command
Major Patrick Forbes

Salisbury Column Contingent
90 Men with Captains Maurice Heany and John Spreckley
One Mule drawn Maxim under Lieutenant Tyndall Briscoe. R.N.

Victoria Column Contingent
60 men under Major Allan Wilson.
One horse drawn Maxim under Captain Lendy R.A.

Tuli Column Contingent
60 men under Captain Coventry (but subordinate to Commandant Raaff.

Bechuanaland Border Police
90 Men under Commandant Raaff
Two horse drawn maxims
One mule drawn seven pounder under Captain Tancred

Bibliography

Archives

United Kingdom
The National Archive (TNA) CO, Africa (South) No 358, 5633, No 5
TNA CO 879/30/369/, no. 65. encl. 372
TNA CO 119/514 Administration of Oaths to Judges; Basutoland Affairs; Enquiry into Loss of a Military Patrol on Shangani River; Native Regulations; Private Conversation with President Kruger (April 1893); The Tati Concession Company
Parliamentary Archive (PA) C 284 Correspondence Respecting the Death of Two Indunas at Tati, October 1893. No. 3 Enclosure 6. Moffat to Loch including Ingubogubo's Statement, 24 October 1893
PA C 7284 W.H. Sawyer's Report upon the Circumstances Leading to the Death of Indunas on 18 October 1893. Dated 9 January 1894 (Sawyer Report)
PA C 7290 Further Correspondence Relating to the Affairs in Matabeleland, Mashonaland, and the Bechuanaland Protectorate; Sir John Willoughby's Account of the Battle of Shangani, 24 November 1893 (Willoughby's Account)
PA C 7555 I Report by Mr P.J. Newton upon the Circumstances Connected with the Collision between the Matabele and the Forces of the British South Africa Company at Fort Victoria in July 1893 (Newton Report)

South Africa
NZA, Cape Town Office of BSAC. CT 1/14/3 Court of Inquiry; Pursuit of Lobengula by Forbes, 20–27 December 1893
University of Witwatersrand Historical Research Papers Archive, ZA HPRA A77 *Maund Papers*

Zimbabwe
Zimbabwe National Archives (ZNA) CR: 2/1/1 Interviews with Siatcha, Ginyalitsha and Ntabeni Kumalo
ZNA HC 3/5/30/6 Office of the High Commissioner for Southern Africa, Section.H.C. 3 (Correspondence) H.C. 3/5/30 (Matabele War) H.C. 3/5/30/6 Sir Henry Loch's Memorandum on the Report of the Inquiry into the Patrol under Forbes, 12 March 1895
High Court of Matabeleland Civil Records, Case No. 275 *Regina v. Daniel and Wilson*

Official Printed Sources

Aberdeenshire Council Historic Environment Record - Moray - NJ35NW0061 - WILSON MEMORIAL, FOCHABERS
BSAC, *Rhodesia: South Africa Company 1892* (Cape Town: BDA, 1909)
Colonial Office, *South Africa: Copies and Extracts of Correspondence to the British South Africa Company in Mashonaland and Matabeleland* (London: HMSO, 1893)
Hansard, House of Commons Debate, Vol. 18, cc. 543–627, 9 November 1893
Her Majesty's Government, *Charter of Incorporation*, 28 October 1889

Secondary Sources

Altham, Edward, *Some Notes on the Life of Major Patrick William Forbes (late 6th Inniskilling Dragoons)* (London: Warren & Son, 1928)

Ash, Chris, *Matabele: The War of 1893 and the 1896 Rebellions* (Pinetown: 30 Degrees South, 2016)

Ash, Chris, *The If Man: Dr Leander Jameson – The Inspiration for Kipling's Masterpiece.* (Solihull: Helion & Co., 2012)

Baden Powell, Robert, *The Matabele Campaign* (London, Stevens Publishing, 1896)

Blake, Robert, *History of Rhodesia* (London: Eyre Methuen, 1977)

Brassey, Thomas, *The Royal Naval Artillery Volunteers* (London: Longmans, Green & Co., 1874)

Bulpin, Thomas Victor, *The White Whirlwind* (London: Nelson, 1961)

Burnham, Frederick Russell, *Scouting on Two Continents* (New York: Garden City Co., 1926)

Cary, Robert, *A Time to Die* (Cape Town: Howard Timmins, 1968)

Cary, Robert, *Charter Royal* (Cape Town: Howard Timmins, 1970)

Chilvers, Hedley A., *The Seven Lost Trails of Africa* (London: Cassell & Co., 1930)

Cloete, Stuart, *African Portraits* (London: Collins, 1946)

Colvin, Ian, *The Life of Jameson* (London: Edward Arnold, 1922)

Cooper-Chadwick, John, *Three Years with Lobengula, and Experiences in South Africa* (London: Cassell & Co., 1894)

Creswicke, Louis, *South Africa and the Transvaal War*, Vol. 1. (Edinburgh: T.C. & E.C. Jack, 1900)

Davidson, Apollon, *Rhodes and His Time* (Pretoria: Protea Boekhuis, 2003)

Donovan, Charles H.W., *With Wilson in Matabeleland: Or Sport and the War in Zambesia* (London: Henry & Co., 1894)

Du Toit, Stephanus Jacobus, *Rhodesia: Past and Present* (London: Heinemann, 1897)

Forbes, P.W., 'From Sigala Mountain to the Shangani', in Wills & Collingridge, *The Downfall of Lobengula*

Forbes, P.W., 'Leaving Mashonaland for the Front', in Wills & Collingridge, *The Downfall of Lobengula*

Forbes, P.W., 'Organising the Forces', in Wills & Collingridge, *The Downfall of Lobengula*

Forbes, P.W., 'Retreat from the Shangani River', in Wills & Collingridge, *The Downfall of Lobengula*

Forbes, P.W., 'The Downfall of Lobengula', in Wills & Collingridge, *The Downfall of Lobengula*

Forbes, P.W., 'The Loss of the Wilson Patrol', in Wills & Collingridge, *The Downfall of Lobengula*

Forbes, P.W., 'The Occupation of GuBulawayo', in Wills & Collingridge, *The Downfall of Lobengula*

Forbes, P.W., 'The Pursuit of the King', in Wills & Collingridge, *The Downfall of Lobengula*

Fort, G. Seymour, *Dr Jameson* (London: Hurst & Blackett, 1903)

Fripp, Constance. E. and Hiller, V.W. (eds), *Gold and the Gospel in Mashonaland* (London: Chatto & Windus, 1949)

Fry, W. Ellerton, *The Occupation of Mashonaland* (Open source)

Galbraith, John S., *Crown and Charter: The Early Years of the British South Africa Company* (Berkeley, CA: University of California Press, 1974)

Gale, W.D., *One Man's Vision: The Story of Rhodesia* (GuBulawayo: Books of Rhodesia, 1976)

Gann, Lewis Henry, *A History of Southern Rhodesia from Early Days to 1934* (London: Chatto & Windus, 1965)

Gibbs, Peter, *A Flag for the Matabele* (London: Frederick Muller, 1955)

Gibbs, Peter, *Blue and Gold: The History of the British South Africa Police, Vol. 1* (Salisbury: BSAP, 2009)

Glass, Stafford, *The Matabele War* (London: Longmans, 1968)

Goold-Adams, Hamilton, 'Goold-Adams Report, 21 November–18 November 1893', in Wills & Collingridge, *The Downfall of Lobengula*

Hemsley, Howard, *The History of Rhodesia* (London: William Blackwood & Sons, 1900)

Hensman, Howard. *History of Rhodesia: Compiled from Official Sources* (London: Blackwood, 1900)

Hepburn, J.D., *Twenty Years in Khama's Country: And Pioneering among the Batauana of Lake Ngami* (London: Hodder & Stoughton, 1894)

Heyer, A.E., *A Brief History of the Transvaal Secret Service System from Its Inception to the Modern Times* (Cape Town: William Taylor, 1899)

Hiller, V.W., 'The Commission Journey of Charles Dunell Rudd, 1888', in Fripp & Hiller, *Gold and the Gospel in Mashonaland*

Hole, Hugh Marshall, *The Making of Rhodesia* (London: Macmillan & Co., 1926)

Hole, Hugh Marshall, *The Jameson Raid* (London: Philip Allan, 1930)

Johnson, Frank William Frederick, *Great Days: The Autobiography of an Empire Pioneer* (London: G. Bell & Son, 1940)

Johnston, Harry, *The Story of My Life* (London: Chatto & Windus, 1923)

Jones, Neville, *Rhodesian Genesis* (Bulawayo: Rhodesia Pioneers' and Early Settlers' Society, 1953)

Keppel-Jones, Arthur, *Rhodes and Rhodesia: The White Conquest of Zimbabwe 1884–1902* (Montreal: McGill-Queen's University Press, 1983)

Knight-Bruce, G.W.H., *Memories of Mashonaland* (London: Edward Arnold, 1895)

Laband, John, *The Battle of Majuba Hill: The Transvaal Campaign 1880–1881* (Solihull: Helion & Co., 2017)

Leonard, Arthur Glyn, *How We Made Rhodesia* (London: Keegan Paul, Trench, Turner & Co., 1896)

Lockhart, John G. & Woodhouse, Christopher M., *Rhodes* (London: Hodder & Stoughton, 1963)

Marston, Roger, *Own Goals, National Pride and Defeat in War: The Rhodesia Experience* (Rothersthorpe: Paragon, 2010)

Mason, Philip, *The Birth of a Dilemma* (Oxford: Oxford University Press, 1958)

McGuire, James & Quinn, James, *Dictionary of Irish Biography* (Cambridge: Cambridge University Press, 2009)

Meredith, Martin, *Gold, Diamonds and War: The British, the Boers and the Making of South Africa* (London: Schuster & Schuster, 2007)

Millais, John Guille, *Life of Frederick Courtenay Selous, D.S.O.* (New York: Longmans, Green & Co., 1919)

Millin, Sarah, *Rhodes* (London: Chatto & Windus, 1933)

Michell, L. *The Life and Times of the Rt Hon. Cecil John Rhodes* (London: Arnold, 1910)

Norris Newman, Charles, *Matabeleland and How We Got It* (London: Fisher Unwin, 1895)

O'Reilly, John, *Pursuit of the King* (GuBulawayo: Books of Rhodesia, 1970)

Pakenham, Thomas, *The Scramble for Africa* (London: Abacus, 1992)

Preller, Gustav, *Lobengula: The Tragedy of a Matabele King* (Johannesburg: Afrikaanse Pero-Boekhandel, 1963)

Radziwill, Catherine, *Cecil Rhodes, Man and Empire-Maker* (London: Cassell & Co., 1918)

Rorke, Melina, *Her Amazing Experiences in the Stormy Nineties of S. Africa's Story* (London: Harrap, 1939)

Rotberg, Robert, *The Founder: Cecil Rhodes and the Pursuit of Power* (Oxford: Oxford University Press, 1988)

Rouillard, Nancy (ed.), *Matabele Thompson – His Autobiography* (Johannesburg: Central News Agency, 1957)

Sauer, Hans, *Ex Africa* (London: G. Bles, 1937)

Schowalter, A. (ed.), *The Memoirs of Paul Kruger as Told by Himself* (New York: Century Co., 1902)

Selous, Frederick Courtenay, *Travels and Adventure in South East Africa* (London: Rowland Ward, 1893)

Selous, Frederick Courtenay, 'Introductory Review of the War', in Wills & Collingridge, *The Downfall of Lobengula*

Smit, A.J., *The Shangani Story* (GuBulawayo: Allan Wilson Technical Boys High School, 1952)

Snape, David, *The Rescue They Called a Raid: The Jameson Raid 1895–96* (Warwick: Helion & Co., 2021)

Strage, Mark, *Cape to Cairo: Rape of a Continent* (New York: Harcourt Brace Jovanovich, 1973)

Tanser, G.H., *A Scantling of Time: The Story of Salisbury, Rhodesia (1890–1900)* (Salisbury: Stuart Manning, 1965)

Wilcox, John, *The Shangani Patrol* (London: Headline, 2010)

Wills, W.A. & Collingridge, L.T., *The Downfall of Lobengula* (London: Simpkin, Marshall, Hamilton and Kent & Co., 1894)

Wrey, Phillip B.S., 'The Collision at Victoria', in Wills & Collingridge, *The Downfall of Lobengula*

Journals

'History of Banking in Zimbabwe', *The African Spectator*, 3 February 2015. https://africanspectator.blogspot..com

Anon, 'The Skull of Lobengula', *Time Magazine*, 10 January 1944

Edington, Alexander, 'South African Horse Sickness: Its Pathology and Methods of Protective Inoculation', *Proceedings of the Royal Society of London*, No. 67, 1900

Glass, Stafford, 'James Dawson, Rhodesian Pioneer', *Rhodesiana*, 16, July 1967

Jeacle, Ingrid, 'The Bank Clerk in Victorian Society: The Case of Hoare and Company', *Journal of Management History*, Vol. 16, 2010

Roberts, R.S., 'The Treasure and Grave of Lobengula: Yarns and Reflections', *Heritage of Zimbabwe*, 23, 2004

Snape, David, 'The Failure of the Shangani Patrol'. *The Bulletin of the Military Historical Society,* Vol. 71, No. 283, February 2021

'"I consider Dawson to blame for the whole occurrence" The Tati Incident 1893', *Soldiers of the Queen, Journal of the Victorian Military Society,* Issue 182, Spring 2022

Woolford, J.V., 'The Matabele War', *History Today*, Vol. 28, Issue 8, 1978

Newspapers and Magazines

Black and White, 25 October 1895

The Cape Times, 1 June 1894

Glasgow Herald, 12 September 1893

The Graphic, 1893 & 1894

Illustrated London News, 1893, 1894 & 1896

Johannesburg Star, 23 December 1893

Pall Mall Gazette, July 1890

Penrith Herald, 29 December 1917

The Queenslander, 3 February 1894

Review of Reviews, 1891

Rhodesia Herald, June 1894

The Sketch, November 1893

South Africa Magazine, 5 May 1894

The Star, 5 June 1923

The Sydney Mail, 28 July 1898

The Times, 10 February 1894

The Truth, 8 February 1894

Vanity Fair, 1 March 1904

Westminster Budget Magazine, 1894

Index